Stickier
Marketing

Also by the author

Sales Therapy: Effective selling for the small business owner

Sticky Marketing: Why everything in marketing has changed and what to do about it

SECOND EDITION

Stickier Marketing

How to win customers in a digital age

Grant Leboff

KoganPage

LONDON PHILADELPHIA NEW DELHI

First published in Great Britain and the United States in 2014 by Kogan Page Limited

2nd Floor, 45 Gee Street	1518 Walnut Street, Suite 1100	4737/23 Ansari Road
London EC1V 3RS	Philadelphia PA 19102	Daryaganj
United Kingdom	USA	New Delhi 110002
		India

www.koganpage.com

© Grant Leboff, 2014

Sticky Marketing is a trade mark of Grant Leboff
Stickier Marketing is a trade mark of Grant Leboff
Problem Map and Problem Maps are registered trademarks of Grant Leboff

The right of Grant Leboff to be identified as the author of this work has been asserted by him in accordance with the Copyright, Designs and Patents Act 1988.

ISBN: 978 0 7494 7108 8
E-ISBN: 978 0 7494 7109 5

British Library Cataloguing-in-Publication Data

A CIP record for this book is available from the British Library.

Library of Congress Cataloging-in-Publication Data

Leboff, Grant.
[Sticky marketing]
  Stickier marketing : how to win customers in a digital age / Grant Leboff. — [Revised edition].
    pages cm
  ISBN 978-0-7494-7108-8 (pbk.) — ISBN 978-0-7494-7109-5 (ebook)   1. Marketing.   2. Internet marketing.   3. Information technology–Social aspects.   I. Title.
  HF5415.L362 2014
  658.8'72—dc23
                                                                                        2013044131

Typeset by Amnet
Printed and bound in by CPI group (UK) Ltd, Croydon CR0 4YY

CONTENTS

LIST OF FIGURES
AND TABLES

LIST OF ABBREVIATIONS

API   Application programming interfaces
CEO   Chief executive officer
CEP   Customer engagement point
CMR   Customer managed relationships
CRM   Customer relationship management
FD   Financial director
GPS   Global positioning system
MD   Managing director
MMS   Multimedia messaging service
NFC   Near field communications
ROE   Return on engagement
ROI   Return on investment
RSS   Really simple syndication
SEO   Search engine optimization
SMS   Short message service
UGC   User-generated content
USP   Unique selling proposition

PART ONE
Prologue

What the Sex Pistols taught me about marketing

It was a mild autumn day in 1999. I was in the UK, in Brighton, at a recording studio belonging to a friend of mine, Paul Mex.[1] We were having a chat about the state of the music industry, because in the summer of that year Shawn Fanning had started Napster, a music file-sharing site that gave people the ability to share music with each other all around the world.

The music industry later had Napster closed down. At the time, however, there were many people who were infuriated that consumers were now sharing music across the web, for free. The music industry's business model was based on the fact that they controlled the distribution of music and charged the public to access it. In 1999, this was mainly by way of CDs.

Paul and I were having a discussion about the future of the music industry, and how they were going to approach this new development. While we were having this debate, Paul suddenly stopped the conversation and told me he wanted me to listen to a recording he had. At the back of the studio was a cupboard full of tapes, records, cables etc, and Paul rummaged in there for what seemed like an age. He eventually returned waving a cassette. He sat me down and told me to have a listen.

He explained that it was a tape of a live phone-in with Paul Cook and Steve Jones from the Sex Pistols, Paul's favourite band, which took place in the summer of 1978 on KSJO Radio in the United States. He pressed play on the tape recorder and we sat back and started to listen. About two minutes into the recording, Paul indicated that the section he wanted me to hear was coming up.

At that moment, a woman listener came on the air. She was decidedly unimpressed with the Sex Pistols and had phoned in to tell them so. She was given her opportunity to speak and started, 'I just wanted to say that I don't think the Sex Pistols have any right to cut down the Queen until they learn how to be musicians first.' At that point Steve Jones interrupted, replying: 'It's got nothing to do with music, you silly cow!' Paul then stopped the cassette player.

I looked at him, puzzled. 'Did you get it?' Paul asked.

'I think so,' I replied, decidedly unsure.

Paul made an MP3 file of the interview. I saved it to my desktop and every so often I would have a listen. As broadband became ubiquitous and the web was having a greater influence on our lives, Steve Jones's comment back in 1978 seemed to resonate with me more and more. Eventually, I could not get it out of my mind. I soon realized that this one comment seemed to summarize much of what I was trying to say in the speeches I was presenting and in the work I was undertaking with clients.

It may have been a flippant comment made 12 years before the invention of the world wide web, but Steve Jones had opened my eyes to what I observed was happening at the dawn of the 21st century and he was right... 'It's got nothing to do with music, you silly cow!'

Stickier Marketing is not about how to conduct an e-mail marketing campaign or the intricacies of search engine optimization (SEO). Rather, it presents a new way of thinking in the digital age. This book will provide the narrative as to how and why the old paradigms of marketing, with which we lived for so long, are no longer relevant. It will uncover the 'new rules' by which companies must now operate in order to be successful.

By ensuring they have the correct mindset and adopting the principles contained in this book, businesses will be able to ensure their marketing is effective in this web-enabled digital age. *Stickier Marketing* will explain how companies can become attractive, which in turn will lead prospects to their door. It will detail how to create competitive advantage in a world where customers seemingly have a plethora of choices and where standing out appears to be increasingly difficult. Ultimately, *Stickier Marketing* will explain the principles and the steps that need to be taken in order to become 'sticky'. In so doing, a business will emerge that prospects and customers alike will want to engage with. The result is that a company will acquire one of the most precious resources available, and the one that all companies require in order to be successful. That is: customer attention.

PART TWO
Setting the scene

Printing press to world wide web

> *When I became President in 1993, there were only 50 sites on the worldwide web – unbelievable – 50. When I left office, the number was 350 million and rising.*
> **(PRESIDENT BILL CLINTON, 2001[1])**

As alluded to by President Clinton, it is the pace at which change has taken place since the invention of the world wide web that has made understanding its effects so difficult. Many established companies failed to grasp quickly enough how the landscape was altering. Consequently, they have been left behind by new companies that have filled the void.

For example, *Yellow Pages* was a concept and brand known throughout the world for over 100 years.[2] In whichever country you lived, it was often your first point of reference when looking for a product, service or supplier. Quite simply, *Yellow Pages* dominated search. Surely, therefore, any of the major companies that owned *Yellow Pages* were in the best position to establish themselves as the major search tool on the web. In the UK, *Yellow Pages* was owned by British Telecom,[3a, 3b] a huge company with vast resources. Yet, it was Google that became the major search brand online: a company with no history, launched in 1998 from a garage in California by two computer graduates.[4]

Similarly, *Loot* magazine, first published in the UK in 1985,[5] was a market leader if you had unwanted items that you wished to sell. Therefore, one could argue, certainly in the UK, that it was in the best position to establish this market online. However, it was eBay, founded 10 years later in 1995,[6] that established itself as the major provider of this service.

Whether it is Amazon, usurping all major book retailers, or the failure of any large telecom provider to be the first to develop a service like SKYPE, now the biggest carrier of international calls in the world,[7] there is a litany of examples of established companies failing to grasp the opportunities, or to see the risks to their business, that the revolution in technology and communication has brought.

It is the old analogy of the frog in water that is put on to boil. As the water heats up, it cannot recognize the subtle changes in its surroundings. By the time it understands that the water is boiling, it is too late. Similarly, many companies have failed to grasp the changes that are taking place around them. They have tried to bolt the web onto their existing business models, failing to realize that the web is not merely a new communications vehicle, but rather represents a fundamental change in the rules of engagement.

Stickier Marketing explains how and why the rules changed, and what businesses need to do in the digital age in order to win customers and be successful.

The development of communication

It is unbelievable to think that when Bill Clinton was being inaugurated as the 42nd President of the United States, there were only 50 sites on the web. In fact, it was only in December 1990 that the first web client–server communication took place over the internet.[8] Yet, despite its relatively short existence, Sir Tim Berners-Lee's creation is now proving itself to be the biggest revolution in communication since the invention of print.

Having invented the technique of printing in the 1450s,[9] Johann Gutenberg published the first real book, a version of the Bible. Gutenberg introduced the world to the first one-to-many mass medium of communication. In other words, from the pen of one, the written word could be distributed to the many. This allowed for the wider dissemination of knowledge.

Printing enabled people to publish their ideas throughout the world. Once the power of this communication was unleashed, life was never the same again. The Protestant Reformation, the Renaissance and the Scientific Revolution were unlikely to have occurred without printing allowing ideas to spread. Thus, the revolution in communication, signified by Gutenberg's first printed book, helped to change the course of history.

Of course, there have been many other developments in the world of communication that have impacted on our lives. The 20th century saw dramatic changes in communication as new inventions started to affect the way we live. The influence of cinema,[10a] radio[10b] and television[10c] can in no way be underestimated. In TV's heyday, families would schedule their week around the popular programmes of the day. It was these shows that also set the tone for many of the conversations that took place around the coffee machine at work the following morning. Cinema, radio and television, however, still represented the transmission of ideas from one to many.

It was print that changed all the rules, by making mass communication possible. The other developments merely made the one-to-many medium more efficient. For example, television made it possible to communicate simultaneously with much larger audiences. However, although cinema, radio and, in particular, television did change the game of communication, they did not change the rules by which the game was played.

In other words, print allowed for the mass marketing of products via advertising, mail order catalogues and direct mail pieces. Using television, the mass marketing model may have reached a bigger audience than traditional direct mail. This was because many of the big TV shows would have larger audiences than an average direct mail campaign. One could also argue that having sound and pictures delivered directly into people's homes gave those communications greater influence, although this is certainly debatable. However, the reality is that the principles were the same. The audience were still passive receivers of communication, with no right of reply. These broadcasts were generated by those who had the money to use the distribution channels available.

Let me explain, using a tennis analogy: the game of tennis changed when players migrated from the old wooden racquets to those made of graphite.[11] The new racquets gave players power with unprecedented accuracy. The game became faster and the serve became harder to return. These developments undoubtedly changed the game. They did not, however, change the rules by which tennis was played.

Similarly, print was the revolution in communication because it changed the rules. It made mass communication and the spreading of ideas possible. Meanwhile, cinema, radio and television, like our graphite racquet, merely changed the game by creating an increasing variety of potent channels through which to reach the audience. The game may have become faster and more furious, but nevertheless, the rules of mass communication remained the same.

The invention of print and the other forms of one-to-many communication changed the world in which we live and influenced the way our society has developed. However, the limitations of these forms of communication have been as important to our development as the benefits.

The limitations of traditional communication channels

Because these vehicles of communication are one to many, they did not allow for mass discussions to take place. Authors, producers and programme makers could put their message across to millions, but the majority of their audience did not have the means with which to reply. Of course, people could discuss a particular message with friends. Certain individuals, such as journalists, could react when writing reviews. Books, television programmes and films could even inspire other authors and creators to write something new in reaction or reply to a piece of work. However, the number of people who were able to respond and be heard was severely limited. The one-to-many form of communication in itself is not capable of facilitating a discussion.

For example, when the Beach Boys released their groundbreaking album *Pet Sounds* in 1966, individual journalists could write reviews and reactions to the album. Paul McCartney himself acknowledges that *Sgt Pepper's Lonely Hearts Club Band* was, in part, the Beatles' reaction to the *Pet Sounds* album.[12] Meanwhile, although millions of music fans may have had one-to-one conversations about the record, they were unable to be heard by a wider audience. This left the average fan a mere passive observer in the discussions taking place between the few voices with the means to grab their attention.

This highlights another limitation of the one-to-many platform, in that distribution was in the hands of relatively few. Anyone could write a book or record a song, but without access to a publisher or record company and its distribution network, it was unlikely that many others would know of its existence.

Whether it was newspapers, films or TV, it was media conglomerates that owned the distribution channels necessary to reach a wider audience. Therefore, few voices would be heard. Meanwhile, those who had control over the distribution of the information exerted enormous influence on our lives. Certainly in the arts it was the big film, record and publishing companies, and those they employed, that chose which acts were financed and which were never to see the light of day. Without being signed by one of these large companies it was unlikely that an artist, author or filmmaker would have any success at all.

We can acknowledge the existence of pirate radio stations, independent filmmakers and underground magazines that have been successful. However, these are exceptions rather than the rule. In the main, those with the means of distribution were heard, with everyone else unable to communicate their message beyond friends, colleagues and family.

In business, companies would gain access to distribution through money. For example, a company could produce television or radio advertising and buy airtime. Alternatively, it was possible to design messages for newspapers, billboards and magazines and purchase space. Companies could also go to the expense of designing, printing and posting their own direct mail. Whatever the vehicle, without money it was impossible to obtain distribution and, therefore, to be heard. Generally, it was the larger companies that could afford to take advantage of these tools of communication. Smaller businesses would have less access to the media, owing to lower budgets.

Consequently, our lives were shaped by the big media magnates and companies that could control the means of distribution and the large companies that had the money to buy access to that distribution network. In the main, the individual was reduced to being a passive recipient. While one-to-many communications inspired billions of one-to-one discussions among friends, family and colleagues, most people had no means by which to be heard beyond their own immediate circle.

The web's impact on communication

The creation of the web is now changing all the rules of communication. As with the invention of print, it has radically altered the way in which we react to and disseminate information. Just as print was the first one-to-many form of communication, the web is the first many-to-many medium.

No longer do individuals need to own a large media network or have access to money to be heard. Using the web, anyone can broadcast their message. This, in turn, means that individuals are no longer reduced to the role of passive recipients. Everyone is now able to react to others' messages in real time. As this process escalates, a conversation ensues between tens, hundreds or even thousands of people, as comments and reactions can be added to a discussion on an ongoing basis. Thus the web is capable of facilitating a dialogue among potentially millions of people in a way that no previous media outlet could.

While it is possible to use the web as a one-to-many communication tool, it is impossible to prevent your audience from having a right to reply.

Therefore, although many companies have tried to use the web to broadcast their one-to-many messages, these have often turned into many-to-many communications, as empowered individuals take it upon themselves to exercise their right to react. For example, even if a company broadcasts its message without allowing a direct reply on that page, anybody can post a comment in a relevant forum, chat room, blog or social network.

Before the invention of the web, the majority of the public had very few vehicles with which to voice an opinion. For example, we could write a letter to a newspaper column, but few would ever be published. Also, the time lag between writing and posting a comment, and its subsequently being received and printed, meant that often it would lose some of its potency.

Compare that with today, when we can send a message immediately, reacting to a story we have just seen. Many of us now have our own distribution networks. Whether these are our friends on Facebook or Google+, connections on LinkedIn, subscribers to our blog or newsletter, or followers on Twitter, an increasing number of us have a ready-made audience to which we can impart our thoughts and feelings. Apps on our mobile phones such as Vine, Instagram and Bambuser allow us to distribute video and pictures in a few seconds. Media such as YouTube, iTunes, Squidoo and Vimeo offer anyone the chance to distribute their message to a mass audience. In other words, people can now voice their opinions and broadcast a message in written, audio and visual formats and enjoy immediate distribution at virtually no cost at all. What we have witnessed is the empowerment of the individual and the democratization of information.

A famous example of this is musician Dave Carroll.[13a] He claimed that his guitar was broken while flying in the United States with United Airlines. When he failed to make a claim in the pre-requisite 24-hour time frame, United Airlines told him he was ineligible for compensation. After nine months of failed negotiations, Dave Carroll wrote a song, *United Breaks Guitars*, about his experience. To date this YouTube video has had over 13 million views.[13b] This is a situation I am sure United Airlines would have rather avoided.

This phenomenon also means that we no longer solely rely on the established news networks to deliver us information about current events. When US Airways flight 1549 landed in the Hudson River in January 2009,[14] it was Jim Hanrahan on Twitter that broke the news four minutes later. During the events of the Arab Spring in 2010–11 when leaders in Tunisia, Egypt and Libya, amongst others, were deposed, there were times when more relevant information could be obtained from social platforms than established news networks.[15] And it was an IT consultant, Sohaib Athar, living in Abbottabad, who unknowingly tweeted details of the US operation on Osama Bin Laden's compound as it was happening.[16]

In fact, media organizations are now embracing the change. For example, in 2013, the *Guardian* newspaper launched 'Guardian Witness',[17] which is available both online and as a mobile phone app. The aim is to encourage the public to supply *Guardian* journalists with videos, photos and stories around breaking news and events.

Forums and discussion groups that proliferate on the web invite us to comment and be heard, and we have been utilizing these platforms for a while. During the 2009 inauguration of President Obama, there was an average of 4,000 status updates every minute through the CNN.com live Facebook feed.[18] These were people commenting and reacting to each other's observations, in real time, throughout the entire broadcast. Three years later, when Barack Obama was re-elected in 2012, a picture he posted of him hugging his wife Michelle with the tagline 'four more years', was, at the time, the most re-tweeted picture in history. It was re-tweeted over half a million times in one night.[19]

This ease of distribution also means that we no longer react to information in the same way. We are often willing and able to share, with our friends, messages that we find particularly interesting or funny. Before the creation of the web we might have torn an article out of a newspaper or magazine and shown it to a few select people, or mentioned a particular programme to a few friends. Now we can share content with our entire address book or social network, at the touch of a button.

It is not just the ease with which we can contribute and distribute ideas that has empowered us. It is also the access to information provided by the web that has been liberating. Before the web, finding information was often a time-consuming, laborious and difficult process. Now, we can go online and find the knowledge that we require, almost immediately. Whether it is news, reviews, products, facts, instructions, schedules or reports, there are very few situations where we are unable to find the information we require.

However one chooses to define marketing, at its core is the communication of ideas. The web is the biggest revolution in communication since the invention of print. This being the case, if the rules of communication have changed, doesn't it make sense that the rules of marketing must also have changed?

The web's influence on global change

The web has also helped accelerate other game-changing factors. There is no doubt that even before the web, the world was becoming a smaller place. Trade amongst many nations was becoming increasingly free; for example, the creation of the Common Market,[20] which subsequently became the European Union, brought the nations of Western Europe closer together both politically and economically. The fall of the Berlin Wall[21] has opened up the world and the phenomenon of globalization has emerged.[22]

However, the web has broken down borders even further. We can now read newspapers, listen to radio and watch news broadcasts and TV programmes from many different countries. We can have discussions with people throughout the world via blogs and forums or through communities and social networks with common interests. In this way, information and ideas can now be shared globally with ease. We can also source products and services internationally. The web means that geography is no longer the boundary it once was.

In order to save costs, technology has also made possible the outsourcing of labour to other places in the world. For example, you can staff a call centre in India and be taking calls from customers in the United States or United Kingdom. The web makes it easier for people in different countries to access the same piece of information. Culturally, the web is also breaking down barriers, as we are increasingly engaging with people from all corners of the earth. This has resulted in people becoming more comfortable dealing with other countries than perhaps they once were.

Technology has also made it easier for people to work for themselves. The capital outlay that was once necessary to start a business is no longer required. Online access is all you need. The web, together with e-mail, allows you to engage and communicate with prospects and customers relatively inexpensively.

This has led to a proliferation of small businesses, with an increasing number appearing all the time. Not everyone today is an entrepreneur, although there are many more than there once were. However, with capital outlay no longer a barrier, and in a knowledge economy, people no longer see the need to work for others. This is especially true as one of the major reasons for seeking employment was job security. In today's market, this is something that even the biggest corporations do not seem to be able to offer in the way they once did.

Big businesses still exist, but the dynamics of the marketplace have changed. Whereas in the 1970s or 1980s you might not have considered buying from a one-person business working from home, you probably would now.

In short, we live in a world where people have been empowered. Anyone can produce content relatively cheaply and easily and have the means with which to distribute it. Companies, however small, can communicate directly with their customers in a way not previously possible. Meanwhile, consumers can now give direct feedback to companies and, perhaps more importantly, can talk to each other, cutting the company out of the communication completely. These peer-to-peer conversations have given the general population a voice they never had before. In short, this means that today everyone is a marketer. For every single individual has the ability to communicate an opinion about the products and services your business offers. As one of the biggest influencers on human behaviour is social proof, these opinions can determine whether people choose to buy from you or not.

Stickier Marketing takes into account the changes that have taken place, and that we continue to experience. It provides a new set of rules for effective communications in a world that has been impacted by advancements in technology and the web:

- customers have changed;
- communication has changed;
- marketing has changed;

Stickier Marketing provides you with a compelling response to the change. Read on, and find out how to win customers in the digital age.

Key point summary

- The web is the biggest revolution in communication since the invention of print. It is not merely a new communication vehicle but represents a fundamental change in the rules of engagement.
- The web is the first many-to-many medium. It is capable of facilitating a dialogue between potentially millions of people in a way no previous media outlet could.
- Using the web, anyone can broadcast their message. Therefore, individuals are no longer reduced to the role of passive recipients.

- Today, many individuals have their own distribution networks, whether these are friends on Google+ or Facebook, connections on LinkedIn, subscribers to a blog or newsletter, or followers on Twitter.

- The access to information that the web provides is liberating. Information and ideas can now be shared globally with ease. Geography is no longer the barrier it once was.

- The web has resulted in the empowerment of the individual and the democratization of information.

- Today, everyone is a marketer. For every single individual has the ability to communicate an opinion about the products and services your business offers. These opinions can determine whether people choose to buy from you or not.

Scarcity to abundance

As technology and the web play a greater part in our lives, we are seeing a shift in the dynamics of scarcity and abundance. Think back to 1990, the year the first-ever communication took place over the web.[1] At the time, most people probably thought that they had a lot of choice and access to information. Yet, relative to where we are today, this was not the case. For example, here are some of the ways in which UK consumers were limited in choice at that time:

- Sky TV was less than one year old, having started on 5 February 1989.[2] It had only a million subscribers, leaving virtually the entire UK population with a choice of only four terrestrial television channels.

- The European air industry was going through deregulation, a process that did not finish until 1 January 1993.[3] EasyJet was not to launch until 1995[4] and although Ryanair flew its first low-budget flight in 1986,[5] the choices in low-cost air travel that we enjoy today were not available.

- There were only two landline telephone providers, BT and Mercury, with the latter enjoying only 3.5 per cent share of the residential phone market.[6] Therefore, almost everybody's telephone was provided by British Telecom.

- The only gas supplier was British Gas. Full competition in the gas supply market did not exist until 1998. Full competition in the electricity supply market did not exist until 1999.[7]

- The financial services market had only been deregulated in 1986;[8] therefore, the array of choices we have today were only just starting to emerge.

In 1990, we had relatively little access to information:

- Only 1.14 million people owned a mobile phone,[9] representing only 1.9 per cent of the UK population.[10]
- There was no SMS text messaging. This wasn't introduced until December 1992.[11]
- There was no web and so it was not easy to find potential suppliers of products and services. Most of us relied on the *Yellow Pages* or specialist and trade magazines.
- The adoption of e-mail in business, and later by consumers, did not take place until providers like Demon launched in the UK in 1992[12a] and AOL started to connect their proprietary e-mail systems to the internet in 1993.[12b]

So in 1990, compared with today, there was a scarcity of both choice and access to information. However, it was relatively easy to grab our attention at that time, as there were only four terrestrial TV channels in the UK. On coming home from work, many people would be switching to one of the four channels on their TV sets. Since 1990, viewing figures for the top 10 TV programmes in the UK have been in steady decline,[13] as they have in other countries where the media has fragmented, such as the United States. It is in this context that traditional TV advertising is proving a less potent form of communication than previously. Budgets are increasingly being diverted to online digital media.[14]

In the UK, in 1990, of the four terrestrial television channels available, only two were commercial stations. Therefore, if a company wanted to relay a message to the wider public, paying for advertising on one of these two channels was deemed good value for money as it would reach an extremely wide audience. Moreover, viewers did not have the array of distractions and variety of channels to which to flick during the commercial breaks. Whether it was advertising on television, direct mail through your door or individuals calling on a telephone, essentially companies would pay to shout messages at us. This proved an effective form of communication.

In a world before the web, consumers did not have easy access to information. Therefore, while companies would shout to enable them to sell their products and services, consumers were prepared to listen. Where did you go to find out about a better mortgage product, the latest technology or a new service that might be available locally? In this environment, when direct mail shots were posted through your door, the telephone rang from a sales call or the advertising came on television, then, assuming it was well written and well put together, we were willing to pay attention. Although consumers were well aware that companies were trying to sell to them, these messages were often a valuable source of information. It was in their interest to give time to these messages as much as it was in the company's interest to create them.

In a world where both choice and information were scarce, the old marketing model worked on an unwritten contract between company and consumer. A business would pay money to interrupt what we were doing and shout its message at us, but if the messages were well presented and of good quality, consumers were prepared to watch, listen or read, as there was value in it for them.

For example, one of the highlights of the year for many people, and therefore an important purchase, is their annual holiday. It is not only the money they will spend, but also the importance of being able to have quality time with the people closest to them. However, before the web, how did most people choose their holiday destination?

Generally, they would go to their local shopping centre or high street, and pick up the sales brochures supplied by their local travel agent. They would then flick through them and choose a place to go. Unless one had a friend or a family member who had been to the destination previously, there was no way of validating the purchase. However, what were those travel brochures if not the marketing material of companies looking to sell holidays? They were certainly not put together to provide the public with useful information and an enormous sense of well-being! Yet, people would go out of their way to obtain these sales brochures. In a world where there was a dearth of information, culturally people were used to relying on the marketing and advertising of companies to inform them of what was going on and products that were available. Now, if you look at where we are today, there is an absolute reversal.

The abundance of choice and information

In most facets of our lives, rather than a scarcity of choice we are now presented with an absolute abundance in almost everything. Whether it be food, clothes, suppliers for our business requirements or ways to spend our leisure time, we are usually faced with a plethora of options. Obviously there are exceptions. For example, there has traditionally been a shortage of housing stock in the United Kingdom. We also have the challenge of the limitations of many natural resources.

I sometimes think that a contributory factor to our cynicism about politics is the fact that it is one of the few areas of our lives where we are limited in our choice. For example, both the United Kingdom and United States operate what is essentially a two-party system, limiting our alternatives. However, our normal experience in our day-to-day lives is having a vast array of options.

Not only do we have more choices than ever before, but the web gives us the wherewithal to identify them both locally and globally. For example, think about buying a television. Before the web, you would most likely visit a few local stores in order to make a purchase. If the model you required was unavailable, it would have to be ordered and another visit to the shop would have to be made, often weeks later. Moreover, the selection on offer was often limited by what we saw on the shelves in the few places that served our locality.

Today, via the web, we have easy access to almost all the choices available. We are no longer limited by the stock that our local provider carries. In fact, in many cases, we can research, choose and pay for items and have them delivered within 24 hours, without ever leaving the comfort of our homes or offices.

This access to information on the web allows us to compare products and services from a larger array of providers than was previously possible, thus enabling us to make a more informed choice. Rather than physically having to make contact with every provider, today most of the information we require is at our fingertips. The abundance of both information and choice means that in most areas of our lives we are now confident that we will not only be able to find what we want, but that we will also be able to make the purchase at our convenience.

This situation has been compounded with the successful development of mobile technology. Back in the 1990s when the web was in its infancy we had to 'dial in' for it to be used. Then as broadband took off in the year 2000,[15] we started to get used to the web always being on. However, since 2007 smartphones have become ubiquitous. It was in this year that Apple launched the first mass consumer smartphone with its iPhone product.[16] Consequently, we are now used to carrying all the information that we will almost ever need, in our pockets with 24/7 access.

However, the one resource that has always been scarce, and has become increasingly so, is our time. We have a finite number of hours in any given day and it is widely accepted that technology has made our lives busier than ever before. People now attend to e-mails on the train, text friends and communicate via social networks while queuing, and make telephone calls from their cars. The natural downtime that existed in the normal ebb and flow of life has all but disappeared.

With time so scarce, our lives so busy and an increasing number of messages and amount of information making demands upon us, we are having to become more efficient at screening out unwanted and unnecessary communications. It is this reality that has meant that our unwritten contract with those companies that are shouting at us has been broken.

How many people:

- regularly read their direct mail?
- take cold calls and are pleased to receive them?
- frequently watch and remember TV commercials?
- don't flick to other channels when advertising messages appear?
- watch their programming on digital recorders or online, enabling them to bypass advertising?

Many companies still perceive that there is value in shouting at their potential customers as a way of encouraging them to buy their products or services. The problem for these companies is that there is little value in consumers receiving this information any more.

The 'shouting' lost its value

Although it is impossible to prove, I have substantial anecdotal evidence that years ago many of us would have a cupboard in the hallway, or a drawer in the kitchen, where we would store useful direct mail pieces and leaflets. With access to information so difficult, it seemed worthwhile keeping literature that might be useful at a later date. With the possible exception of takeaway menus, who keeps this material now? With all the knowledge that we require available to us at the stroke of a key, most direct mail finds its way straight into the bin.

As customers, we have all been empowered. We are now confident that when we require a product or service, we will be able to find it and make a purchase. Previously, we were prepared to put up with the shouting and unwanted messages because they often proved to be a useful source of information. Frequently we did receive value from these communications. When messages were not useful, we were fairly ambivalent about them. However, today this has changed. We have plenty of access to the information we require, which we can obtain at our convenience rather than when it suits a company to shout at us. These communications, therefore, have become a major inconvenience. Because they no longer provide value, they now, for the most part, have become irritating.

We are now:

- irritated by the amount of direct mail that we receive;
- irritated by the number of spam e-mails that monopolize our inbox;
- irritated when we answer a cold call;
- irritated when we are interrupted by advertising when we are busy trying to do something else.

Because this kind of marketing works on repetition – continually e-mailing, continually cold calling or continually advertising – companies that still pursue this form of marketing are set to continually irritate their potential customers; not, perhaps, the best way of communicating their message.

Any form of direct communication – for example e-mail, direct mail or telephone calls – that can be considered intrusive by a prospect and has not been requested, will damage your brand. In a world where customers have both the access to knowledge and the array of choices to make their decisions at their convenience, these communications, far from being welcomed, are likely to be seen in an extremely negative light. Of course, there will always be exceptions to the rule. However, it is an extremely tenuous marketing strategy to spend valuable resources attempting to be one of the exceptions.

While it is possible that an advert may resonate with a prospect and over time lead to a sale, one has to question whether this model is the most efficient way of reaching potential customers. With the fragmentation of the media and subsequently the declining reach that any single piece of advertising has, we are moving towards a world where the return on investment does not make sense for any but the biggest brands and companies within their sector. When observing companies that still insist on shouting at their potential customers, I am reminded of something Robert Stephens[17] said: 'Advertising is a tax for having an unremarkable product.'

Consumers no longer use advertising in the way they once did: as a major resource for gaining knowledge about new products and services available in the market. Today, customers have all the access to information they need, at their time of choosing. Moreover, when advertising was used as an information source, it had a great influence on our thinking as it was a form of social proof. This is because we give a certain amount of credibility to sources that provided us with new knowledge. In other words, we believed that the adverts reflected what our contemporaries thought.

Where customers now go for information

Today, as we have become more cynical, sophisticated and savvy, and live in a more connected world with tablet computers, smart phones, apps, text messaging, blogs, forums, wikis, instant messaging and social networks, we take more of our social proof directly from each other, thus reducing the influence that advertising once had. Word of mouth from our peers is now much more influential than any single piece of advertising. Think about it. If you want a new product or service today, there are probably only two places you will go: you will search on the web or you will ask your network.

By network, we are talking about family, friends, colleagues and connections in the online communities to which you belong. Between your network and the information available on the web, you will probably have all the information about possible suppliers that you need to move your purchasing decision forward. It is unlikely that you will need to go anywhere else. This being the case, does it mean that the only marketing that matters now is online and word of mouth? Moreover, as an increasing number of people use the plethora of social platforms available to provide others with their opinions, 'word of mouth' and the online world are increasingly merging into one channel. That is not to say that word of mouth offline will disappear. Of course, it will not. However, more people are using online platforms to tell others what they think.

Both online search and word-of-mouth marketing put the customer firmly in control. It is up to people themselves whether they aid your word-of-mouth marketing by talking about you or referring you to others. Meanwhile, when prospects search online, they will browse and explore the sites and information of their choosing. In fact, the web is the worst vehicle for finding a new customer. If you enter into the Google search bar 'I would like a new customer', nothing of value will be produced. The key to being successful online is for you to be where prospects look. At that juncture, you can communicate with them, providing resources and information of value, and, in this way, hope to start a worthwhile engagement.

Whether it is word of mouth by referral or online search, both these routes require your customer to come to you. This is in contrast to the old model of marketing where you shouted very loudly at prospects to grab their attention, hoping to gain a worthwhile response.

Today, customers have created barriers. They screen out the shouting because it no longer provides them with any value. With an abundance of choice and easy access to information via their networks and the web, customers will find you at a time of their choosing. This being the case, is it not time we created a new marketing model to embrace the new world of digital technology and the web?

Key point summary

- As technology and the web play a greater part in our lives, we are seeing a shift in the dynamics of scarcity and abundance.

- In a world before the web, consumers did not have easy access to information. Therefore, while companies would shout to sell their products and services, consumers were prepared to listen as these messages were often a valuable source of information.

- Consumers now have access to the information they require at their convenience. Consequently, receiving intrusive communications from companies, at the convenience of a business, has become increasingly irritating.

- As consumers live in a more connected world, with smart phones, tablet computers, apps, text messaging, blogs, forums, wikis, instant messaging, social networks etc, they take more of their social proof directly from each other. This reduces the influence that advertising once had.

- Most people today will rely on only two sources when looking to make a purchase: searching on the web and asking their network. Both these channels of online and word of mouth rely on customers approaching your business at a time of their choosing.

- As an increasing number of people use the plethora of social platforms available to provide others with their opinions, 'word of mouth' and the online world are increasingly merging into one channel.

Transactions to engagement

03

The shift from scarcity to abundance has huge implications for marketing. Ostensibly it means that the traditional model of marketing, and the way in which companies acquired new customers, is broken.

Previously, marketing operated as a funnel (Figure 3.1). It worked by companies paying a lot of money to 'shout' at their potential customers. The more money they had, the more often they tended to shout, via vehicles such as direct mail, cold calling, leaflet drops, advertising etc. Some people reacted to the shouting. That action was referred to as response. In business-to-consumer marketing, it was hoped that this response would result in a direct increase in sales. In business-to-business marketing, this increase would come by following up the response, with prospects being qualified out, until eventually there were some paying customers at the end. Thus, a process that could have started with 20,000 direct mail shots might end with 20 paying customers; hence the funnel. As long as the income generated by the paying customers covered the cost of the campaign, with some left over for profit, a company would have made a return on investment and the marketing would be regarded as a success.

The funnel worked in a world of scarcity of choice and information. This model of marketing was completely transactional; it was a means to an end.

FIGURE 3.1 Transactional marketing funnel

It was all about the company selling its products and services. Businesses were concerned only, initially, with the response and ultimately with the transactions that their marketing generated. Customers put up with the shouting because it provided them with information to which they had no other access.

As we have seen, however, the web and the ubiquity of the technology by which it can be accessed, has now provided almost all the information customers require and at their convenience. Consequently, they are less tolerant of companies shouting at them in the way they once did.

Companies that still resort to using the funnel model create a mismatch between the way they market themselves and the way their customers look for a new supplier. Previously, customers had limited access to information and were also very restricted by locality. Consequently, a buyer would have easy access to only a handful of options. Therefore, continual shouting at a potential customer had some intrinsic value for a company. Statistically, at any one time, the majority of consumers would not be in the market for a particular product or service. However, because of the limited choice available, there was a very good chance that, when ready to buy, they would remember your shouting, and subsequently your company. As a result, over the long term, there was the potential for a business to achieve a healthy return on investment from its shouting. Companies would shout via advertising, direct mail, inserts in newspapers, telemarketing, trade press etc, but these were the very resources customers would use to acquire much of their information; hence, materials were often kept, to be referred to at a later date.

Today, this is simply not the case. Consumers are no longer limited by the handful of suppliers they had previously. In most areas of our lives we now have thousands of options. Most people access these alternatives in two ways: first, via their network, consisting of friends, family, colleagues, online connections and companies with which they are already engaged, or second, browsing the web. Companies can shout frequently. However, it is far less likely today that this shouting will lead a customer to its door at the appropriate time. Sending out a direct mail will not generate a word-of-mouth referral and a business can send thousands of e-mails and still not be found when a potential customer is browsing the web. The funnel was more about the supplier than it ever was about the customer. This approach does not work in a world where the customer has been empowered. Today, customers expect more from you than just being shouted at.

Interestingly enough, the exception that always proved the rule was that of local takeaways, such as pizza, Chinese and curry. This is one of the rare occasions where we are extremely limited by locality, as most people are unwilling to drive too far to pick up a takeaway. Because there are very few options available, most people were prepared to rely on the menus that were put through their doors, rather than going online to find something, which traditionally was more of a hassle than referring to a leaflet. The menus provided householders with value, as they were a reliable source of information and, therefore, were kept for when they became relevant. However, with most people now having easy access to the web from their smart phones, this is changing. For example, over 50 per cent of Domino's Pizza orders, in the UK, are online and 20 per cent are now from mobile apps.[1]

The limitations of traditional 'relationship marketing'

The funnel model of marketing, which results in shouting at customers, is failing because it no longer provides any value for those it is targeting. Creating more value was first addressed by Leonard Berry, who in 1983 coined the term 'relationship marketing'.[2] Relationship marketing emphasized the role marketing played in not just acquiring clients, but retaining them over the long term. It recognized the enduring value of keeping customers and the significant impact it could make to a business's success. In fact, relationship marketing was not intended as a process for acquiring new customers at all. Rather, it was a mechanism for client retention. In other words, many of the businesses that advocate relationship marketing are still using transactional marketing and the traditional funnel to obtain new customers. Only once these customers are acquired is the relationship approach used to retain them.

The introduction of relationship marketing led to companies becoming increasingly concerned with providing good customer service. It also encouraged them to have a better understanding of their clients. This meant that companies took a more analytical approach to figuring out customer preferences and consequently targeted consumers with increasingly relevant messaging. This was aided by the advances in computer technology that made a more comprehensive database marketing approach viable. While many of these developments were positive, most companies' understanding of relationship marketing was unsatisfactory. Essentially, it amounted to companies continuing to shout at their database of clients, only this time the message was more targeted, and they used your first name. When analysed, the way most businesses implemented relationship marketing had little to do with developing any kind of relationship whatsoever.

Instead, as companies developed a greater knowledge of their customers, more targeted and personalized messages enabled businesses to up-sell and extract more value from them. Most companies, however, contacted their customers only in order to sell them something. While a more efficient approach to up-selling might have increased the number of customer transactions, this did not necessarily mean that a relationship was being developed. Essentially, for most businesses, what was called relationship marketing was ultimately a more sophisticated transactional approach to selling to a database of existing clients.

Moreover, acquiring a client through the transactional model of marketing makes the switch to a true relationship model difficult. This is because the company, inadvertently, has set the wrong tone for the relationship. After bombarding potential customers with a plethora of e-shots and mailings, it is no easy task to switch from the megaphone to the more intimate frame necessary to develop a relationship. The transactional approach to marketing, however it is dressed up, is about return on investment and getting customers to buy. Inherent in this is the implication that the deal is more important than anything else.

The mere fact that a business chooses to shout at its potential customers, despite the reality that most people find this increasingly obtrusive, speaks volumes about the company's regard for its potential patrons. A sudden switch from this to the suggestion that the relationship is paramount and that as a company you care is not perceived as genuine in the eyes of the customer. In other words, shouting at your clientele creates a barrier to subsequently developing any meaningful relationship, an impediment created by the company itself. In a world before the web, where most businesses shouted and customers were not empowered, this less than authentic approach was accepted. Basically, people had no other expectation. However, with the plethora of choice and information at everybody's fingertips today, consumers see through this less than genuine approach by which many companies continue to address them.

Striving for 'relationships' is not enough

So, in reality, relationship marketing has been a more targeted, cleverer transactional approach to existing customers. In a world of the web, digital technology and increased consumer empowerment, we need a more value-based model. However, most businesses have failed to do this. Many companies would acknowledge the requirement to give customers more value and strengthen relationships. Their lack of success in achieving this is because the term 'relationship' itself is unhelpful and misleading.

Allow me to explain. We all use a plethora of companies on a regular basis, with which we do not want a relationship. For example, I use Google for searching online, Tesco for shopping, MBNA for my credit card and O_2 for my mobile phone. Not a week goes by when I do not use the services of all these providers. However, I do not want a relationship with them, although they may want one with me. Being a regular user of these companies' services, I would imagine that, in marketing parlance, they would regard themselves as having a relationship with me. How do they measure that relationship? Is it when I make another transaction? Is it because I regularly use their product or service?

In our private lives, personal relationships are reciprocal; I like you and you like me. Over time, this evolves into a deep connectedness between two people. However, most companies' dealings with a customer are purely transactional. It just isn't the same. They give me something I want because I am paying for it. There is nothing more than that. As these companies learn more about me and my buying habits, I may be tempted with more relevant and enticing offers. This may mean that I spend more with them. This amounts to a sophisticated transactional approach, which is what relationship marketing has become. Having more data on me, and therefore being able to deliver increasingly relevant messages, does not constitute having a relationship.

For example, before switching to O_2 as my mobile provider, I had previously been with another company for a number of years. I used its service every day and spent a considerable amount of money with it. Occasionally I would call its customer service team with a problem or enquiry, and every year I entered into a dialogue when it came to upgrading my phone and renewing my contract. To all intents and purposes, this company would have assumed that it had a relationship with me. However, having decided there were better offers to be had elsewhere, I left the company in one phone call. I never complained, or gave any indication that this was about to happen. After years of patronage, I ended our perceived relationship in under five minutes.

It is hard to imagine a scenario where, after years of friendship with another human being, you would be prepared to end that relationship in a five-minute phone call, without any prior warning or indication that the relationship was in trouble. Personal relationships are not transactional in nature. They are entered into voluntarily by both sides and we generally place a great value on them. In my example with the mobile provider, this was simply not the case. The relationship was transactional. I was paying for the service that I received. Therefore, when I decided I could get better value elsewhere, I felt no obligation to my previous supplier. Having always paid for the service, I felt no duty of care. This being the case, in business the term 'relationship' is an unhelpful gauge for strategically understanding your company's position with its customers.

Understand, I am not suggesting that relationships in business do not matter. On the contrary, one-to-one interactions with customers take place in many companies. Whether you are a business owner, salesperson, customer service representative, receptionist, account manager or anyone else, it is important that you develop good relations with clients and prospects. The old adage, 'people buy people', is true. Therefore, it makes sense that any person who interacts with customers should be personable and provide their client with a pleasurable experience. Repeated contacts with an individual can lead to a relationship developing that will add value to a customer. In turn, this will increase the likelihood of customers spending more and staying with the business.

Not all companies have the opportunity to have a personal dialogue with their clients. Where applicable, these personal relationships are extremely important. When a company knows that these interactions take place, it should ensure that its staff are well trained and have the ability to handle these interactions effectively. These personal relationships become part of the way a company interacts with its customers. They are part of its strategy. *However, these relationships do not define the strategy.*

'Relationship' is a very passive word. Ultimately, all it means is being connected. Of course, every business is connected with every customer by the mere fact that they have bought something. The word 'relationship', though, is not helpful in defining a strategy for retaining customers. Being connected is not enough. Companies need a gauge for being able to measure just how connected they are. Relationships are the wrong measure for this. On the one hand, it is too passive a term. Being connected, in itself, is meaningless. On the other hand, it is inappropriate. With few exceptions, customers are not looking for the type of connectedness they obtain through personal relationships with friends and family. What we require is a term that measures connectedness based on value, which is the very basis for any interaction that takes place between company and client. Judging this by 'relationship' is not the right criterion.

Moreover, relationship marketing is not, and never has been, a strategy for acquiring customers at all. The world has moved on. Customers have more choice and access to information than ever before. Businesses have unprecedented technology, giving them the wherewithal to deliver better value to prospects and customers than they had previously. Today, in order to acquire new customers, companies need to leave the traditional funnel model of marketing behind. Companies need a framework more robust than relationship marketing for understanding the value they provide in order to retain their customers.

Introducing 'customer engagement' marketing

The model that answers these challenges is customer engagement. 'To engage' means to keep busy. Engagement implies that I am occupying my prospect or customer. Of course, they will participate only if they perceive they are receiving value. Thus, customer engagement is reciprocal. When we provide value to prospects and customers they, in turn, respond by giving of their time. This is an effective measure, because it means that a company is appraising the exact criterion that a consumer subconsciously uses to decide whether to interact with that business.

In order for customer engagement to be an effective strategy, companies must have a clear understanding of what we mean by the term 'value': value is simply when the cost of having or doing something is *less* than the cost of not having or doing it. In other words, I am better off spending my time or money doing this than not doing it because, by not doing it, I am missing out and consequently putting myself in a worse situation.

For example, I will deem it worthwhile spending two dollars on an ice cream if I perceive that, at that moment, my life would be worse off if I did not have the ice cream and I kept the two dollars. Similarly, a business may see value in spending $50,000 on a new IT infrastructure because without this spend it may fear that it will be unable to compete within its market and will therefore be worse off. In customer engagement terms, value can be ascertained with one simple question: 'If I were my customer, would I give up my time for this?'

Customer engagement involves finding value for your prospects and clients around the product or service that you provide. Today, simply concentrating your marketing on the product or service you offer is not enough. For example, if you run a recruitment company, simply talking about the services you offer will be of interest only to those people who currently require new members of staff. Your marketing, therefore, will have relevance only to those looking for a candidate now, which is exactly what happened in the transactional model of marketing. Everyone else would screen the message out as irrelevant.

Alternatively, by understanding the value you can provide, which relates to your product or service, you can widen your appeal and engage with those potential customers who currently have no interest in your actual product or service. So, for example, the recruitment company might produce tip sheets on subjects such as 'how to ensure you retain your best members of staff' or '10 ideas for improving staff morale'. These tip sheets would not be designed to promote their service but be of generic value to any company with employees.

Relationship marketing became a more sophisticated transactional approach because communications tended to relate directly to a purchase. Customer engagement is not based on an immediate transaction – it is purely value led. By offering potential customers and clients something worthwhile, on a frequent basis, a business builds trust and credibility with its audience. When a customer is ready to buy, it is likely that, at the very least, you will be one of the businesses to which they look as a potential supplier. When you have taken the opportunity to demonstrate your expertise and give value to a prospect, they may very well be predisposed to want to use you.

From 'return on investment' to 'return on engagement'

In the digital world, one of the scarcest resources available is customer attention. The demands of modern life, with e-mails, texts, phone calls, social networks, apps, 24-hour news, a multitude of television channels and a plethora of websites all available at any place and any time, mean that getting customers to take notice of you is extremely difficult. Of course, this means that it is equally challenging for everyone else, including your competitors. Once you have your customers' and potential customers' attention, you are much more likely to win their business at the appropriate time. The battle in the marketplace is no longer for transactions. Rather, it is for attention. Quite simply, those companies with customer attention win. Therefore, we need to replace the old model of marketing, which was measured by ROI (return on investment), with a new model based on ROE (return on engagement). For, if you are engaging with your audience, it means that you have their attention and, ultimately, this will lead to business growth.

The customer engagement model of marketing is a complete reversal of the traditional funnel. In fact, we turn the funnel 180 degrees so that it is completely on its head. What you are left with is the narrow spout at the top with the wide base at the bottom (Figure 3.2).

The narrow spout represents where prospects start engaging with us. We are no longer going to shout at them, for example by sending out 100,000 e-mails. Instead, they are going to come to us. It is far more likely that prospects will come to us: one, five or ten at a time. It is extremely unlikely that we will be approached by 100,000 people at once. Therefore, the spout at the top is very narrow, representing the far fewer prospects with whom we begin to engage at any one time. Once a prospect has, metaphorically, raised their hand and indicated that they would like to engage with us, they drop through the narrow spout into the wider base. In an ideal world, this base continues to grow wider and wider.

The reason the wide base is forever expanding is because, unlike the traditional funnel, we are not interested in qualifying anybody out. The scarcest resource for businesses today is customer attention. Those companies with the attention of their potential customers win. Therefore, the more attention we have, the better it is. Marketing today requires us to keep as many people engaged as possible.

Firstly, the more people we have engaged, the more customers we will eventually acquire. For example, if over time you ascertain that, statistically, 15 per cent of your engaged audience buy, then, of course, 15 per cent of 100 engaged prospects is a lot fewer than 15 per cent of 1,000. Secondly, people

FIGURE 3.2 Engagement marketing funnel

will engage with your business only if they are receiving value. Even if they do not become paying customers, some of these prospects will tell others about your company. Although many of your engaged audience will not be customers, some of them will be responsible for attracting new prospects and, therefore, delivering new customers and growing your business.

The cost of engagement before the ubiquity of modern technology would have been prohibitively high. Attempting to give value and stay in contact with potentially thousands of people would have been beyond what most companies could sensibly afford. Concentrating on transactions was the only option open to most businesses. However, utilizing all aspects of modern communications, distribution and advanced customer relationship management tools means that even the smallest business can engage with potentially millions of prospects at negligible cost.

In fact, not only does the customer engagement model of marketing not require prospects to be qualified out of the funnel, but ideally no prospect or customer would ever leave. Thus, the base would become increasingly wide. Of course, there will be natural attrition. In a business-to-consumer scenario, customers move away and disappear. In business-to-business, companies merge, are bought out and go bust. However, aside from this natural attrition, ideally a business will give enough ongoing value to keep all its prospects engaged.

This can be monitored. For example, website analytics packages can be used to track who visits your website, where they come from, what they look at and for how long etc. Social media monitoring software can make you aware of the online conversations involving your business and your market, and will allow you to track the reactions your company receives to the activities it undertakes. It will also allow your business to respond to the comments being made. In addition, customer relationship management software enables you to keep a detailed history of any interactions made directly with a customer. In so doing, you will gain insights as to how you will be able to offer and provide further value in the future.

Moreover, the development of 'social CRM', whereby the customer relationship management software brings up the public information about a person, means that whether it is from Twitter, Facebook, Google+, LinkedIn or wherever, you will obtain a more detailed understanding of individual customers. From being able to ascertain their age, their marital status, their interests or what football team they support, the information can be enlightening. It will help any business provide a more personal experience, as well as assist in understanding how value can be created. This can be used at an individual level as well as allowing you to observe the patterns that emerge regarding the client base as a whole.

If a company identifies that there is a certain point in their journey when people leave, then it would be required to do everything it can to prevent this from happening in the future. By asking consumers, a company should be able to realize why it is no longer able to provide value at this juncture, and then do its best to rectify this situation.

Engaging on your customers' terms

There is a myriad of platforms available with which to engage customers. Some may choose to access content from your website or blog, while others may choose to subscribe to e-mail newsletters or RSS feeds (Really Simple Syndication) of your content.[3] Meanwhile, others may choose to follow you on Twitter, enter into dialogue on a LinkedIn forum or industry website, 'hangout' with you on Google+ or connect with you via Facebook or another platform. The key is to identify the places that your prospects and customers like to visit and be available in those places. This could be a particular industry forum or a popular social network. Offline, this could translate into being present at the major industry events or belonging to a particular association. The point is that customers and prospects want to interact on their terms. By making yourself available on all the different platforms that your various customers and prospects enjoy using, you will make it easy to engage. Wherever they are is where you should be. If you offer the path of least resistance, it is much more likely that they will choose to take it.

A company may host offline seminars or online webinars. Alternatively, it may produce white papers, tip sheets or 'how to' articles. It may write powerful think pieces, create games, hold competitions or any number of alternatives. It is up to individual businesses to ascertain what combination of options will be of most value to their audience. Similarly, they will decide how often new ideas and material will need to be created in order to keep their public interested while at the same time not overloading them.

Of course, how often a business should engage with its customers will vary across companies and different groups of clients. However, the following three examples may provide a useful benchmark for the frequency and mechanism for engaging.

My local supermarket

My local supermarket engages with me every week. While for many businesses this would be far too frequent and become irritating, for my supermarket it does not seem out of place. This is because most people's interaction with their supermarket of choice is weekly. Generally, whether it is online or a visit to the store, most people will do a weekly shop. Therefore, even though every week may seem excessive, it still fits with the consumer's agenda.

In the main, the communication I receive from the supermarket is by way of coupons that discount products that I buy, or is directly related to purchases that I make. My use of its loyalty card ensures the supermarket is aware of the goods that I buy and, therefore, it sends me relevant offers. Although this is a very transactional way of engaging, with a supermarket, it makes sense.

This is because the nature of my interactions with the supermarket is solely transactional. My visit to the supermarket, whether online or offline, is a necessary weekly chore. I want to get in and out as quickly as possible. The way I relate to the supermarket is, therefore, also purely transactional. It does not seem inappropriate or too direct for the supermarket to take a transactional approach. Of course, if the supermarket sends me coupons for money off goods I was going to buy, this does provide me with value and encourages me not to explore alternative stores. By occasionally sending me related offers, the supermarket may also be able to gently nudge me into sometimes trying new product lines and spending a little more than I intended.

My intellectual property law firm

As an international speaker, author and consultant, my business often requires me to trademark certain terms and ideas. To this end, I use a law firm. If my law firm were to contact me every week I would go nuts! I do not have the desire or time to hear from them on a weekly basis. The nature of my work requires me to deal with my law firm, on average, on a quarterly basis. As the nature of my interaction with them is once in 13 weeks or so, how often can they contact me? I would suggest that if they were to contact me every six weeks, that would not be invasive. Of course, the communications would have to provide me with value.

If however, like the supermarket, they sent me money-off coupons, for example $10 off my next phone call, I would think they were mad. Although I obviously pay for the services they provide, my interactions with my law firm are not purely transactional. Rather, I look to them for expertise, consultancy and advice. It would therefore be more in keeping for them to engage me in this way. So, if I were invited to attend a relevant webinar on changes that will affect my business that are currently taking place in Europe, or they deliver an article on new developments for trademark owners in the United States, this would be far more appropriate.

My insurance broker

I buy a few products from my insurance broker each year, including house and car insurance. These are distress purchases, in that I have to buy them and I hope they are never used. On the basis that I only interact with my broker two or three times a year maximum, how often can they contact me? If my interactions are roughly every four months, I would suggest that it may only be appropriate for them to contact me four to six times during the year at most.

If my insurance broker tried to entice me with a webinar on the changing face of car insurance or a white paper on the developments in the house insurance market, I might think it was a joke. Although I don't like it when they try and explain why my premiums have gone up, I am not interested in the intricacies of their marketplace. For me insurance is a necessary purchase, which I want to buy as cheaply as possible. I also want the reassurance of knowing that, if it is needed, it will meet my expectations. Therefore, providing me with special deals for placing all my insurance needs with my broker or sending me 10 ways I can reduce my house insurance premium will most likely resonate.

Of course, this is not an exact science. Different customer groups may be treated differently within one organization. Meanwhile, there may be companies that find a way to engage more frequently with their prospects than my examples would suggest. If you find a cost-effective way to provide your clients with *real value* on a more frequent basis that really engages, then that is excellent. Moreover, companies should be providing value all the time by producing videos, podcasts, articles, webinars, games, offers and anything else that is appropriate. These should then be placed across the web on their own website, blog, company pages on social platforms, in forums and other relevant places.

Many customers and prospects may choose, of their own accord, to engage with these communications on a very regular basis. However, we are referring to the times when a business proactively looks to communicate with its own database via e-mail, phone call, text message etc. Even if these communications provide value, if they are too frequent, people will screen them out as they will not have the bandwidth with which to deal with them. Worse, if they do not provide value they will be deemed spam and your business will have lost that customer's attention, possibly for good. How often have you initiated an engagement with a business only for their efforts to permanently end up in your spam folder? Too many businesses send irrelevant newsletters that are never read, as a lazy attempt at 'staying in touch' with their clients and prospects.

One of the keys to making engagement work as a marketing strategy is to listen intently to the conversations your prospects and customers are having online and in the forums and networks in which they participate. This can be achieved by using social media monitoring software. In so doing, you will gain an understanding of your prospects and customers. When this is combined with what they tell you directly, it will enable you to ensure that all your communication is value led.

In this way, over time, your audience will be encouraged to sign up on your website, register on your blog, connect with you on Google+, Facebook or LinkedIn or follow you on Twitter. Engagement can work only if, over the long term, people reveal themselves to you. The more you can learn about your customers and prospects, both anecdotally and by asking questions, the more value you can deliver. Good data capture is essential. Without the ability to understand customer behaviour, likes and dislikes, and preferences, it will be extremely difficult to provide value on an ongoing basis.

Data capture is a long-term strategy. An attempt to ask customers for too many personal details when they have just discovered that you exist is likely to deter them. Rather, you can attempt to get a greater understanding of your customers and prospects gradually and over a long period of time. For example, if a visitor to your website is encouraged to sign up to receive access to an informative video and you ask them too many questions, they may very well not bother. Instead, on initial sign-up, you may simply require a name and e-mail address. Several months later, they may be interested in a variety of webinars. It could be that at this juncture it is relevant to ask them for a company name and the market sector in which they operate. If your business subsequently chooses to run some offline activities it would then be reasonable to ask them for a geographical location in order to inform potential clients of when you will be in their area. You can see that, over time, an enormous amount of data can potentially be collected, but this should not be attempted all in one go and on the first point of contact.

Similarly, customer behaviour can also be monitored. If certain pages of your website are never visited or are looked at infrequently and for a short period of time, it is possible that they are failing to give value and should be replaced. If a high proportion of your customers and engaged prospects regularly watch your videos but do not access many of your articles, that may be an indicator of the way in which they like you to communicate. The more knowledge and understanding you gather, the more relevant you can be and the increased value you can give. Thus, a virtuous circle is developed.

Becoming a trusted source of information

Giving value and engaging with prospects will eventually lead to business in a world of increased choice. Previously, when people were limited by the number of suppliers available, they would often see most or even all of them. In other words, if there were three major suppliers in my area for a particular service, it would make sense to see all three and then make a purchasing decision. Today, with very little effort, searching online can often uncover tens, hundreds or even thousands of suppliers when looking for a new service. The challenge is not finding what we want, but making sense of the inordinate amount of choice that we face. This is coupled with the fact that most of us are extremely time poor. In short, we rarely have the time to research extensively and educate ourselves about any particular market. In these circumstances, we rely on trusted sources of information.

If you are engaged with potential customers and providing them with value on a regular basis, you will have already built a certain amount of credibility with them. Over time, you become one of their trusted sources of information. When looking for a particular product or service that you supply, it is very likely that your engaged prospect will be predisposed to using you. In some cases, they may not even look elsewhere. In other cases, they may consider a few alternatives so as to benchmark what you provide. However, having regular engagement increases your chances of winning their business. Of course, this does not guarantee that you will obtain the order in every situation. However, by engaging with your prospects, giving them value and, therefore, winning their attention, you put yourself in an excellent position to acquire their business at the relevant time.

In a world of so much choice, the other source of reliable information is often our personal network – our friends, family, colleagues and online connections. When looking for a new supplier, we will often ask for our network's recommendations. These referrals come from trusted sources. Coupled with the fact that we are short of time, we are often predisposed to giving the business to those companies to whom we are referred. If they come across well and meet our expectations, we are very likely to use them. Word-of-mouth referrals are an extremely important source of new business. The more people we engage with, the more people will know about us. Some of those with whom we have built credibility and trust will provide us with referrals over time.

Finally, the more people with whom we engage, the more we will be talked about. This also increases the likelihood of content and materials that we create being shared. Online, these conversations and links to content make us easier to find on social networks and in the search engines. Engagement marketing aligns with the major ways that buyers look for and source new providers. Whether they are searching online, asking their networks or depending on reliable sources of information in order to make sense of the plethora of choices available, engagement marketing will raise the possibility that your business receives these enquiries.

The transactional funnel model of marketing was based on shouting very loudly in order to find clients to buy your wares. In this model, marketing was a means to an end. Return on investment was measured. It was purchases that counted.

The customer engagement model focuses on giving value around the product or services you deliver. This value is not tied to any purchase but is interesting to your audience in its own right. In this way, you become 'sticky' or attractive. When you do this on an ongoing basis, customers and prospects will keep wanting to interact with you. 'Sticky marketing', therefore, is a fundamental underlying principle of customer engagement.

In this model, marketing is not a means to an end; it is an end in itself. Value encourages people to interact with your business on a regular basis. Consequently, you will have their attention, a scarce resource but vital to a business. The new measurement is ROE (return on engagement). As long as your business is engaging with an increasing number of prospects and customers, this hard-won attention will result in your company thriving.

Key point summary

- Customer engagement marketing requires prospects and customers to participate. If you provide them with value, they will respond by giving of their time. Value can be ascertained with one simple question: 'If I were my customer, would I give up my time for this?'

- Value is created around the product or services that you provide. Today, merely concentrating your marketing on the product or service itself is not enough.

- The new marketing model is based on 'return on engagement'. If you are engaging with prospects and customers, it means that you have their attention. The new battle in marketing today is for customer attention.

- Unlike in the traditional funnel, the new model of marketing is inclusive. We do not wish to qualify anybody out. Many engaged prospects will contribute to word-of-mouth recommendations and, online, may contribute to helping us to be found through links, mentions etc.

- A good customer relationship management tool, incorporating 'social CRM', a website analytics package and social media monitoring software, is essential in enhancing your understanding of customers and prospects alike. This, in turn, will enable you to add value and engage with your clientele.

- One key to successful engagement is to identify the places that your prospects and customers like to visit, for example particular industry blogs, industry forums, social networks, events and industry associations. Having done this, you should have a presence in these places.

- The plethora of choice that consumers face means that we all rely on trusted sources of information that we use as filters. By regularly engaging with your clientele and providing them with value, over time you become one of those trusted sources.

- Marketing is not a means to an end; it is an end in itself. Value encourages people to interact with your business on a regular basis. Consequently, you will have their attention, a scarce resource today that is vital to business success.

PART THREE
Developing an effective marketing strategy

Benefits to problems

In 1961, at his inaugural address, President John F Kennedy famously said: 'Ask not what your country can do for you, but what you can do for your country.' This sentiment could be used to describe what marketing should be delivering today: 'Ask not what your marketing can do for you, but what your marketing can do for your customer.'

Becoming 'sticky' and adopting the customer engagement model of marketing, ie turning the funnel upside down, requires a change in approach from other traditional marketing conventions. Among these is the way in which messages are produced. Marketers have routinely focused on conveying the benefits of their product or service to potential buyers. This type of messaging is, by definition, transactional in nature.

Benefits are benefits only when you are ready to buy. For example, a human resources consultancy may communicate an array of benefits in using its service. It may emphasize the protection it can provide for your business against litigation, therefore keeping your business safe. It could stress its ability to make sure your company is compliant with current rules and regulations, mitigating the chances of receiving fines or facing other difficulties. Finally, it could articulate the work it undertakes in establishing efficient practices, saving both time and money. However, if you are not currently in the market for any HR service, or already have a supplier, these benefits are likely to be of little interest. In order to become 'sticky' and engage prospects and customers, you have to stop focusing on transactions and find value around the product or service you deliver.

Your product or service itself will only be of interest at the point someone is looking to buy. Moreover, once they have bought, information about what you do will have little relevance until such time as they are looking to make another purchase. In order to have dialogue both before a purchase is considered and after it has been made, the focus must be on the value surrounding your offering, rather than the offering itself. On this, benefit messaging completely fails.

An example of transactional marketing

For example, an owner of a car dealership offers to host a Chamber of Commerce event as a gesture of goodwill to the local business community. This, in itself, is a good example of engagement marketing. The owner provides great value for provincial companies by facilitating the hosting of an exciting event in their area. This action assists in beginning to establish a degree of credibility and trust. Meanwhile, an offshoot is that more people will have the opportunity to become familiar with the existence and location of the showroom as well as to see some of the products close up.

The head of the Chamber of Commerce asks the dealer, as the host, to welcome everybody and at the same time take the opportunity to say a few words about the showroom. Unfortunately, at this juncture, our dealer resorts to more traditional marketing conventions by introducing the audience to an attractive PowerPoint slide of the latest family saloon. During the welcome, the dealer spends just a few minutes speaking about the benefits of the car.

Our dealer presents the fact that it is the most fuel-efficient car in its class, which means that it is inexpensive to run and leaves more money in your pocket, and that it has the lowest emissions of any car currently on the market, which means that you can have a beautiful new saloon and still be adhering to environmental recommendations. The dealer proudly states that it has been voted the safest saloon in all the European tests, which means that it is the best car available to keep your family safe.

By concentrating on the benefits of the new car, the presentation is customer focused in that it relates to why the car will improve a customer's driving situation. However, it is also a transactionally focused presentation. It is all about why the car would make a good purchase. Benefits are benefits only when I am ready to buy. If I am sitting in the audience and am currently not looking for a new car, the presentation is irrelevant and, therefore, boring. As, statistically, most people will not currently be in the market for a new car, then isn't the welcome a waste of time?

It is highly likely that most of the audience will go home and simply forget about the presentation. This is a missed opportunity in a world where customer attention is so precious. It is possible, though, that the presentation may actually have had a detrimental effect. Forcing visitors to listen to irrelevant sales messages may result in the loss of some of the goodwill obtained by providing the car showroom to the Chamber in the first place.

The success of our dealer's speech relies solely on timing: ie someone in the room currently looking for a new car. Unless an individual makes an enquiry, very little will have been gained from the event. Knowing this, our dealer, a really good transactional marketer, also decides to hold a prize draw. On entering the venue, patrons are encouraged to place their business cards in a hat for the chance to win a bottle of champagne, thus allowing the car showroom to collect personal details of the attendees. This enables the dealer to follow up an unsuccessful presentation with a variety of spam e-mails. Anyone who left the showroom either apathetic or even with some goodwill is likely to be left disgruntled on receipt of repetitive, unwanted e-mails. This campaign is an example of transactional marketing. That is, shout at people about the benefits of your products and hope that someone buys. If a purchase was made as a result of this campaign, it would probably be deemed a success. Little consideration would be given to everybody else who is likely to have been left with a slightly sour taste in their mouths.

The alternative approach: providing value around your product or service

The customer engagement model of marketing would take a completely different approach. The focus would be on providing value for the customer rather than any short-term transaction. This cannot be done by concentrating on benefits, which by definition are about the product or service you sell.

Instead, this time our car dealer would think about the challenges and issues that all car drivers face. For example, they are confronted by increasingly high insurance premiums. They worry about road safety, especially those drivers who are transporting younger members of their family. Compliance and changing regulations, such as the laws regarding mobile phone use, provide other questions that need to be answered. Finally, the running of the vehicle and car maintenance matters; for example, how to achieve the best fuel consumption and minimize the wear on your tyres are perennial concerns.

All of these subjects could provide our car dealer with valuable material for a short presentation. He or she could talk about factors that will help reduce your car insurance, or the five top tips, unknown to most drivers, that would make them safer on the road. Alternatively, the dealer could chat about new regulations and mistakes people inadvertently make that are actually against the law, or could decide instead to convey expert recommendations about obtaining the optimum performance from your car.

No matter what subject our car dealer chooses to cover during the two-or three-minute welcome, the nature of the presentation changes completely. By getting information that is useful to all drivers, the audience gains value and is therefore more likely to regard the car brand and showroom in a favourable light. The car dealer, by presenting this material, demonstrates the firm's knowledge in its field, which in turn helps to build trust. In so doing, it increases the likelihood that next time a member of this Chamber of Commerce requires advice about a car, they will visit this showroom.

Moreover, by providing the audience with value, our car dealer can offer as a follow-up something more substantial than a bottle of champagne and spam e-mails. By creating a tip sheet and announcing its availability on the firm's website, our dealer gives members of the audience a reason to engage further. In fact, our car dealer could produce other tip sheets on different subjects, which can also be downloaded from the site. Those attendees who provide their e-mail address in order to receive the download would have initiated the beginnings of customer engagement. Not only is it possible that some people may choose to share these tip sheets with others, but they can also be used as mini articles that can be placed on other websites and in magazines, with links back to the showroom's own website. The presentation could even be recorded and posted on a platform like YouTube, eg 'The best way to improve your vehicle's fuel consumption'. Dealing with universal problems that drivers face gives the material wide appeal, making it more likely that it will be watched and shared.

Thus, a short presentation can be the catalyst for starting valuable customer engagement with a number of members of the audience, as well as providing an array of other opportunities to use the material. By imparting good information and providing consistent value, our car dealer's content will be used and shared, and its base of engaged customers will grow. As this engagement develops, it will become a trusted source and filter of information about 'all things cars' for this particular group of people. Over time, some of these people will buy from the dealer, while others may refer this particular showroom to individuals in their network. A presentation with this result could never be created by concentrating on benefits.

The shortcomings of benefit messaging

Benefits will not help you understand the value around what you do or provide an insight into the universal issues that your customer experiences. Benefits merely focus on the transaction, dispensing reasons as to why a customer should buy a particular product or service. Thinking in terms of benefits will not help you in looking at the wider concerns of a prospect and so being able to take a more holistic approach. A focus on benefits will not help a business establish a customer engagement approach to its marketing. Our car dealer's successful presentation was arrived at by understanding the challenges and problems that the audience faced. Benefits are benefits only when I am ready to buy. Challenges and problems are more universal. For example:

- I may not be in the market for a car right now, but I would like to achieve better fuel consumption with my current vehicle.
- I may not want to buy a brand new suit today, but I would like to know how to make the best of my existing wardrobe.
- I may not be looking to change my accountant, but I am interested in benchmarking their performance and seeing if I am paying too much tax.

Not only does a problem approach allow you to understand the value around your product or service, it more accurately reflects the way in which people search online.

In fact, in the main, people have two iterations when making a purchase. In the first instance, they will undertake research: that is, browse the web and ask friends and colleagues, in order to gather information and obtain a better understanding of the market. Once they have made a decision on the product or service they require, and the price they are willing to pay, a second iteration will be to look for a supplier that meets the purchasing criteria upon which they have decided.

By creating value around the purchase, it is more likely that a business will be able to engage clients when they are researching the market. In helping to educate a prospect, a company has a chance to influence that individual's criteria for purchase. In turn, this makes it more likely that the company will be a desirable supplier later down the line. Moreover, by being able to provide a prospect with value at the beginning of the purchasing journey, a business has a chance to build some credibility and trust with a potential customer.

Of course, this does not guarantee that a company receives the business. It does, however, make it much more likely that it will be considered when the prospect is ready to purchase. This is all anyone can ask of their marketing. If every time a potential customer is making a purchase, your company is one of the considered suppliers, then your marketing is working.

A website solely dedicated to the benefits of a product or service is far less likely to engage at the first iteration of search: that is, the information-gathering stage. Therefore, it makes it harder for the company to influence the purchasing criteria or elicit any credibility and trust. Even if the prospects revisit the site, or find the site at the second iteration when they are ready to purchase, at that juncture the supplier is engaged in much more of a commodity sale based on criteria such as price. The opportunity to add value and create differentiation is more likely to have dissipated.

It is also important to understand people's mindset when they search. Many will have particular preferences for websites they use to catch up on news or use for entertainment. However, when people search online, looking for something new, it is more often than not that they have a problem in mind. For example:

- I may search cinema listings: *Issue?* Where am I going on Friday night?

- I may search for the weather: *Issue?* What am I going to wear tomorrow?

- I may search on traffic reports: *Issue?* What time do I need to leave my house in order to arrive at my meeting on time?

So, for example, people could be searching the web for local accountants. There may be a variety of issues on their minds. It could be that they feel dissatisfied with the current service they are receiving and want to know what else is available. Alternatively, they may be unhappy with the level of tax they are paying. Of course, it could also be that they are looking for an accountant for the first time and are researching to learn about the possible options. Landing on a home page that details the benefits of a particular firm is unlikely to resonate with a potential client. For example, typical messages may focus on:

- the personal and friendly service this particular firm provides;
- its aim to save you money on your tax bill;
- the formidable range of expertise and experience it can provide.

These messages, however, are merely platitudes. No accountancy firm is likely to claim that it provides an unfriendly service, doesn't wish to save you any money or has no experience or expertise to offer its clients. Therefore, these messages are bland and meaningless. Moreover, it is unlikely that the primary aim of any search is to find the friendliest accountant or the one that makes the most outlandish claims with regard to how much money it may be able to save.

Ask the right question

A far better approach, therefore, is to focus on the issues potential clients are likely to have when initiating their search. So, for example, a home page may ask three pertinent questions, with links the user can click to find the answers:

- Are you receiving a good service from your accountant? Click here for the 10 top deliverables that all accountants should provide.
- Are you paying too much tax? Answer our online questionnaire for an immediate idea as to whether you might be overpaying.
- Looking for a new accountant? Here are the five questions you should be asking every potential supplier.

It is far more likely that this approach will engage a new visitor to the site. It does not provide platitudes or meaningless promises in which a customer is not interested. Rather, the content aligns itself with the type of questions prospects are likely to be asking themselves. Of course, by talking with clients and using web analytics that will provide details of the links visitors click on and the ones they ignore, you can constantly strive to perfect the messaging on your website. The principle, however, is sound. By thinking about the problems that your customers face, it is far more likely that your communications, whether online or offline, will align with any potential buyer's thought processes. In so doing, it will be much easier to engage with that prospect.

It is only by thinking in terms of problems that you will understand the wider value you can provide for a customer, built around what you do, rather than focusing on the product or service itself. It is this added value, not based on transactions, that will engage potential customers and enable you to build an ever-widening group of people who regularly interact with your business. This will allow you to turn the funnel on its head, engaging with a growing number of people, some of whom will share your content and refer you to others. Moreover, when they are ready to buy, it is more likely that, at the very least, you will receive an enquiry. The irony is that in a world where there is an abundance of choice, it is impossible to research all the options available. In this scenario, time pressure often means that, on many occasions, people do not exercise their choice at all. Therefore, if you have built up credibility and trust with a customer with whom you are regularly engaged, there is a very good chance that when they are ready to buy, you will receive the sale.

Problem Maps®

This being the case, a mechanism is required for being able to identify the issues that you solve for a customer and the value that can be created around these challenges. This can then be used as the basis of your customer engagement model. So let me introduce you to Problem Maps.[2]

Problem Maps are exactly this: they are a way of being able to understand the issues that start to lead a customer towards a purchase. They will also enable you to understand the value around your product or service in order to then come up with ideas and messages that will work within the customer engagement model. So let me explain how a Problem Map works.

First, you need to draw a 16-box matrix as seen in Table 4.1. Alternatively, these can be downloaded from our website, stickymarketing.com.

You start filling out a Problem Map by considering four headline problems your potential customers may have and that you know you can solve. This is not about you; it is an exercise focused solely on your customer. It forces you to put yourself in your customer's shoes. These headline problems are issues that perennially challenge many typical prospects and customers. All four headline problems must be different.

Once you have entered these four headlines, you then need to identify three issues that result from each of the initial headlines. In every vertical column, the three resulting problems under each headline must also be different. In other words, once completed, each vertical column will contain four unique issues. However, resulting problems may be repeated under different headlines in other vertical columns. Therefore, although there are 16 boxes in your Problem Map grid, you will have fewer unique problems. As a guide, a typical Problem Map will contain 10–13 unique issues.

TABLE 4.1 Problem Map® template

	Headline Problem #1	Headline Problem #2	Headline Problem #3	Headline Problem #4
Headline Problem				
Resulting Problem 'A'				
Resulting Problem 'B'				
Resulting Problem 'C'				

© Grant Leboff

Table 4.2 is an example of a Problem Map for a company we will name Jellybox Call Answering Service, a company providing call-answering services for businesses.

You can see that we have the four headline problems across the top, which are all different, and then underneath we have the three resulting problems. In every vertical column all four problems are different. However, in the horizontal 'Resulting Problem' columns, there is some overlap. So although, potentially, there could be 16 unique issues, in this case there are only 14.

When you are preparing a Problem Map it is important not to be lazy and merely repeat the same resulting issues in various columns, because the result will be only seven or eight unique issues. On the other hand, you should expect there to be some overlap. Inevitably these problems are going to be connected, and that should result in some repetition.

Looking at the Problem Map, there are certain key areas we can identify where Jellybox adds value:

- It is a solution for small businesses to maintain a professional image and to better manage their time.
- It is a solution for bigger companies to save money, manage their resources more effectively and, therefore, become more competitive.

TABLE 4.2 Jellybox Problem Map®

	Headline Problem #1	Headline Problem #2	Headline Problem #3	Headline Problem #4
Headline Problem	I sometimes miss calls because we are a small company and not always available.	I am spending more money on receptionists than I would like.	I need my calls screened, but cannot afford a PA.	I struggle to deal with peaks and troughs in my business.
Resulting Problem 'A'	People get the answerphone, which makes us look amateur.	I end up wasting company resources on staff I don't need.	I end up wasting valuable time on calls I shouldn't take.	I end up wasting company resources on staff I don't need.
Resulting Problem 'B'	Opportunities go missing, because some people do not like leaving a message.	I have less money to divert into other areas of the business.	I miss important calls, which annoys my customers.	Sometimes we miss opportunities because we are unable to cope with the call volume.
Resulting Problem 'C'	I struggle to manage my time properly in the day as I am often distracted.	We carry a bigger overhead, so it is harder to be more competitive in the market.	I struggle to manage my time properly in the day as I am often distracted.	It affects other areas of the business, as members of staff are diverted away from important tasks.

- It is a way for any company to be able to manage the dynamics of their business cycle.

Competing with bigger companies, managing time better, saving money, becoming more competitive and managing the dynamics of the business cycle are perennial issues that many people are concerned about all the time, not just if they are in the market for call-answering services.

The Problem Map presents all sorts of opportunities for Jellybox to start engaging with companies within its target market areas. For example, it can produce a series of tip sheets, podcasts, videos and articles called 'How to present your small company in the right way'. By partnering with other providers of services it could produce some really engaging material that many small business websites, publications and associations would be happy to promote and distribute to their own members because it would add value. In turn, all of this may encourage people to engage with Jellybox and visit its website in order to receive other valuable material. It is even possible that some prospects will consider using a call-answering service, even though it had not previously occurred to them.

Using other providers and partnering with them, it can organize a seminar or a webinar online, aimed at finance directors and procurement departments, providing many ways of cutting costs off the bottom line. It could also partner with relevant associations and industry bodies who would invite their members to participate in this webinar or seminar. Therefore, no shouting needs to take place in order to get attendees there and give value.

Jellybox could employ a market research firm to do some investigation into how businesses, in certain industries that are seasonal etc, cope with the peaks and troughs of the business cycle. It would uncover the challenges they have and the solutions they employ. Relevant research like this can often create a story that leads to successful PR and articles being written for various publications. This is because independent research such as this carries credibility. This research would then be available for download on the Jellybox website, another way of initiating customer engagement.

Once you have a Problem Map, you can really understand the value you can deliver around your product or service, and use this as the start of your customer engagement strategy. The key is always to put the customer first and make sure you are relevant and providing value.

Using Problem Maps® as the basis for engagement

Using Problem Maps provides you with a mechanism for understanding your product or service through the eyes of a customer. This insight then enables a business to create value around its core offering, with which to engage prospects and customers alike. We can demonstrate this in the case of a neighbourhood burger bar, which we will call Benny's Burgers.

CASE STUDY   Example case study: Benny's Burgers

Let's set the scene; Benny's Burgers is an independent burger bar run by a husband and wife team. Their vision is to produce burgers and chips, offering fast food but in a very healthy way, using fresh organic meat, fresh salads etc, the idea being that parents can feel good about taking their children there. They open up in a local market and start their marketing by leafleting the area. Their messaging is entirely 'benefit' led:

- Fresh organic meat – you get a healthy meal that tastes great!

- Variety menus – three-course meals that don't break the bank!

- A large car park and easy access – so it is a stress-free experience!

Now of course, unless I am in the market for burger and chips at that very moment, this messaging – in my day-to-day life – is probably not that relevant. It is very transactionally based. Shouting about their new bar does not get them very far. People don't come, and the owners become disillusioned when customers fail to appear. It is time for Benny's Burgers to take a customer engagement approach by turning the funnel on its head. This process necessarily starts with a Problem Map.

Marketing solutions to the problems

Looking at the Problem Map in Table 4.3, it becomes clear that Benny's Burgers is a children's brand. Most of the problems involve feeding, occupying or marking special occasions with the kids. However, Benny's Burgers is unknown. It is also not the only brand in its area that provides activity displacement for children or ways to mark special occasions for the family. So how can it give value and engage its customers? One possible way is by leveraging partnerships.

TABLE 4.3 Benny's Burgers Problem Map®

	Headline Problem #1	Headline Problem #2	Headline Problem #3	Headline Problem #4
Headline Problem	I need to feed the family and I'm just too tired to cook today.	The weather is lousy and the kids are driving me nuts!	I'm pushed for time and the kids need feeding.	How do we mark a special occasion for the whole family?
Resulting Problem 'A'	I become even more irritable and tired as I have to cook the dinner.	I am becoming increasingly short tempered as I have run out of things that we can do together.	I end up running late for an activity or meeting.	I don't want a bad atmosphere because someone isn't having a good time.
Resulting Problem 'B'	I start to feel a bit depressed as the chores never seem to end.	I am scared that someone is going to get hurt soon because the kids are getting increasingly wild as they become more frustrated.	I end up cooking a microwave dinner, which I really want to avoid.	I need to find somewhere affordable. We can't keep spending loads of money when going out. It becomes prohibitive.
Resulting Problem 'C'	My mood is having a bad effect on the rest of the family.	I am sure we are going to have a family argument in a minute and there is going to be a bad atmosphere because everyone is just pent-up and stuck indoors.	I'm getting stressed out and this is leading to arguments in the house.	I don't want the occasion to pass by and do nothing.

It is springtime. Benny's Burgers draws a 20-mile radius from its restaurant and investigates all of the activity-displacement provision for children in its area. It approaches all of the providers and proposes to promote their activities to its own customers if the right special offers can be agreed. Having decided on promotions with 10 particular companies, Benny's Burgers produces an attractive flyer entitled '10 things to do with your kids this summer', which focuses on the particular area in which it is based. This flyer contains offers that can be redeemed by way of coupons. For example: visit the zoo and a second child gets in free, one free regular popcorn when you visit the cinema for a children's matinee, £10 off a family ticket for the theme park on Mondays and Tuesdays etc. This flyer is then posted on its website and optimized in order to be found by the online search engines. This is achieved by using key words based around children's activities in its local area.

Benny's Burgers also successfully obtains coverage in the local paper. Each week of the summer holidays, the paper prints one coupon with a small feature related to the particular activity. At the bottom of each article it mentions that more offers like this can be downloaded from Benny's Burgers' website. Also, some of the companies with whom Benny's Burgers partners are happy to carry links on their website to Benny's Burgers' website, as are some local interest and community sites.

In order for parents to be able to cut out the coupons and use them at the appropriate destinations, they are requested simply to provide a name and e-mail address, and then the flyer is sent to them via e-mail. While the 10 offers have nothing to do with Benny's Burgers, there is a bonus, offer Number 11, which provides special discounts at Benny's Burgers' restaurant. This promotion leads to numerous downloads of the flyer. Word of mouth is also generated as parents start to tell others about the availability of the coupons. The owners of Benny's Burgers start to see new customers visiting their restaurant and redeeming some of the vouchers.

This campaign benefits Benny's Burgers in a number of ways. It starts to position itself as a leading children's brand in its local area, generating a lot of goodwill with customers because of the enormous value it is imparting. By being associated with more established brands in its locality, it starts to gain credibility and trust, far exceeding what a new restaurant in its area would expect. The campaign attracts customers and engages many people. However, this is not about burgers and chips. This is about understanding the problems that its customers face and engaging customers by providing them with value associated with these issues.

Creating value

This example sees the funnel model being turned upside down. Benny's Burgers shouted at no one. Instead it has become attractive by creating value within a niche market and being discovered through search engines, the local paper and by word of mouth. As more people download the offers, thereby engaging with Benny's Burgers, its funnel becomes wider and wider.

By the end of the summer, Benny's Burgers has developed a large permission-based e-mail list. At this juncture, many companies would be tempted to send out regular special offers for the burger bar. This, however, would be a step back into the old world of transactional marketing. Messages relaying special offers are of no value unless you want to purchase a burger and chips at that moment. Moreover, however attractive the offers, regular receipt could become tiresome to even the most loyal of customers. Instead, Benny's Burgers continues with the customer engagement model. It commissions a designer to put together a series of mini activity booklets containing puzzles, quizzes, colouring, word searches and other exercises for children. During the winter, when the weekend weather report is bad, Benny's Burgers e-mails its booklet for parents to print off and be able to spend some time with their children. Although each activity booklet does contain a coupon with an offer for Benny's Burgers, that is not the focus of the communication. It is not about promoting burgers and chips, but providing value for the client.

These booklets are not just found on Benny's Burgers' website, but are also placed on some local community sites. As parents mention these booklets to others in conversation, and as children see them at friends' houses, some word of mouth is also created. The upside-down funnel continues to get wider. Benny's Burgers keeps its customers engaged and attracts new ones by focusing on providing value.

It is establishing itself as a major children's brand in its area, and its restaurant is becoming busier. Its marketing, however, is not a means to an end, a way of just selling more product. By creating value, it engages customers, but the special coupons and activity booklets can be used without any purchase ever taking place. In other words, the marketing is an end in itself. It creates its own value. It is no longer about burgers and chips, or alternatively, as Steve Jones of the Sex Pistols said in 1978, 'It's got nothing to do with music, you silly cow!'

Key point summary

- 'Ask not what your marketing can do for you but what your marketing can do for your customer.' Marketing is now an end in itself. It must create value in its own right.

- Benefits merely focus on transactions, dispensing reasons as to why a customer should buy a particular product or service. They will not help in creating value around what you do because they do not provide an insight into the universal issues that your customer experiences.

- When people search for information online, they normally have an issue in mind. For example, they may enter cinema listings into the Google search bar, but their concern is what they will be doing at the weekend.

- When you think in terms of problems that your customers face, it is far more likely that your communication will resonate with them. In so doing, it will become much easier to engage.

- Problem Maps® provide a mechanism for understanding your product or service through the eyes of a potential customer. This insight then enables a business to create value around its core offering, and so to engage customers and prospects alike.

- The key to engagement is always to put the customer first, by making sure that all communication is relevant and provides value.

Products to experiences

Before the Second World War, the Western industrialized economies were product economies. More people were employed in the making of products than any other sector of the market. Differentiation, when purchasing, was mainly based on the quality and characteristics of the product. There was very little else to be taken into consideration when making a purchase. In a world of limited choice, customer expectation was relatively low.

After the Second World War, the Western industrialized countries began to develop into service economies. By the end of the 1950s more people were working in the service sector than anywhere else.[1] As the availability of products increased, and subsequently prices declined, they became increasingly commoditized. It was, therefore, the service delivery around these products that became more influential when making purchasing decisions. This new emphasis was borne out by companies that started to change the focus of their business. For example, IBM consciously repositioned itself from a manufacturer of products to a service company delivering business solutions.[2] Customers were less concerned with the quality and features of a particular product as the offerings became increasingly similar. It was other aspects of the purchase, such as free delivery, home installation or the availability of post-sales support, that became important when deciding on which item to buy.

Today, technology and the web are changing where the perceived value in a purchase lies. Technology has enabled individuals to start businesses with very little capital investment. This is compounded by the new economic realities of the world in which we live. One of the major motivations in working for others was job security. Today however, even the biggest corporations cannot offer the job security and guarantees of yesteryear. The result is that one of the major barriers preventing people from starting their own business, ie the perceived risk involved, has, to a large degree, been removed. There are, therefore, more people starting companies at home or working from small offices than in any previous age.

With an increase in suppliers, and therefore more choice for customers, services have largely become commoditized. This has led to companies offering their customers progressive levels of convenience, speed, support etc, the result being that customers' expectations rise as profit margins fall. This has led to whole areas of service being outsourced. Outsourcing is a way for companies to provide services for their customers, for example 24-hour telephone support, while still making healthy profits, because it lowers the cost of delivery.

Offshoring is another trend attempting to achieve the same outcome. For example, many Western companies started to base their call centres in countries such as India. However, in many ways this has accelerated the commoditization of service. As more companies outsource services to similar business-processing outsource companies across the globe, their focus is on delivering acceptable levels of service at an affordable cost, rather than creating anything special. Thus, over time, whole market sectors are delivering a similar service, from a similar provider, thousands of miles from where their customers live.

The web has, perhaps, been the final stage of this commoditization of services. The speed and convenience that the web provides makes it a primary resource for the sourcing and purchasing of both products and services. However, the web also creates commoditization as both products and services are distilled into similar, easily accessible promises that make the same claims regardless of the company.

With the emergence of comparison websites, products and services are condensed into comparable tables of analytics: in other words, delivery, date, availability, colour, price etc. The web has also, in many cases, lowered the cost of delivery. The result of all of this is that customers put less value on good service; it becomes merely something that they expect.

For example, with the emergence of sites such as Amazon, service delivery has become incredibly efficient. Customers can choose to pay for 'next day delivery' or, alternatively, wait a few days at no cost. Whatever the option, customers can follow the progress of their package online. From the moment the product is ordered to its dispatch and its progress through the system until its final delivery, your package can be traced at all times. Once service delivery becomes this efficient there is nowhere else to go. As an increasing number of companies deem it necessary to offer this level of service, it becomes expected and commoditized. With the amount of choice customers have, they know there will always be a supplier, somewhere, who will deliver what they require. As companies try to compete online, the effect of all this is that often the only clear differential on the web is price.

The move from selling products to services did not affect the traditional transactional model of marketing. Instead of shouting about a product's benefits, companies merely emphasized the service delivery aspects of their offering, in order to entice people to buy. The messages, however, were still about the transaction: 'this is what you will receive when you buy.'

'Sticky marketing' does not work by shouting about the benefits of a transaction. Instead, the funnel is turned upside down and customers are attracted to your business. Once attracted to you, engagement can take place and, over time, many prospects will become customers. However, in order to attract prospects, value that relates to the products and services you provide must be created. Communications are not merely about the transaction itself.

Whether you sell burgers and chips, accounting services, management consultancy, jewellery or anything else, people will be no more interested in your service than they are in the product unless they are in the market to buy. Ultimately, understanding how I will be looked after as a customer matters only at the point at which I want to find a provider.

The value is in the experience

In short, while products have been commodities for a long time, technology and the web have commoditized services. This has led to a shift in what customers now hold in high regard. The value is no longer in the product or service that you deliver to your customers, but in the experience that they receive when engaging with your business.

For example, a restaurant in an amazing location and with a wonderful view will be able to charge more than an equivalent restaurant that lacks these other assets. Although the food and service may be the same, the experience will not be. The restaurant providing the view will be able to charge more for giving its customers a superior experience – and customers will be willing to pay for it.

Take passengers who fly business class. They still arrive at the same destination at the same time as those flying economy. Is it worth paying significantly more money simply to receive extra legroom? But of course, this is not what customers are paying for at all. Business-class passengers receive a faster check-in and a quiet lounge. Once on the plane, they enjoy a comfortable seat with more legroom and a better quality of food and drink. On landing, they disembark first and their luggage receives priority, thus minimizing their wait. Customers are paying for a whole experience that leaves them less tired and more relaxed than many of the passengers in the economy-class cabin.

Of course, one could argue that paying for better views in restaurants or for a superior flying experience has been happening for many years. This is true. The difference, however, is that today the experience is the primary aspect that matters. It is where the value exists. In a world before products and services were commoditized, the main concern of most people was being able to 'join the party'. In other words, when Henry Ford offered customers a car only in black,[3] they didn't care. By reducing the cost of production, Henry Ford gave many Americans an opportunity to own a car, something they could not have done previously. In this context, the aesthetics of colour were of little concern.

With the commoditization of products and services, this is no longer the case. In the Western industrialized world, apart from the most disadvantaged in our society, the majority of individuals can attend 'most parties'. For example, going abroad for a vacation is no longer the prerogative of the rich. In Europe, since 1992 low-cost air travel has been available to most people. The difference between flying with a no-frills airline or a more expensive alternative is not about the destination one can visit. For example, they both fly to Madrid. Neither is it about safety, because both airlines comply with the same safety regulations. The difference is whether one is given an allocated seat, the amount of legroom assigned, whether the chair reclines, the in-flight service of food and drink, the availability of facilities such as films and entertainment, and the offerings of newspapers and magazines. In other words, the difference between the two is the experience.

Whether it is being able to buy modern technology such as computers and mobile phones, or being able to enjoy leisure activities such as meals out and visits to the cinema, price is no longer a barrier for most people. There is normally a solution available in all price brackets. Moreover, many similar products or services charge very similar prices. The difference between these today is more subtle.

For example, with mobile phones and computers it may be the aesthetics and usability of the particular device. In leisure activities, it may be the comfort of the seats, the view on offer or the quality of the ingredients. In other words, there is no value in merely enabling us to partake in these activities; most of us can. The value comes from the nuance within the offering; in other words, the experience provided.

Developing the experience

So, in order to avoid being commoditized and to be able to embrace the new engagement model of marketing, companies need to move away from products and services into delivering experiences. For example, take our two similar restaurants. Merely communicating the benefits of the food and service will not engage a customer. These aspects become interesting only when people are looking for somewhere to eat, having made an active decision to buy. Moreover, it is likely that both restaurants will make very similar claims about the quality of their food and service, making it difficult to tell them apart. However, the magnificent grounds in which the first restaurant is located may make it a wonderful setting for a romantic meal. It may be this aspect that the restaurant decides to deliver to its patrons: 'give your partner the ultimate romantic experience.'

By focusing on this, the restaurant will then concentrate on achieving the right ambiance, using lighting, décor, music etc. However, the need to deliver a proper experience becomes all-encompassing. The romantic idea will necessarily influence everything from the food that is served (more meals for two to share) to the names of the dishes. Whether it is what the staff wear or their training in interacting with the clientele, everything must be taken into consideration. It is only by looking at all aspects of the restaurant's communications with its customers that it can ensure the idea is executed well.

Once the restaurant defines itself by delivering the ultimate romantic experience, it can then look to create value around this offering. The restaurant could position itself as a hub for romantic experiences in the area. It could provide tips, articles and fact sheets giving people ideas on how to mark important occasions for that special someone. These could be made available on its website. It may also be able to supply this information to other businesses that would find it valuable for their customers. For example, local beauty salons and spas may be willing to carry some information by providing articles or tips in their waiting rooms. By partnering with flower shops, beauty salons, chocolate suppliers, jewellery stores, luxury spas and agents for romantic holidays and weekend breaks, the restaurant could make it easy for customers to act on its suggestions.

Moreover, the restaurant could host themed evenings featuring ideas such as live music, chocolate indulgence or romance from other cultures. In this way, the restaurant would have content and offerings with which it could build an active engagement with a growing customer database. This experience, however, would not be merely about the food or service that the restaurant provides. In today's world of choice, they *have* to be good. On their own, though, they are not enough to ensure the restaurant's popularity. For the engagement model of marketing to work, an experience must be delivered. From this, wider value can be created that provides a reason for customers and prospects to want to interact with a business.

The importance of strategic partnerships

This example highlights another aspect of the engagement model of marketing: that is, you do not have to, and you probably cannot, do it alone. Partnering with other companies enables you to deliver value and maintain an engagement with prospects and customers alike. By taking this approach, engagement can be continued at very minimal cost. Meanwhile, your strategic partners have their own opportunities for business development, which otherwise would not have existed.

This is in stark contrast to the old model of marketing. Traditionally, a company would have products or services to sell. Having identified a target audience, it would then shout at these people. Those who became customers might then, in the future, receive special offers. However, all of this messaging tended to be transactional. It revolved around purchases being made.

This transactional model of marketing relied on capturing attention at the moment a prospect was ready to buy. However, the ubiquity of available products and services, together with the access to information that we all enjoy, means that these marketing messages provide us with less value than ever before. Modern technology has increased the channels of communication available to us all. It has also meant that communication is no longer isolated to when we are behind our desks or in our homes. People make phone calls from their cars, send e-mails from the train, text while walking down the street and surf the web while standing in queues. Customers no longer simply react to the marketing messages that are 'shouted' at them. The customer journey today is more likely to start with individuals undertaking a search at their convenience. Consequently, the most precious resource a company can now acquire is customer attention. The companies that receive regular attention from prospects and customers will be the real winners in this digital age. Whereas traditional marketing valued the transactions that could be made as a result of a campaign (return on investment) today, successful companies should measure the ongoing engagement they have with their prospects and customers (return on engagement).

Therefore, partnerships are a vital ingredient in making your marketing 'sticky'. They allow a business to provide more value to its customers and prospects. This increases the likelihood of their remaining engaged. In turn, this becomes a self-fulfilling prophecy. The more engagement and attention any one company has from its customer base, the more value it can bring to potential partners, who will therefore be more receptive to entering into an alliance. This provides a business with two opportunities: 1) you can keep adding value, through strategic partners, at little cost; 2) there is potential to earn passive income from any transactions a partner makes through your business. Of course, this would depend on the nature of any deal established.

Experiences are not limited to any one aspect of a company's offering. Whether it is engagement with a prospect before any purchase has been made, or interaction with a customer during or after a sale, experiences need to be delivered. For example, Amazon allows you to rate the books it sells on its website. This adds another dimension to a customer's reading experience. It provides purchasers with a platform to deliver their own personal view and response to reading a book. Merely giving customers this platform demonstrates that Amazon believes that its clients matter. This sharing of opinion also provides a better experience for potential purchasers of a book. Would-be customers, on the Amazon site, have the opportunity to learn from the wider community before making a purchase. This development of providing experiences, by supplying customers with a platform to become involved, is not confined just to the web.

For example, some of the most popular television shows of the past few years, such as *Big Brother, Britain's Got Talent, American Idol* and *X Factor*, all have one aspect in common. The audiences are encouraged to have their say by voting for their favourite contestant. In other words, the outcome is decided by the viewers rather than by TV producers. This involvement, however, is not restricted merely to voting on the programme. Both during the show and afterwards, viewers remain engaged, commenting on blogs, forums and on social networks such as Twitter and Facebook.[4]

In fact, television is increasingly becoming a 'two-screen experience'. While viewers watch the television on one screen they will use a second screen (such as a smart phone or iPad) to browse relevant facts, make comments and contribute in some way to the programme and watching experience. For example, in 2011 Heineken successfully launched its 'Star Player App', which allowed viewers of European Champions League football games to speculate when goals would be scored, predict other match outcomes and answer related questions to the game. This all happened in real time while the game was taking place. Participants could then see how they were doing against others using the app around the world, or create their own league to play against friends. In so doing, Heineken, turned viewing football into an even more engaging experience.[5]

Embracing the idea of providing experiences

The delivery of experiences is not confined to any particular type of business. Nor does it matter whether you are working in the business-to-business or business-to-consumer marketplace. All companies need to embrace the world of experiences if they want to flourish in this brave new world in which we find ourselves.

For example, our car dealer from the previous chapter wanted to engage with the local business community. It is for this reason that it volunteered the use of its showroom for a Chamber of Commerce gathering. The event, with guest speakers and networking amongst the different models of car, was an experience in itself. The real challenge for the car dealer, however, is to make an everyday visit to the showroom an experience. The following example is one way in which this can be achieved.

Every day, our car dealer has fresh Danish pastries and coffee delivered. Not only does this make the showroom smell great, but it also creates a very welcoming environment. WiFi is also installed. Every person who enters is offered refreshments and the opportunity to sit with a coffee and catch up with any work. The showroom has a large car park, which is under utilized. Our car dealer decides to invite the local business community to use the facilities at their convenience and free of charge. This offer is open to anyone, not just customers. As word of mouth grows, local business people pop in, enjoy a coffee and Danish, and do a little work. This is, of course, a great way of starting an engagement with a prospect. Not every person who uses the showroom will buy a car from this dealer, nor is it expected of them. However, it is very likely that any business person who has used this showroom will at the very least have this dealer in mind, when contemplating the purchase of a new car. Moreover, the goodwill and trust developed between the dealer and the business community will mean that more people will be predisposed to purchase from this showroom than would otherwise have been the case. Of course, it is not just the local business community who enjoy the showroom's facilities. When bringing their car in for a service, existing customers can also utilize the comfortable surroundings. This factor may be taken into consideration when making a purchasing decision.

On buying a car, customers are welcomed to one of four quarterly cocktail events, during the early evening hours, at an exclusive local hotel. They are invited to bring a guest, which introduces new potential customers to the showroom. As people meet and talk at these events, they will naturally exchange business cards; they remain in contact. To help people stay in touch, regular networking events are held in this car showroom. These events are open to the wider business community in order to network and meet local business people. As a result, there is real value in the experience that this car showroom provides. Customer interaction is no longer only about the cars, or the service, that this dealership offers. Or, as in our prologue, 'It's got nothing to do with music, you silly cow!' Rather, it is the whole customer experience that people enjoy and value. It is much bigger than just the purchase of a car.

Participation

Delivering experiences makes engaging with customers before, during and after a transaction easier. The major difference between a service and an experience is simple: a service is something that is done to you or for you. An experience, on the other hand, is something that is done with you. In other words, the customer becomes integral to the solution offered.

Without the customer's participation, the offering would not be as good. In the UK, a football match has always been an experience because the fans' participation is integral to the event itself. First, there is the tribalism of fans walking towards the stadium, parading their team's colours. Once in the ground, there is the roar of the crowd when the teams appear, and the distain and euphoria exhibited about the different refereeing decisions. Whether it is the banter between the two sets of supporters or the cheers when a goal is scored, the event would not be nearly as exciting without the participation of the crowd.

Similarly, the difference between a good meal and a great meal at a restaurant is often not the food. At some establishments, aside from ordering the food, we may feel that we are almost superfluous to everything else that is happening around us. This makes the food merely a service for which we have paid. Alternatively, there are other times when we will feel engaged and very much part of the ambiance and atmosphere around us. This is when a meal can turn into an experience for which we will return on another occasion.

Delivering an experience requires customers to participate and become involved with your business offering. Whether it is reviewing a book, voting on a television show, stopping at our car showroom to have coffee and Danish and make use of the WiFi, or attending an event, experiences require customers to actively participate. Today, this is reinforced by our increasing use of the web to undertake our day-to-day activities. The web itself is a medium that requires participation in a way that communication channels such as radio, cinema and television never did.

The web encourages participation

The web is the first many-to-many communication tool. It empowers all of us to 'get involved'. Unlike with previous communication channels, on the web people do not want to absorb information passively. Rather, they want to comment, contribute and share. In other words, participate. Therefore, in order to engage with customers in any meaningful way, companies need to visualize the experience they provide, rather than thinking only in terms of the product or service they deliver.

There is a vast number of ways to develop experiences. Holding events around your product or service, like our car dealer, is one way of creating an experience. For some businesses, starting a club that provides events and special offers, and connects different members, could also be a way of delivering an experience. Clubs create a sense of belonging and community that, if utilized properly, can be extremely powerful. User-generated content (UGC) – ie allowing and encouraging customers to contribute content to your website by giving them the wherewithal to comment on blogs and forums, or post their own articles, podcasts and video – is another way of engaging customers. Alternatively, giving customers an increasing influence over the products or services your company offers becomes part of the experience itself. This can be voting on an outcome, as in a reality TV show, or providing ideas that contribute to the next offering that your company provides.

Not only does participation move your business into the realm of experiences, but it also makes it more probable that you will be well received by customers. People are much more likely to embrace solutions to which they have contributed. Moreover, it is more probable that you will be talked about, and therefore will achieve more positive word of mouth. Because experiences are internalized, they are emotional in a way that products and services are not. They are therefore much more likely to affect a customer. It is because they feel personal that they develop into a story and narrative more easily than do products and services.

Imagine going into our car showroom, buying a car and driving it away. You may tell a few people that you bought a new car, especially if you are pleased with your purchase, but it does not develop into much of a story. However, this changes once the showroom delivers an experience. Being offered fresh coffee and Danish, while sitting and catching up with a few e-mails and realizing that other people use the showroom as a business hotspot, becomes more of a talking point. Being invited to an event with food and drink at an exclusive hotel starts to provide you with a narrative that you are more likely to relate to others. Experiences, by their very definition, should be memorable. They have a greater impact on us than do products or services because they affect our feelings. Because they are more emotional, interesting and story based, we are more likely to talk about experiences than we are to mention a product or service.

Today, the two main ways in which people source new products or services are online and by word of mouth, asking their network, friends, family, colleagues etc. It is hard to have much control over passive word of mouth – that is, people mentioning your business because they are pleased with the work undertaken. Providing experiences for your customers creates a reason for them to talk about you, thus making awareness of your business by word of mouth much more likely.

Marketing's move from tactics to strategy

This highlights another important change between the old transactional funnel model of marketing and today's engagement model advocated by 'sticky marketing'. Because the traditional model of marketing was solely about the transaction, it was largely approached tactically. In other words, marketing departments would spend money on particular campaigns. An individual campaign might utilize TV, radio, billboards and mail shots. All of these channels might have delivered a consistent message for the campaign's duration. After the campaign was over, and having reflected on the results, new tactics would be employed, with some successes repeated. The same process would be undertaken at all companies, whatever their size. However, while big companies could afford to utilize channels such as television, smaller companies, especially in the business-to-business environment, would make more use of the letterbox and trade magazines.

Today, however, although occasional tactics can still be employed, marketing is no longer tactical but strategic. When people are buying experiences, the marketing is no longer something that you decide upon after the product or service has been developed. Rather, it has to be built into the design of your product or service. In a connected world where people have a plethora of channels through which to communicate, word of mouth is of the utmost importance. Moreover, with an ever-increasing amount of dialogue happening online, on social platforms such as Google+, Twitter and Facebook, word of mouth and online marketing are becoming one and the same. As word of mouth increasingly happens on the web – with its greater reach and, therefore, potential for influencing purchasing decisions – word of mouth has become even more important than ever before. Therefore, a key question that needs to be answered in a modern marketing strategy is: How do you enable people to share whatever it is you do?

This is not something that can be bolted onto a product or service after its design. It has to be integral. It means allowing people to participate and get involved. For example, Amazon allows people to share their experience of books. YouTube also has word of mouth built into its offering. Because anyone can upload content for free, people accept the YouTube branding on the screen. This means that as people share their content, they are also spreading the word about YouTube.

In order to make your marketing 'sticky', it has to be truly aligned with, and part of, the business strategy. This was not always the case. Years ago, the leaders of a business would agree their strategy and the parameters of their product or service offering. Marketing would then be brought in to promote the offering using certain tactics. Today this is no longer effective. In order to be 'sticky' and engage prospects and customers, the promotion and selling of the product or service must become part of the experience.

For example, when our restaurant with the magnificent view decided to position itself as the ultimate romantic destination within its locality, this was as much a marketing decision as it was a product and service offering. Subsequently, partnering with beauty salons, spas, florists etc, as well as producing tip sheets and ideas for romancing a loved one, has as much to do with delivering an experience as it does with marketing. In other words, the two are seamlessly intertwined and are not two separate entities.

The changing dynamic between sales and marketing

This approach also renders another old rule redundant: that is, the splitting of the sales and marketing department. Traditionally, directors and senior management would set a strategy and decide the company's products and services. Marketing would then be brought in to communicate the virtues of the product or service to a particular target audience. Salespeople would then be sent out into the field, to follow up the leads generated by the marketing activity. They would also capitalize on any market awareness generated by the campaign. This may appear to be a little simplistic, but in the business-to-business world, in essence this was how it worked.

Today, marketing is integral to the business strategy. The experience ties up so many facets of the company's offering. Both the core products and services and strategic partnerships will affect the experience delivered. However, other decisions, such as how customers share what you do and how they can participate, will also contribute to the experience they receive. It is hard to distinguish between the different aspects that contribute to the experience, and the marketing is necessarily tied up in all of this.

'Sticky marketing' – that is, cultivating a model of customer engagement – requires companies to attract prospects to them. Hence, the top of our upside-down funnel is narrow. The days of shouting at hundreds, thousands or even millions of people, in order to make them take notice of your offering, are disappearing. The logic of this is that traditional salespeople are no longer required. These are the staff who would go out and, metaphorically, knock down doors looking for opportunities in the market. They were often known as 'hunters'. In many ways, the 'hunters' were an extension of, or were sometimes used instead of, traditional shouting.

The 'farmers', those salespeople who were better at nurturing relationships over the long term, may still be required. This will depend on the nature of the business and whether it is cost effective to employ what amounts to account managers in the field. Where this is applicable, these 'farmers' become more of an extension of the marketing department. In other words, there may be a point where initial customer engagement naturally leads to the need for a face-to-face meeting. This requires marketing and sales to work much more closely together than has often been the case. In fact, when engaging customers by delivering value over a long period of time, it will not always be clear where marketing stops and selling starts.

The lines between marketing and sales are now blurred in a way that they were not previously. In order to do a good job, both functions have to understand the other and work closely together. Today, so much customer engagement takes place online that you can often take a customer right through from initial interaction to a sale, and over time up-sell and cross-sell as well, just on your website. For example, a prospect may stumble upon the Amazon website while looking for a particular book on a given subject. In the first instance, it may be the book reviews that provide value and draw the customer in. Providing this value may lead this particular person to make an initial transaction. Over time, because of its sophisticated backend, Amazon may up-sell other relevant books to this particular customer. As the company establishes credibility and trust with this client it may, in turn, cross-sell an electrical item such as a digital camera. Marketers involved with the web interface of any business will need to have a deeper understanding of selling than they once did.

Meanwhile, a salesperson's role will need to change in order to repeat the customer engagement model in person. While marketing must ensure it is 'sticky' and engage customers via media channels, a sales executive must achieve this person to person. Salespeople, too, must become 'sticky' and engage customers around the value and experience they can provide. In order to do this, they must be subject experts and, therefore, a useful resource to prospects and customers alike. Word-of-mouth recommendations, referrals and new customers will result from this approach.

Without understanding business strategy and marketing strategy, salespeople will be unable to fulfil this role properly. So much of the customer engagement model requires the giving of value to customers around the transaction. Traditionally, salespeople were focused only on the transaction. This requires a mind shift and change of emphasis in a salesperson's role. If it is relevant for your company to employ salespeople, they are on the front line talking to prospects and customers every day. Their feedback and market intelligence can make a significant contribution in keeping your customer engagement model fresh and relevant. In other words, today sales and marketing should be working within the same department, taking on different roles, but utilizing the same strategy and working closely together. What has been, in many companies, an adversarial relationship has to change to become highly collaborative, to the point that there should not even be two departments, but one. Today, sales has a large marketing function within its role, and marketing a large selling one.

The role of delivery mechanisms

The move from products and services to experiences requires a company to rethink the way it conceives the offerings it provides. It also makes it necessary for a business to reassess the role of both its sales and its marketing functions. It is also vital that a company considers the mechanisms by which it delivers the experience to its clients. When buying a product, whether one buys it at the store or orders it via a catalogue, the product itself remains unchanged. However, if businesses are no longer selling products or services but experiences, the way in which a particular experience is delivered changes the nature of the experience itself.

For example, if you arrive home from work one night and do not fancy cooking, you may decide to get a takeaway. You will then make up your mind whether you want, say, Chinese, Indian, pizza or fish and chips, which may be the options available in your area. What is unlikely is that you decide to get a pizza and only then make up your mind whether you want a takeaway or to eat it in a restaurant. A more probable scenario is that you will decide whether you want to go out to eat, pick something up to bring home or have something delivered. In other words, in this example the delivery mechanism is more important than the product. Once you have decided how you wish to receive your food, only then will you decide on the particular meal. In a world of abundance of choice, we no longer buy products or services, but experiences. In this context, the delivery mechanism becomes a vital part of the experience. So:

- Some customers would like to buy in shops; others will want to buy online.
- Some will do research in shops and buy online; others will research online and buy in a shop.
- Some people will buy a whole album; some people will want only a single song.
- Some people will want a physical CD with artwork; others will require a digital file.
- Some people may want to buy a book; others may want only one chapter.
- Some people may not wish to own the book but will pay a small fee to read it.
- Some people may not want to read the book at all but will buy the audio version; others may be happy having access only to edited excerpts.

In other words, by making your offering accessible in as many ways as possible, you can appeal to a wider market. Although the product being delivered may be the same, the experience will be different. Because of the low cost of distribution created by the web, it is often possible to distribute a product in a number of different ways.

For example, management consultants may deliver their knowledge face to face with their clients. However, they could also offer a more general version of their expertise via phone seminars and webinars. It may also be possible to offer the principles that they espouse through a distance learning course sent via e-mail or accessed with a special code on a website. Other media channels such as podcasts and videos could also be exploited to impart some of their wisdom.

The general principle is this: while the knowledge stays the same, it can be packaged in a number of different ways. This enables people to access the information in a form, and at a price, convenient to them. Some people may not wish to pay for face-to-face advice, but will be happy to part with less money and undertake a distance learning programme. Others may not be inclined to listen to podcasts but may be very willing to watch videos. A management consultant can take the same knowledge and, by packaging it in a variety of ways, can begin to deliver a very different experience to an array of customers. The web allows for the distribution of all these distinctive products at minimal cost. However, by being able to take the same knowledge and turn it into a number of separate experiences, management consultants can maximize the revenue they are able to generate through their expertise.

The move to experiences is a direct result of the ubiquity of products and services. We are all faced with a plethora of similar choices, to which the web has provided us easy access. It is in these circumstances that customers change their perception of value. With wide availability, consumers have stopped focusing on the products and services themselves. With regard to these, they have an expectation level that is already set extremely high. Rather, today, the real value is in the nuances that a company delivers. These subtleties, however, are not about product features and service deliverables, but in the experience a customer enjoys.

Once businesses focus on providing experiences rather than products and services, opportunities to engage with prospects and customers arise. This, in turn, allows a company to create value around its core deliverable and become attractive to its marketplace. Once a company realizes that its focus should be on providing experiences, it requires new questions to be considered and answers to be found. While these fresh challenges may make individuals feel somewhat uncomfortable, the opportunities that the move to experiences affords provide businesses with exciting prospects for the years ahead.

Key point summary

- Value is no longer in the product or service that you deliver for customers, but in the experience that they receive when engaging with your business. The only way to avoid commoditization, and to be able to engage with your clientele, is by delivering experiences.
- Strategic partnering with companies will help enable a business to deliver value and maintain engagement with prospects and customers

alike. Partnerships allow a company to create more value around what it does, which aids the process of becoming 'sticky'.

- Delivering experiences makes engaging with customers before, during and after transactions easier. An experience is something that is done *with* the customer. In other words, the customer becomes integral to the solution offered.

- User-generated content (UGC) – that is, allowing and encouraging customers to contribute content to your website by providing the wherewithal to comment on blogs and forums or post their own articles and videos – is a great way of engaging customers.

- Giving customers an increasing influence over the products or services your company offers can become part of the experience itself. This can be voting on an outcome, as in a reality TV show, or providing ideas that contribute to the next offering your company provides.

- Today, marketing is integral to the business strategy. When people are buying experiences, the marketing is no longer something that you decide upon after the product or service has been developed. Rather, it has to be built into the very fabric of the offering.

- When buying a product, whether one buys it at the store or orders it via a catalogue, the product itself remains unchanged. However, if businesses are no longer selling products or services but experiences, the way in which a particular experience is delivered changes the nature of the experience itself.

Unique selling point to customer engagement points

The idea of the unique selling point[1] or the unique selling proposition (USP) started to be used in advertising in the 1940s. It was finally written about and explained by Rosser Reeves, an advertising executive working for Ted Bates and Company, an advertising agency on New York's Madison Avenue. In his 1961 book *Reality in Advertising*, Reeves explains what the USP is and how it works.

In simple terms, a USP is a unique benefit that will attract customers. It is 'unique' because it is supposed to be an offer that no one else in the marketplace has. Therefore, it is a way of gaining a competitive advantage.

In the 'transactional funnel' approach to marketing, the USP was a great idea. If you were going to shout at people about your product or service, having something unique, and therefore special, gave you a greater chance of catching a prospect's attention. Moreover, your advertising, direct mail, leaflet drops etc, were designed to capture people who were currently in the market to buy. Having a USP gave them a reason to buy from you.

In a world where there was relatively little choice, it was easier to come up with a benefit that was truly unique. With many services being restricted by geography, it was also possible to copy what a company was doing somewhere else, but still be unique within your own locality. However, the abundance of products and services, and access to knowledge and choice, that technology and the web have provided has now rendered the USP completely and utterly irrelevant.

The USP, in reality, is just another benefit of your product or service, albeit a unique one. However, benefits are benefits only when a person is ready to buy. Therefore, for most people, at any one time, your USP will be completely irrelevant. The result is that it is almost impossible to engage prospects around your USP. Meanwhile, trying to compete on a USP, by definition, means making your offering transactional. It is also an easy way to get into a competitive race within your market, which can lead to commoditization as competitors make greater promises to customers in order to attract business.

This highlights another problem with the USP. Today, there are hardly any truly unique offerings. With very few exceptions, there is almost nothing that you can conceive that a competitor cannot duplicate. The web and the speed of communication allow ideas to be copied very quickly, resulting in your having no competitive advantage at all. Often in fact, all companies are left with are the additional costs of the new promises they made to prospects.

For example, in 2008 one or two companies came up with the concept of selling mobile phone packages by giving away free Netbooks as an enticement.[2a, 2b] However, the idea spread quickly across the globe, to the point that it took very little time before there was no competitive advantage at all. Quite simply, what started out as a USP soon resulted in another customer expectation as people knew there would be someone offering a free Netbook when looking for a new mobile package. Not only did this not result in any significant increase in competitive advantage, but the aftermath was that companies incurred additional costs, however minor these may have been.

James Dyson patented his invention of the bagless vacuum cleaner. However, there are a variety of bagless vacuum cleaners manufactured by other companies available in the marketplace today. Microsoft owns Windows, but there are plenty of other office suites of software that one can obtain. The Apple iPad is widely credited as being the device that saw the coming of age of tablet computers. It was launched on 3 April 2010.[3] Yet by 2 September of that year, Samsung was exhibiting its Samsung Galaxy Tab, its alternative to the iPad, at the International Radio Exhibition in Berlin.[4] Original ideas spread and are rewritten, changed and regurgitated by others. In other words, there are very few occasions when a company will have a USP for very long.

Moreover, it used to be possible to copy a USP and deliver it in your own locality. Today, with the web breaking down geographical boundaries, companies increasingly find themselves competing with businesses from further afield. The result is that even delivering something unique in your own area is becoming more difficult.

Why the USP will not sell experiences

The unique selling proposition requires a company to define its offering in a single idea: that is, a unique benefit that will attract customers. This is unhelpful in an experience economy. Experiences are more three dimensional than products or services. Rather than being defined by one single idea, experiences often weave together a tapestry of ingredients that, as a collective whole, then deliver something special. However, each constituent part may *not* be unique in its own right.

So, as discussed earlier, Benny's Burgers developed a strong identity as a children's brand and became a hub for kids' activities in its local area. Similarly, our car showroom became a focal point for local business people. Experiences allow companies to create powerful market positions for themselves. Over time, this results in providing a business with competitive advantage. This is because, once a company has engaged a client base around a particular experience, a competitor has to be able to offer something significantly better in order to move that client base from the current supplier. This is not easy. The reason is that the more engaged a customer becomes, the more a business learns about the preferences of individuals and the customer base as a collective. This, in turn, allows the business to develop ever more personal experiences and relevant offerings for its customers.

This is an important development in new marketing. The digital environment, in which we operate allows organizations to collect and monitor information about customer behaviour and preferences. In so doing, a business can use this data to deliver ever more relevant and personal communications to its customers. In a digital world, where people are more in control of the flow of information they receive, customers have become less tolerant of communications that do not reflect their personal preferences or are deemed irrelevant. Therefore, constant customer engagement creates an ever-increasing barrier to market, as the minimum offering a competitor has to provide becomes harder to deliver from a standing start, because it has less information about the customers. The development of an experience allows a company to become special and attractive to customers. This is not achieved, however, by trying to produce a defining USP.

For example, I am a user of Moonpig.com, the online greeting card company. When I send a card to family or friends, the site offers to remember the occasion and sends a reminder a few days before the event the following year. Over time, it has built up an extensive catalogue of dates and addresses, which means that no matter where I am in the world, I never forget a special event. Now, although a competitor site could offer a similar service, it would take a complete year of events for it to be able to offer me the level of service that Moonpig already delivers. Because of this, it is unlikely that I will leave unless I become particularly dissatisfied with Moonpig. As long as it continues to deliver, I am unlikely to look elsewhere. Meanwhile, because Moonpig allows me to personalize cards, altering the wording and adding pictures, it turns a very standard purchase into more of an experience.

As products and services become increasingly commoditized, the value in an offering is in the experience provided. Companies can no longer define themselves by a single USP. For example, is there anything a solicitor can offer its clients in terms of product or service that cannot be copied by another firm? Probably not. In the old transactional model of marketing, the USP was fundamental to the offer being made to prospects. It was *the* reason to do business with you rather than anyone else. Today, 'sticky marketing' requires the focus to move from transactions to customer engagement. Businesses have to start thinking in terms of experiences provided, rather than products or services delivered. Companies previously attempted to gain attention by developing an irresistible USP. Today, companies must become attractive by using entirely different criteria. We must move from thinking in terms of unique selling points (USPs) to creating a vision based around customer engagement points (CEPs). Customer engagement points are a way of transforming what you do into a multidimensional, tangible entity that engages customers in a number of ways and on a number of levels.

The journey to customer engagement points

However, in order to arrive at the customer engagement points, we are required first to answer a different question. A business will be able to introduce compelling CEPs only by undertaking a process that will enable it to reach the right answers. The first part of this process is the completion of a Problem Map, as introduced in Chapter 4.

It is vital to understand that every purchase solves a problem at the point at which it is made. It may be that, later on, a customer regrets buying a particular item or service. However, at the actual time of acquisition, a problem will have been solved. This could be a practical purchase such as buying milk so that one can have a cup of tea or buying petrol to run the car. Alternatively, it could be an emotional purchase: for example, buying an expensive watch to solve the problem of establishing or maintaining status, or a luxury car that enables the owner to demonstrate success. Shopping has also become a displacement activity in modern times; in other words, the mere act of going to the shops to buy something solves the problem of not having anything to do or anywhere particular to go.

The Problem Map is a mechanism for understanding both the emotional and practical challenges that your potential customers will face. Once a Problem Map has been completed, the starting point for making your business attractive is to ask the following question: Why are we best placed to solve the problem? The answer to this question requires you to look at your Problem Map and think about the following four areas:

- What is the actual problem that you solve? Although your Problem Map will cover a wide variety of issues, there will be key themes and problems that continually recur. These will indicate what the fundamental and overriding problems are. It is these issues on which you must focus your attention at this juncture.

- For *whom* are you best placed to solve these problems? This question will help you distil who your likely customers will be. You must consider the people who are most likely to face these issues. You should also contemplate for whom the solving of these challenges will be most compelling. By understanding this, you will be able to identify the particular clientele for whom you can add the most value. In order to be able to achieve the right answers, you must also consider when these problems are likely to occur, and where these people are likely to be at that time.

- What are the current dynamics of the market? It is important to identify the sectors and localities in which you wish to operate and the offerings that already exist within those places. By understanding the choices already available, you will be able to carve a distinctive path for your own business.

- Is there anything special about you? Whether they are a one-person business or a vast organization, companies have to assess if they already possess experience or expertise that makes them particularly attractive to certain types of customers, within specific market sectors or locations.

Having clarity in these four areas is fundamental to any marketing strategy. If you do not know why you are best placed to solve the problems for a specific set of customers, *they* will never know. It will be impossible to define your customer engagement points properly because you will not have the clarity around whom you should engage and why.

CASE STUDY   Example case study: an accountancy firm

We can see more clearly how this works by taking an example of an accountancy firm. Having completed its Problem Map, it decides upon the fundamental issues it believes it solves for its clientele. These are:

- *Compliance*: There are a number of obligations a company must fulfil. Failure to do so leaves them vulnerable to severe penalties or even prosecution. Many companies do not have the in-house expertise to deal with these issues.

- *Financial security*: Valuable insights can be gained from understanding the financials of a business. Without these, companies can put themselves at risk by missing fundamentals, such as cash flow, profit margins etc.

- *Missed opportunities*: Companies must constantly evolve in order to maintain competitive advantage. A detailed reading of a business's accounts can assist in identifying new opportunities on the one hand, and areas that are becoming less productive on the other.

Having understood the fundamental problems that this accountancy firm solves, the second question that must be answered is: Who is most likely to have these problems? It is also important to consider when and where these challenges will occur. Our accountancy firm will use the experience of its current customers to enable it to develop its answers:

- *Who*? Chief executive officers, managing directors and finance directors are the main people who face these issues.

- *Where*? Financial issues can play on people's minds wherever they are. However, they are particularly focused upon them in their place of work.

- *When*? These issues will come to the fore at specific times. For example, they will be given particular consideration at year end. Alternatively, other events such as a company not developing as hoped, or a business with ambitious plans experiencing problems with cash flow as a result of rapid growth.

The next area our accountancy firm considers is the dynamics of the marketplace and its role within it. If this accountancy practice is a two-partner firm, it may decide that its market is local. People often like to have their accountants close by. There is also no point in trying to work with customers who are 200 miles away from its office when there are plenty of clients for a two-partner firm on its doorstep. So, it decides that its marketplace is a 30-mile radius from its office. Within this area it understands which other accountants exist, from the corporate firms down to some of the smaller firms like itself. Who are they? What do they offer? What are the profiles of businesses within this 30-mile radius? What do they look like in terms of turnover or number of employees? Are there any particularly strong market sectors within this area?

While carrying out this research, the firm realizes that there are a large number of small accountancy practices and they all present themselves as general practice, all-purpose firms. It also realizes that the majority of businesses in the area are small owner-managed companies without employees. There are also a significant number of small entrepreneurial businesses with a small number of employees.

Finally it looks at itself; what is special about the two partners? One of the partners previously ran her own business and so has a very good understanding of the dynamics of being a small business owner. The other partner has a lot of experience of working with start-ups and helping them grow. The two accountants recognize that their experience is with small entrepreneurial businesses. There are plenty of these within the 30-mile radius in which they are happy to work. They understand, therefore, that their customers are going to be small business owners. Within their 30-mile radius there is no accountancy firm that has positioned itself as *the* accountant for entrepreneurs.

Therefore, the answer to the question 'Why are we best placed to solve the problem?' is that in their locality they are the only specialists working with small entrepreneurial businesses. This is an area in which they have vast experience. The point of the positioning is this: they are not best placed to solve the problem for everyone. In a world with an abundance of suppliers, no one can be.

However, for their target audience of small business entrepreneurs, they are the best placed firm to solve the problem.

This can sometimes be as much about perception as it is about reality. In other words, the core skills required to assist one market may be exactly the same to help another. However, it is vital that you define the market in which you want to operate. In a world of abundance, trying to be all things to all people actually means being nothing to anyone. Faced with so much choice, people will gravitate to a supplier whom they feel is exactly right for their requirements. In a world of so much choice, there is likely to be one. You must, therefore, decide upon your niche.

An engagement strategy means becoming attractive

An engagement strategy is about encouraging prospects to come to you. In order for this to happen you have to be attractive. There are two aspects to being attractive. First, you have to be noticed. It does not matter how attractive you are if no one knows you exist. Second, you have to be desirable. That is, once you are noticed, people must be drawn into wanting to know more about you. In a world of choice, being a small fish in a big pond will not get you noticed. This is the equivalent of trying to be all things to all people where there are so many options available. On the other hand, if you are a big fish in a small pond, you will always be noticed. This is the equivalent of working within a defined market. The more relevant you appear to be to a particular marketplace, the more likely it is that clients will see you as desirable.

Companies often become concerned when defining their market in narrow terms. The feeling is often that they are dismissing potential opportunities out of hand. This is not the case. It may seem counter-intuitive, but the narrower your market focus, the more attractive you become to a particular audience. Moreover, determining a narrow focus allows you to choose a market where you may already have some inbuilt competitive advantage. For example, by choosing to define its market as small business entrepreneurs, our accountancy firm's experience became much more relevant and important. Herein lies an essential lesson for all companies: in a world of abundance of choice, it is necessary to be a big fish in a small pond. Far from being restrictive, this can be liberating. After all, you get to pick the pond.

Of course, why wouldn't you carve up a pond in a way that provides your business with maximum competitive advantage? When finding a niche, the only question a business must ask is: Is the market big enough to sustain our business? As long as the answer is yes, there is little to worry about. In fact, it may even be possible to define the market still further.

Being a big fish in a small pond will mean more word of mouth, more recognition and more customers. Once you dominate the market, if you wish you can diversify by getting representation in offices in other regions, or moving into different vertical sectors. For example, you may start off defining your audience as doctors and slowly, over time, diversify into dentists. You may choose to do this with your existing company name or by creating a different brand.

The principle, however, is this: in an engagement strategy, aim at the narrowest target market to which you can give the best experience and that will sustain your business to the level you require. In our accountancy firm example, working with small entrepreneurial businesses, within a 30-mile radius of its office, provides a large enough marketplace. The other importance of narrowing your market is that it becomes a self-fulfilling prophecy. In our accountants' case, they have identified that their experience is in the field of small businesses and these are the customers with whom they will engage. The more they engage and the more customers they acquire, the more they learn and the more contacts they build in this area. This produces a virtuous circle whereby, as a result of working in this narrow field, they become increasingly valuable to their target market. As they continue to build their experience, knowledge and contacts, they become true experts in their area of specialization and increasingly capable of delivering added value to their customers.

This is also true for their geographical focus. While building knowledge of other businesses, they are able to introduce their customers to other sources of expertise in their locality, such as specialists who can help with the sourcing of funding. Thus their claim of being the best firm to solve the challenges of small entrepreneurial businesses in their area continually strengthens over time.

The importance of a 'narrative'

Once you have answered the question 'Why are we best placed to solve the problem?', there is another consideration before examining your customer engagement points. Part of understanding the experience you are delivering to customers is to explain the narrative behind what you do, how you started or what you are trying to achieve.

For example, you may have a certain methodology that you use when working with a customer, which you may be able to explain in story form. Alternatively, you may be able to recount how you started in a back room somewhere and how you grew. This may be an interesting journey that a customer will enjoy and that builds your credibility. Conversely, you may have really ambitious goals for what you are trying to achieve, whether it is feeding the starving or stopping the homeless problem. Building a story around these ambitions can help bring them to life and enable people to understand where you are coming from.

A narrative can become part of the experience for a prospect or customer. A compelling story can be engaging in itself. It allows people to understand you. In turn, this makes it easier for them to feel that they know you and can trust you. Stories often give prospects and customers something to talk about, making it more likely that your message will spread. Is it any wonder that the most successful book of all time, the Bible,[5] contains some of the best stories and narratives ever told?

Moreover, a narrative helps people internalize what you do. It has the ability to affect them on a deeper level than simply stating facts about your product or service. It enables them to feel part of your business, rather than simply being bystanders. In this way, your offering becomes more personal. If companies need to deliver experiences, having a narrative sitting behind them will also make it much easier to deliver consistently, time and again.

Having understood the problems that you solve for a customer, you then define your market in order to ensure that, within your niche, you are well placed to be the solution provider. By being strategic in determining the markets in which you operate, you become a big fish in a small pond. This is the first stage of ensuring that you are attractive; that is, being noticed. The second part of attractiveness is becoming desirable. Desirability is achieved by imparting value. It is this that will encourage prospects to engage with your business. 'Sticky marketing' requires ongoing engagement with prospects and customers alike. In a world of abundance, we are all overwhelmed and distracted by the choices we face. Consistent engagement means having the attention of our prospects and customers. This makes it very likely that when they are ready to make a purchase we will, at the very least, be considered and on many occasions we will win the business. This return on engagement model requires a system for developing engagement strategies, just as the USP provided a mechanism for developing effective ways of shouting at prospects in a previous age. Customer engagement points (CEPs) provide businesses with this formula.

Introducing customer engagement points

Customer engagement points comprise four areas:

- partnerships;
- content;
- market positioning;
- emotional selling proposition.

Partnerships

While partnerships, alliances, associations etc, are as old as business itself, the purpose of these is now changing. In the old, traditional transactional marketing model they had limited use. They existed when both parties felt they could achieve more sales when working together than on their own. Partnerships were also about maximizing profit. So, for example, the alliance between McDonald's and Coca-Cola gave McDonald's a competitive advantage of serving the world's leading cola brand in its restaurants.[6] It gave Coca-Cola access to a huge audience on which it might otherwise have missed out. Both parties found the arrangement highly profitable. This agreement, however, was not about engaging the customer; rather it was transactional. The fact that Coca-Cola is available in McDonald's is only of interest to me when I'm thinking about buying a fast-food meal. While it may influence my purchase at the time, it will not engage me at any other moment.

Today the abundance of choice and information available, together with the fragmentation of media and communications, has rendered attention a scarce resource. This means that companies already enjoying prospect and customer attention need to find new ways of providing value in order to keep them engaged. This can often be achieved by partnering with aligned businesses. The focus of these partnerships, however, is in creating value in order to maintain customer engagement and keep their attention. For companies that do not enjoy the attention of their potential marketplace, partnerships give the opportunity to leverage a business that has succeeded in this area. Therefore, a win–win situation ensues. While one company can use partnerships to add value and keep its customers engaged, another can use these partnerships to develop some initial interaction with future customers. While, indirectly, both companies will hope that this partnership increases sales over the long term, that will be an indirect result of the alliance. The initial criterion for determining the partnership will be to create customer value, which in turn will encourage both prospects and customers to engage.

Understanding who to partner with takes you right back to your Problem Map® and the issues that you solve. For example, in Chapter 4, Benny's Burgers realized that it was not in the business of burgers and chips but in the business of activity displacement for children. Therefore, it looked for other companies that were in the activity displacement for children business. This led to a partnership with the local zoo, leisure parks, cinema etc. Engaging customers around burgers and chips was almost impossible. People would be interested in its offering only at very specific times. However, having activities to amuse your children is a perennial and universal problem. Benny's Burgers could not fix the problem on its own, but by partnering with other businesses it widened the solution it could deliver by offering vouchers for these other activities. It also broadened the experiences that it could assist in bringing to its clientele. Vouchers, in themselves, are not an experience. However, by enabling the different experiences at the zoo, cinema, bowling etc, to happen, Benny's Burgers became a small part of the occasion and benefited from some of the goodwill generated. Partnerships allowed it to deliver value and become a hub for parents looking for things to do with their children. Thus partnerships are an important element of an engagement strategy.

Similarly, our accountants working with small entrepreneurial businesses could look at partnering with a solicitor, an HR consultancy, a marketing company or other service providers who also have small businesses among their clientele. With these partners, our accountancy firm could offer money-off services, fact sheets and top tips and hold seminars, all relating to assisting the small business owner. Thus engagement can take place by creating value through partnerships. This example with our accountants brings us to our second customer engagement point.

Content

Understanding the problems that you solve for a client can lead you to appreciate the sort of content that can be delivered and will create value around your core product or service. For example, Benny's Burgers solved the problem of activity displacement for children. It partnered with other companies that solved the same issue and created offers for each of the activities. This was then turned into content, a flyer containing all the vouchers that could be downloaded from its website. Then, after the summer, Benny's Burgers created more content of value by distributing activity booklets for kids, via e-mail, on weekends when the weather report was not favourable. Imparting value like this helped to keep both the parents and the children engaged. It was never, however, directly about burgers and chips; or, as Steve Jones so rightly said, 'It's got nothing to do with music, you silly cow!'

Our accountants could use partnerships in order to create great content for their clients, together with their HR, marketing and legal partners. If you are a service provider with a vast amount of expertise, you can create your own material. Alternatively, you can partner with other firms in order to create something of real value for your clients. Suppliers may also be an important resource that you can utilize.

For many businesses, the most important contributors of all can be the customers themselves. On Amazon, for example, the content of real value is the reviews written by customers. These reviews offer useful insights when making a buying decision. However, this content would not be nearly as respected if it was produced by Amazon itself. The credibility and value come from the fact that contributions are made by regular readers. Moreover, by giving customers a platform on which to participate, a service turns into an experience as consumers are able to become involved.

Content can be made accessible on your own website or delivered by request directly to prospects and customers via e-mail, RSS feeds, etc. However, accessing content on your website relies on visitors coming to you. There is no doubt that your website can be a powerful engagement tool. However, many opportunities will be missed if a business depends solely on this channel of distribution. You should not simply expect prospects and customers to visit your site.

Rather, a far more powerful strategy is to take your content to the places your prospects and customers already visit. This can be achieved by utilizing public platforms used by your customers, such as Google+, YouTube, Facebook, LinkedIn, Twitter, etc. It can also be accomplished by partnering with other businesses and associations. For example, a tip sheet full of great ideas produced specifically for small businesses by a solicitor may be uploaded onto the firm's website. However, because the content delivers real value and is not simply a promotional tool, associations like the local Chamber of Commerce and Institute of Directors may also carry the piece in their newsletter, magazine or on their own website. The top tips may also be disseminated individually over the course of a few weeks on Twitter. By taking the content to the places to which small businesses already refer, this content has a lot more chance of being seen and engaging new prospects. Links from the information could direct readers to other sources, such as the firm's website or blog, for those who would like to learn more.

Whether it is creating videos for YouTube, writing serious articles for other people's websites and portals, or encouraging customers to contribute material to your own website, content is an extremely important strand in building customer engagement points. The right content, together with the appropriate strategic partnerships, starts to contribute towards the third part of your customer engagement strategy.

Market positioning

'Sticky marketing' is all about attracting customers to you. With the abundance of choice and access to information that we all now have, there is little point shouting at prospects. People will do things when they are ready and on their terms. Creating an effective market position for yourself and your business is vital in becoming attractive.

Benny's Burgers partnered with other children's brands offering free discount vouchers. It designed and gave away children's activity booklets. It also created an excellent dining experience within its restaurant. In so doing, it became one of the de facto children's brands within its area. It became a hub, a trusted adviser if you like, and the first port of call for parents when it comes to children's activities in the locality.

One of the myths in this world of abundance is that customers now want and demand choice. Consumers actually do not want choice at all. People often feel overwhelmed by the number of options they face when making a purchasing decision. What customers actually desire is the result that so many choices provide: that is, exactly what they want, where, when and how they want it. Therefore, people are becoming increasingly sophisticated about how they search for new products and services, in order to find what they are looking for as quickly as possible.

With so many choices available, people find ways of making sense of it all. They often achieve this by using filters, i.e. ways to screen out all the noise and find what is relevant to them. This, in effect, is what Google does. When you initiate a search, it screens everything else out and delivers the most pertinent results for you. Similarly, posting questions and asking friends on social or business networking sites achieves the same results. The recommendations that come back are delivered by trusted contacts and are therefore credible. By relying on these recommendations, you reduce the market from an overwhelming amount of choice to a few manageable options.

Within their own niche markets, many businesses can deliver this to their patrons through effective market positioning. For example, in its area Benny's Burgers is becoming *the* filter for children's activities. Similarly, our accountants could do the same thing for small businesses within their locality. So they could partner with the right business networks and advisers. By also providing good content and being involved in organizing some interesting local events, over time they could become a hub for small business activity. In order to become a hub, the resources you provide must be highly relevant to a specific group. This reinforces the requirement to be a big fish in a small pond.

Market positioning is more robust than the USP. A USP can normally be copied with relative ease. Once that happens, it does not matter to the customer whose original idea it was. If two companies offer free delivery, do you care which did it first? However, market positioning is different. Benny's Burgers is not the only children's burger bar in its area. It has some very well-known competitors. However, it is Benny's Burgers that has the right strategic partnerships, regularly delivers valuable content to an engaged customer base and provides information about other children's activities on its website.

No business must be complacent. Nor should it take enjoying the attention of many of its prospects and customers for granted. However, if another burger bar in the locality did try to copy Benny's Burgers, while not impossible, it would face an extremely difficult task. Established strategic partnerships, good quality content – like their activity booklets – and an established reputation for delivering accurate and relevant information cannot be cultivated overnight. It is a slow organic process. Over time, the cost of implementing this strategy is minimal, but to try to compete from a standing start is a huge challenge. Moreover, while copying free delivery or a giveaway, or matching a price is relatively simple, trying to copy an experience is that much harder. Not only this, but experiences are internalized. This means that an emotional attachment is created. Therefore, delivering an excellent experience to your customers develops a deeper sense of loyalty than a mere product or service ever can. The importance of emotion in an experience economy brings us to our fourth customer engagement point.

The 'emotional selling proposition'

'Sticky marketing' requires businesses to engage people by creating value around what they do. This is achieved by understanding the problems that they solve. By providing content, working with partners and developing a market position, companies move away from merely delivering a product or service to providing customers with an experience.

An experience is emotional. It is internalized. It is three-dimensional. Delivering an experience can only be done effectively by understanding emotionally what you supply. Identifying the emotion that your company conveys will assist you in being able to produce an experience that is consistent. Do you:

- sell candles or romance?
- sell burgers or escapism?
- provide accountancy or reassurance?

The language on your website, the way your staff dress, your corporate colours, etc, should all reflect the emotion you deliver. The digital age has made word of mouth more important than it has ever been. People only recommend companies they trust. Therefore, in order for people to trust you, they must feel that they know you. By delivering an emotionally consistent message, you will become familiar more quickly, and therefore are more likely to be recommended more readily and more often. Achieving consistency has become increasingly difficult when there are so many channels of communication available to us. Many companies and individuals find themselves in the position of maintaining a website, writing a blog, creating a Facebook profile and company page, having a presence on Google+ and LinkedIn, while Tweeting pertinent bytes of information, etc. Not only this, but within businesses there may be a number of contributors to these channels. How do you maintain consistency across so many platforms? Your emotional selling proposition provides a useful internal benchmark and guide in order to help make this happen.

In order to arrive at your emotional selling proposition you need to ask yourself two questions:

- What do the problems that we solve mean emotionally for people? Does our small business accountancy firm provide peace of mind, reassurance or security?

- How do we want people to feel when they use us? Our small business accountancy firm may want people to feel calm or comforted. It is, of course, quite possible for two accountancy firms to have two different emotional selling propositions. Our small business accountancy firm, whose target market is entrepreneurs, will have a very different offering from another accountancy firm that specializes in preparing audits for public limited companies (PLCs).

Whatever your emotional selling proposition is, it should be one word – for example, hope, reassurance, empowerment, romance – that will act as an internal benchmark for everything you deliver to your customer. It is not something that you share directly with clients; rather, it should come across in every communication and interaction with them. Your emotional selling proposition must be consistent with everything you are trying to achieve as a company, especially with your market positioning.

For example, Virgin is one of the most successful private companies in the world.[7] Although it was conceived over 40 years ago, it is still perceived by many as a fresh and exciting company. Much of this is due to its market positioning. Although it is a large and successful company, it is inevitably the underdog in almost all the markets in which it competes. Virgin Records was not as big as the likes of EMI. In aviation, Virgin was up against national airlines such as British Airways. In mobile phones, Virgin competed against established brands such as O_2 and Vodafone. Virgin, despite its own success, normally appears to position itself as the minnow, attempting to take market share away from much larger corporates. It is because of this that its entry into a market often seems quite exciting. It usually approaches the market with a promise to change the status quo. Therefore, emotionally, it delivers a feeling of being anti-establishment.

This goes hand in hand with the persona of Virgin's famous founder, Richard Branson. We buy into the anti-establishment message because he is an unconventional business leader. While attending business meetings wearing casual clothes may not seem very radical today, it made quite a statement in the early 1970s. Meanwhile, his high-profile activities outside the office, such as attempting the fastest crossing of the Atlantic in a powerboat and his adventures in a hot air balloon, mean that we accept the fact that he is not your typical executive of a large company.

By carefully fashioning a good market position, together with a clear understanding of the emotional selling proposition that your company delivers, you will enable your business to create a strong identity. By providing quality content and leveraging partnerships, the mechanisms will be in place to develop a robust customer engagement strategy. Continually providing value to both prospects and customers alike will keep them engaged. It may then be possible to become one of their trusted filters in your particular area of expertise. With consistent interaction, transactions will happen, over time. The key to success, however, is leveraging CEPs in order to create and maintain successful customer engagement.

Key point summary

- All companies must identify the problems that they solve and the customers to whom they could add the most value with their solutions. This, combined with an understanding of the dynamics of their marketplace and the unique expertise their own business possesses, will start to lead a company towards an effective marketing strategy.

- The narrower a company's market focus, the more attractive it becomes to a particular client base. Determining a narrow focus allows it to choose a market where it may already have some inbuilt competitive advantage. The aim is to be a big fish in a small pond. The key is for a business to pick the right pond.

- Part of understanding the experience you are delivering to customers is to develop a narrative behind what you do, how you started or what you are trying to achieve. A compelling story can be engaging in itself. It can help people feel like they are part of the business.

- Customer engagement points comprise four areas – partnerships, content, market positioning and the emotional selling proposition.

- Partnerships can help create value in order to maintain customer engagement and so keep their attention. They can also assist a business in developing some initial interaction with future customers.

- Content can be made accessible on a company's own website and be sent to customers via e-mail, RSS feeds, etc. A business should not simply expect prospects and customers to visit it. Rather, it is essential that content is also delivered to sites and platforms that a company's prospects and customers already visit.

- Creating an effective market position is vital in order for a business to become attractive. The aim is for a company to become a hub, a trusted adviser, in its own specialist area. In other words, it should become one of the filters people use in order to make sense of the overwhelming amount of information to which they are exposed.
- An experience is emotional. It is internalized. It is three-dimensional. Delivering an experience will be performed more effectively by understanding emotionally what a business supplies. Identifying its emotional selling proposition will enable a company to produce an effective experience that is consistent.

PART FOUR
Communicating the message

Messages to conversations

Before the web, the major forms of communication – print, radio, cinema and television – left the public as passive receivers of information. The few people who had the means of distribution could convey their ideas to the many, and the rest of the populace had to be satisfied with sharing their thoughts with friends, family and colleagues.

Magazines and newspapers had letter pages and radio shows hosted phone-ins, but most people had very few ways of distributing their ideas to the masses. This being the case, it was something that the 'silent majority' accepted ('silent majority' being a well-known colloquialism that reflected this situation). In marketing terms, these circumstances gave companies quite a lot of control in their interactions with prospects and customers alike. Companies would create imagery and messages and then pay for distribution in order to put these in front of their audience. Consumers had very few outlets by which they could respond to this messaging and therefore were unable to voice an opinion.

Moreover, because customers had very little access to information regarding new products or services, commercial messages were often worthy of their attention. The development of technology and the creation of the web has completely transformed this situation. We have come full circle, whereby control has shifted from companies to individuals. The general populace has now been empowered in a way never previously known. We are no longer passive receivers of messages, but active players in the creation of that information.

A good example is the news. Everyone used to glean their knowledge from the same few newspapers, television and radio stations. Now, we obtain information from a plethora of channels, including websites, blogs, forums and social networks. Examples include postings on Facebook during the overthrowing of the Tunisian government during December and January 2010/2011, messages on Twitter when Hosni Mubarak was deposed as President of Egypt in February 2011 and video on YouTube in the aftermath of the large Japanese earthquake in March 2011, or the protests in Taksim Square in Istanbul in June 2013 that were not being generated by news networks but by ordinary people. Because of the volume of material that is being produced in this way, it is fairly easy to corroborate stories and so make sense of what is going on. Thus today, fast, accurate and reliable information is being provided by the masses. Others can, in turn, react to this in real time. This is being compounded with media channels now encouraging this type of citizen journalism. For example, in the UK, the *Guardian* newspaper, launched 'Guardian Witness' in April 2013.[1] This is an app to encourage people to upload pictures and video of news events as they see them occur.

The news is obviously one example, but this phenomenon is happening in all aspects of our lives. Millions of people are now making music and videos or writing articles and books, all of which can be accessed by the multitudes. For example, Park Jae-sang, better known by his stage name Psy, was a little known musician outside South Korea until Gangnam Style went viral. It became the most watched video on YouTube, with over 1.5 billion hits. Consequently, Psy became a global superstar, being asked to speak at the Oxford Union, winning best video at the MTV Europe Music Awards in 2012 and performing with Madonna at Madison Square Garden in New York City. There has, in effect, been a democratization of the production and distribution of ideas. This phenomenon has directly impacted on the effectiveness of the traditional marketing approach that companies take.

Today, all consumers have a voice, and many exercise it on a regular basis. Having been empowered, customers now expect to be involved. The result is that people do not want to be 'marketed to' as they once were. They do not want to be passive. Companies used to be in control but this is no longer the case. Customers are no longer willing to sit back and simply wait to be shouted at by businesses. In fact, many of these messages are being screened out by viewers. Up until 2002, 78 per cent of consumers said that advertising was a good way to learn about new products. By 2006, that figure had already dropped to 53 per cent, according to *Business Week*,[3] and it has been in steady decline since.

Companies used to sell their products and services by devoting large budgets to shouting at people in order to direct them to their particular offering. In the world of technology and the web, customers will look for this information themselves. Predominantly, they will refer to two places. One is their own networks, that is, friends, family, colleagues and other online connections. The second is searching on the web. Whether information is obtained face to face, on social networking platforms or by conducting searches, the knowledge imparted will be dominated by the opinions of individuals. Face to face, this will literally be via word of mouth. Online, this material will be disseminated through comments and postings, in forums and on networks, on blogs and in reviews written by consumers, etc. A company's own messaging will be only a small part of the plethora of information available and may not be accessed at all.

Power to the people

In a world where we all have a voice, a growing number of us are not just passively listening, but partaking: that is, posting ideas, views and comments. This information is then available for everyone else to see. In effect, we are all now marketers, having the ability to communicate our likes and dislikes on a massive scale. Moreover, we are more likely to be influenced by the views of other consumers rather than companies themselves. We identify with other customers because we believe they are like us. Unlike companies, we also assume that they do not have any vested interest in the comments they make.

The web has made information extremely transparent. Because we have so much access to information, we are all savvier and more cynical. The age of bombarding consumers with attractive images and messages that they will passively accept is gone. Information used to be disseminated via publication. Today, an ever-increasing amount of information is disseminated via conversation. The reality now is that more marketing messages are created by the public than by marketing departments. Ultimately, people have more influence on brands than the companies themselves.

It is in the contributions from ordinary people in the form of blogs, postings in forums, reviews, comments on Facebook or other social media platforms, Tweets etc that the real marketing is happening. These conversations are where the communication of ideas is taking place. It is here that people interact, influence purchasing decisions and become influenced by others.

This changes the whole nature of marketing. Customers are no longer pawns to be marketed to, for the sole purpose of generating transactions.

A company's success is no longer down to how attractive a product or service can be made to look by a creative advertising campaign. The public at large now play an enormous part in the marketing of any offering. Previously companies controlled messaging; now the best they can do is help facilitate it.

There used to be an adage that 'the customer is king'. I would suggest that customers are even more important than that. Today, the customer is your partner. This is because, for a product or service to be successful, you now have to market *with* your customers, not at them.

Becoming 'part of the conversation'

Conversations are happening online, whether a business chooses to participate or not. Power has shifted from companies to the public. The access to information and choice that the web provides means customers today are proactive in initiating their buying journey, from information gathering to purchase. In other words, the web is extremely effective in assisting buyers in discovering suppliers. Therefore, the emphasis of so much of a company's activity taking place online should be about customers finding the business at the relevant time. With so much choice available, a company's prospects will probably not have to look too hard for a supplier. This means that a business has to make sure it has a presence where activities are already taking place. That involves participating in the conversation. However, for a company to move from the old system of shouting at people with messages, to the new paradigm of being part of the conversation, they will have to alter the way they undertake their marketing activities.

In the old model of marketing, messages were conveyed to the public by shouting at them through a variety of available channels. Companies may have conducted market research to try to ensure that their shouting would be relevant and well received, but that was often as far as any interaction went. Today, the emphasis is on conversations. These conversations often happen in real time and, like regular conversations, are at least two-way. As in any conversation, there will be subtleties and nuances that must be recognized. This, together with the speed at which messages can travel, means that companies need to be attentive. Businesses, therefore, before participating in these conversations, must be listening. Failure to listen intently can leave companies making inappropriate communications and damaging their reputations. Conversely, listening properly will give companies the opportunity to add real value to prospects and customers, and engage with them in a meaningful way. This engagement may well lead to transactions further down the line.

There are many online tools available that businesses can utilize in order to listen to the conversation. Understanding what is going on in the market will provide an array of opportunities. It may lead to developing new offerings, or delivering specific information, help or advice. All this creates value for prospects and customers. In turn, an engaged market will be more likely to purchase from these companies, at the appropriate time, and be more loyal to a business that always dispenses value in a relevant and timely way.

Starbucks was obviously monitoring the conversation when my friend Mark Shaw took his daughter for a drink in one of their branches. On Tweeting this fact, Mark was delighted to receive a message from Starbucks itself. It was genuinely interested in Mark and his view of the experience it provided. Having exchanged several messages with Starbucks, Mark is now a self-confessed advocate for the brand. Not bad, considering that he was a loyal patron of one of Starbucks' main competitors.[4]

There is a plethora of tools available that one can use to monitor the conversations taking place. A comprehensive recounting of all of these goes beyond the scope of this book. The following information is meant only to provide readers with a guide and an idea of the types of mechanism to which I am alluding. The few mentioned below indicates the wide array of products available:

- http://www.google.co.uk/alerts – provides e-mail updates of the latest relevant Google results on particular queries, eg, your company name, industry sector etc.
- https://www.socialoomph.com/ – helps in managing Twitter, including allowing the tracking of keywords in the public Twitter stream.
- http://hootsuite.com/ – social network management tool, including being able to track brand mentions.
- http://www.tweetdeck.com/ – monitor and manage Twitter.
- http://manageflitter.com/ – Twitter management, including tracking keywords.
- http://socialmention.com/ – provides e-mail updates of the latest mentions of particular keywords, eg company name, your name, industry sector, etc, on a variety of social platforms.

- http://sproutsocial.com/ – social media management, including monitoring.
- http://www.socialbakers.com/ – social media measurement and engagement tools.
- http://www.twilert.com/ – receive regular e-mail updates of Tweets containing chosen keywords.
- http://www.seomoz.org/ – marketing analytics software.
- http://commun.it/ – Twitter management and monitoring.
- http://crowdbooster.com/ – social media analytics.
- http://tweetbeep.com/ – Twitter alerts by e-mail.
- http://argylesocial.com/ – social media marketing solution.
- https://www.ubervu.com/ – instant brand insights powered by social media.
- http://www.sysomos.com/ – business intelligence for social media.

Whether you look for your company name, subject of expertise or product area, you are likely to gain valuable insight into people's opinions, issues and concerns in the market. Monitoring relevant blogs, wikis and forums, as well as interest groups on Facebook, Google+ and LinkedIn, will provide businesses with valuable knowledge. Blog search engines such as Technorati can also be useful tools in understanding what people are saying about your area of interest.

These monitoring tools give companies unprecedented insight into their marketplace. One must remember that consumers also have more knowledge than ever before. Therefore, with fresh opportunity come new risks. Companies that misrepresent their position or tell half-truths about their business are in danger of being exposed very quickly. Businesses that fail to listen to their patrons and provide them with real value will soon find they are ignored. Conversely, the businesses that do provide value, and therefore engage consumers, will benefit from a great reputation, word-of-mouth recommendations and, over time, an increase in transactions.

Companies can no longer simply broadcast messages at prospects and customers as they once did. Today, rather than controlling communications, they can help facilitate them. Facilitation means entering into a partnership with prospects and customers. Businesses can legitimately lead conversations if they have new ideas or research that they want to share. They can make suggestions and ask questions, and in this way help set the agenda.

Businesses must remember, however, that individuals can do the same. They must therefore be prepared for conversations to go in directions that they did not anticipate. If companies operate ethically, are truthful and authentic and have a good sense of who they are and what they stand for, they have nothing to fear. In fact, the opposite is true. Unexpected conversations can often create options for businesses that they did not even realize existed.

The customer is no longer king, but your partner. Having partners means allowing them to have a stake in your business. Although this may sound risky for many, companies today simply have no choice. However, with big risks also come big rewards. Once prospects or customers feel that they have an influence on the company, they will then have an interest in its future. Thus, they are more likely to be loyal to that business. Many customers are willing to spend a lot of time and put in a lot of effort, not for financial reward but because they want to. For many clients, participation is the prize. People no longer want to be passive, they like to have a say. Far from running away from this situation, business should embrace it. By facilitating this involvement companies can, over time, create a very loyal and vocal group of customers.

User-generated content and co-creation

Where appropriate, businesses should encourage user-generated content (UGC): that is, allow and encourage customers themselves to provide useful content that, in turn, helps to create value in your business offering. For example, Sky News adds value to its website by allowing readers to leave comments underneath individual news items. It also allows viewers to contribute by uploading videos and photos of news and stories that they witness. Meanwhile, its trending section allows visitors to the website to immediately see what the most popular stories amongst fellow website users are currently. All this turns the Sky News website into an experience, as people are encouraged to get involved. These comments, photos and videos become a rich resource of the public view on any current event. Of course, Sky News has its own editorial pieces, but its site is much richer for ensuring that the wider public can also contribute. Giving people an active voice is empowering and encourages them to keep using the website. It also means that they are likely to talk about it in the context of their own post, and so promote the website to others.

There are entire websites whose value lies in the content contributed by the public. Both YouTube and Facebook are merely platforms that enable user-generated content to flourish. The value is in the information contributed by the members.

A similar idea to that of user-generated content is 'co-creation': that is, allowing customers to suggest new ideas as well as influencing the products and service that companies introduce themselves. If people are involved in creating and shaping your products and services, they are more likely to tell others. Moreover, by allowing customers to collaborate with your business, you enable them to customize what you do. Therefore, you are more likely to offer exactly what your customers require. Not only does this cut out inefficiency and wastage, but it also increases customer loyalty – customers may reject your solutions, but they are less likely to reject their own.

There are many good examples of companies using co-creation. Lego's digital designer allows people to design their own Lego models, on their website, and share these designs with others.[5] Starbucks's 'my Starbucks idea' is a website dedicated to people contributing new ideas to the Starbucks chain.[6] As well as contributing ideas, individuals can see the suggestions others have made and observe how some of the ideas have been actioned by Starbucks themselves. Meanwhile, Walkers Crisps, both in 2008 and 2013, provided the public with an opportunity to invent a new flavour of crisp.[7]

Co-creation encompasses many elements, from allowing prospects and customers to design products and services from scratch, to enabling them to change aspects of the offer, such as delivery, colour, specification, etc. One of the advantages that user-generated content and co-creation bring is that they encourage people to talk about your business. Those who are actively involved in the creation of a company's offering are more likely to spread the word and become advocates. This is significant. For, if you recognize the importance of the conversation, then a part of any company's marketing strategy is to build word of mouth into its offering. In other words, give people something to talk about.

For example, if you take the time to upload a video to YouTube it is because you want it to be seen. Therefore, most people who upload content to YouTube will send links to family, friends and colleagues. Similarly, no one wants to be on Facebook with no friends. Therefore, on joining, people will invite others to connect with them on the platform.

By creating iconic white headphones, Apple made sure that the marketing was built into the product. Anyone walking down the street with white headphones in their ears is presumed to be listening to one of their iPods or using an iPhone.

Building conversation into any offering is vital in order for it to succeed. Encouraging people to comment by giving them something to talk about or share is fundamental to any marketing strategy. Whether it is user-generated content, co-creation, multi-user games, competitions, etc, every marketer should now be asking themselves: Where is the conversation for this product or service? Why would my marketplace want to talk about it? If the answer is that they wouldn't, something needs to change.

The importance of social platforms

One major place conversations will occur is in social networks. When trying to engage with your market, you cannot expect people to simply come to you. Initial engagement will often have to happen in the places they already frequent online. Consequently, businesses do need to utilize social networking sites, because whether it is Facebook, LinkedIn, Google+, Twitter, YouTube or one of the many others, inevitably their customers will be on them. The offering you provide may determine the platforms that your company chooses to become involved with.

Communities have always existed amongst people with common interests. These were once limited by geography and required membership of a particular organization, eg, a church, a school, a youth club, the Scouts, etc – the biggest of these institutions, of course, being the nation state itself. Now, however, communities can be formed online, across borders and time zones.

Communities previously formed in geographical locations required a critical mass of participants in a relatively small area in order to make the group viable. So, if you had a niche interest, you might have been able to conjure up only three or four people in your area who would want to participate in your group, thereby not making the proposition particularly attractive. Today, without these geographical boundaries, communities can develop more easily around niche interests. Without geographical limitations, even the narrowest interest groups can obtain enough of a critical mass to make them worthwhile.

Within the large social networks such as Facebook, Google+ and LinkedIn, there are many communities, clubs and forums started by people with interests in narrow fields. There are therefore opportunities for companies to engage with all walks of life and also build communities of their own on these platforms. Developing communities within these platforms is another channel open to business that can be used to engage. It becomes another way of creating a hub and facilitating the spread of knowledge and ideas in order to impart value.

Companies that choose to develop communities must understand that, ultimately, they are not about the business at all and how many sales they might make. Rather, they are about the community and the wider value created by everyone within the group. Communities are composed of people who interact and have conversations. Although a company may facilitate these forums and groups, it should not view this as control. It does not own them, and if it thinks it does and abuses its position, it will watch the community disintegrate. The dialogue must be allowed to develop of its own accord without a business trying to police it. Dialogue is necessarily two-way. It is, therefore, as important for a company to listen to what is being said as it is for it to contribute.

Abusing social media and using it to shout at people in the old way, without allowing or caring about the response, is an abuse of what these communities are about. Companies that do this are in danger of ruining their reputation. Social platforms are not forums for transactions. They are more akin to having a conversation in a bar. Transactions result as customer awareness grows, together with the credibility and trust that you earn over time.

Hard selling is not appropriate in a bar, nor is it appropriate in social media. It is not called 'social' for nothing. A good conversation in a bar is more likely to develop if you show an interest in other people. Conversely, if you show blatant disregard for other patrons, they will be insulted and are likely to bad-mouth you to others. Exactly the same will happen on these online platforms.

For example, a company with which I worked used social platforms to engage with curators of museums. Rather than talk about the storage equipment that it actually supplied, its focus was on providing a forum for curators themselves to share knowledge through videos, podcasts, case studies, articles etc. Related associations such as those concerned with antique furniture, coin collections and paintings were also encouraged to share their knowledge and expertise. The idea was to create a hub that curators would regularly engage with. This, of course, did not guarantee that the company would win their business when they required new storage equipment. It did, however, mean that curators were aware of its services and were, therefore, more likely give its solutions at least some consideration. Moreover, the goodwill and trust this company acquired meant that many curators were predisposed to using this provider if possible.

Businesses must understand that marketing today is about providing an experience. That often involves creating value at the periphery of your core offering. As part of this engagement, knowledge can be shared on social media platforms. For example, on business networks such as LinkedIn, where people often ask professional questions, information of value can be imparted. In so doing, however, companies should not try to sell, the same way as they wouldn't in a bar. If you are having a drink in a bar and someone asks you a business question, you will most likely give an answer of value and then say, 'If you want to know more, give me a call and we can have a meeting,' and offer them your business card. You will most probably then carry on drinking and have a good evening with the person, which, incidentally, will make it much more likely that they will get in touch.

The same is true of online social networks. Engage with people and focus on giving value, so that people enjoy their interactions with you. Instead of giving your business card, you can often provide an answer of value and then refer to further sources of information; these may include your website or blog, for example. The irony is that by not focusing on transactions, over time you will probably get more of them.

The importance of the 'social graph'

If conversations are now so important in marketing, with many of these taking place on social platforms, understanding who is having these conversations is an important part of any marketing strategy. One of the keys for doing this is understanding your 'social graph'.

Offline, most people will not treat their prospect and customer base equally. For example, there may be some prospects and customers, whom one would be willing to take to lunch, because the investment of time and money would be deemed worthwhile. On the other hand, there would be other customers who, while you may value their business, taking to lunch would not be considered a productive use of time. In other words, people treat their offline connections differently depending on who they are.

Online however, too many businesses treat everyone the same. Whether it is 'Twitter followers', 'LinkedIn connections' or 'Facebook Friends', many organizations indiscriminately post to these people without being strategic.

For a business to understand its social graph, it needs to analyse and discern who the different people are with whom the organization is connected. Seeing who is connected to the company is the first level of the social graph. Going one step further and identifying those connected with the company's followers can be extremely valuable.

Firstly, there may be people within its social graph who should be singled out. Maybe there are individuals with whom it is worth investing the time to e-mail, call or even invite to a lunch or dinner. This is one way that understanding the social graph at a deeper level can be helpful, but there is another.

'Birds of a feather flock together.' Understanding who the company's connections are, within the social platforms a business engages, provides a channel for that business to generate more conversations with the 'right people'.

For example, I have more professional speakers in my network than most individuals. This is because, as well as a marketing consultant, I am also a professional speaker and spend a significant amount of my working life travelling around the world speaking about marketing and sales at conferences and events. On my travels, I meet other speakers with whom over time I have become friends.

Therefore, if an organization had a product or service specifically designed with the professional speaker community in mind, I would be a good person to engage. If they noticed I was part of their social graph and created content that provided me with value, and which I was encouraged to share and 'talk about' with my network, they would reach a proportionately large number of other professional speakers. For a business, understanding its social graph and using it strategically can be invaluable.

Identifying the 'influencers'

It is not just understanding the social graph that can be of value to a business. In any given marketplace there will be key individuals, who have more influence over potential buyers than others. These people are known as 'influencers'.

Influencers are normally those who are better connected in a given market-place and whose opinion is taken seriously. They can be potential customers themselves or, alternatively, be a trusted third party. For example, account-ants could be regarded as influencers in the purchase of financial software.

Whether these influencers are extremely active in a particular market, eg a well-known and followed blogger, or whether they are well connected or are considered trendsetters by their peers, it is worthwhile for companies to identify who these people are, and how they can possibly work with them.

There may be communities of influencers who, despite not purchasing your goods, may be worth engaging. Some IT consultants, for instance, may be very influential in the enterprise software that a company chooses, even though they will not be buying that software for themselves. If this is identi-fied, a software provider might look to engage the IT consultant commu-nity. Of course, it could only do this by providing those consultants some perceived value. This may be achieved with white papers, webinars or other events. In so doing, the software provider would be able to demonstrate its expertise and gain trust and credibility. This makes it more likely that it will be recommended by the IT consultants at a relevant time.

In identifying influencers, companies may have the opportunity to mar-ket straight to their customers. For example, a customer relationship man-agement (CRM) software provider may identify marketing consultants as being key influencers in the purchase of customer relationship management software. It may strike up a partnership with these consultants and pro-duce material, free trials and downloads that actually sit on the consultants' website. Thus, it is marketing straight to the clients of these consultants. The consultants themselves may receive commission on every purchase as well as feeling that this information provides added value for their own clientele.

Loss leaders can also be used to turn influencers into advocates. These could be in the form of providing them with exclusivity, hosting special events, or even giving your product or service away for free. In turn, if they like it, they may well become advocates and tell others. People who are well networked in an industry or on social networks, an influential blogger or spokesperson in a particular community, will be the type of people for whom this scenario may be given consideration.

For example, when Nintendo launched the Wii this is exactly what it did.[8] Its Ambassador Program identified key market categories. Nintendo subsequently hosted events for each ambassador and their closest friends and relatives. This allowed those ordinary people to play with the Wii for the first time and then to share their experiences.

Years ago, influential journalists could make or break a new product or service with a positive or negative review. The difference today is that we can all choose to be critics in areas about which we are passionate. In the world of old media, most of us did not have the wherewithal to respond to a journalist's article. Today, we can all write reviews and respond to others. Consequently, reviews often become catalysts for conversations to occur. Engaging with influencers can help a business become part of more conversations in more places.

A point to consider is that influencers are not necessarily individuals within your target market. They can also be people sitting outside that group. Consultants, industry bodies, procurement groups, bloggers, spokespeople etc can all have a huge influence on your customers' buying decisions without being part of your potential customer base. It is important that these people are considered in any marketing strategy as they may very well be part of the conversation, whether you choose to engage with them or not.

Working with 'key' influencers

Identifying the 'key' influencers, whether they are in your prospect target group or not, is vital. In any given market there will be people with more influence than others. Influence is measured in two ways, by reach and resonance. Reach, is literally the number of people an individual's message will touch. Resonance, is how much the communications from a particular person influence behaviour.

In the offline world, reach and resonance go together. This is because, in order to reach a vast array of people, a message has to be carried by the traditional distributors of information: TV networks, newspapers, magazines, publishers, record companies, radio broadcasters, etc. These distributors only bother with information they believe will attract an audience. Therefore, reach and resonance tend to work hand in hand.

Online, this is not always the case. It is possible for someone to collect thousands of followers on Twitter or friends on Facebook, yet no one may take much notice of what this individual posts. What provides someone with influence is the combination of reach and resonance. For example, if some-one has 500,000 followers on Twitter, they have considerable reach. If they recommend a video in a Tweet and 200,000 people click on the video link, this would be someone with considerable resonance as well.

Today, there are software products that will enable a business to identify the top 50 or so influencers in their industry and country of operation, etc. 'Influencer marketing software' such as Traackr, Appinions and SocMetrics is becoming increasingly popular, and with good reason. Identifying the influencers in its market sector provides an organization with a number of opportunities.

Firstly, once a company knows who these people are, that provides them with the opportunity to engage with these individuals directly. It may be worth sending a blogger with thousands of readers a product sample for them to review. It may be that these people can contribute content to the company's website. Conversely, an organization can offer to contribute content to the influencer's blog or website. It may just be a case of picking up a phone or sending an e-mail and exploring what opportunities exist between the company and the influencer. The fact is, one of the most precious resources that every business requires to be successful is the attention of its prospects and customers. Engaging directly with someone who has some of this attention has the potential to create opportunities.

The second opportunity in identifying the top influencers is to see what they are writing, recording and posting. Every company today owns media channels, from its website to a YouTube channel, from a Facebook or Google+ page to a blog. All these channels require content, and it is not always easy for a business to continually come up with new and interesting ideas. Being able to see what the top influencers in any industry are currently talking about is bound to provide a company with new and interesting subjects on which it can create its own content.

Moreover, once a business creates content, it should not only be placed on its own online real estate, that is, its website, Facebook page, blog or YouTube channel, etc. The content should also be posted in places that a company's prospects and customers frequent online. A question that every organization should be asking is: 'Where do my customers learn?' In other words, what are the websites, forums, blogs and video channels that a company's prospects and customers use for information? Being able to identify where some of an industry's top influencers post will provide a business with a good indication of some of the places its own content should be placed.

Finally, there are many businesses and organizations, or individuals within companies, to whom it would be advantageous to be seen as an influencer themselves. By being able to track where influencers in their industry, are posting, and what material they produce, one can start to work on one's own levels of influence within a sector.

Being seen as having influence is becoming more important in a world that is increasingly connected. Hierarchies used to be mainly positional. In other words, a CEO was seen as more important than a receptionist. Increasingly, hierarchies are becoming more about how connected and influential an individual is, rather than the position or title they hold.

Software that measures an individual's influence, such as Klout, Kred and Peerindex, is becoming increasingly widespread. I am sure, over time, these types of software will be used by companies when looking for new employees, and by organizations sourcing suppliers and buyers, as a measure of the added value they could possibly bring.

If marketing is about having conversations, then having the right interactions, with the right people, will greatly assist in a company's communications being effective. As well as contributing, it is equally important to listen and learn. Good conversations allow companies to educate their marketplace, provide value, demonstrate their credibility and expertise, and so, over time, elicit trust. The most important salespeople and marketers a company has today are often not those whom it employs but rather those who become advocates. Conversations enable ongoing engagement, which over time leads to sales.

Marketing, however, has moved from solely being a message to being a conversation.

Key point summary

- Today everyone is a marketer, having the ability to communicate their likes and dislikes on a massive scale. It is in the contribution from ordinary people in the form of blogs, postings in forums, reviews and comments on social media platforms that the real marketing is happening. The reality is that more marketing messages are created by the public than by marketing departments.

- Companies have to move from the old system of shouting messages at people to the new paradigm of being part of the conversation.

- Before participating in conversations, businesses must be listening. Failure to listen intently can leave companies making inappropriate communication and damaging their reputation. Conversely, listening properly will give companies the opportunity to add real value to prospects and customers and engage with them in a meaningful way.

- Where appropriate, businesses should support user-generated content: that is, allow and encourage customers to provide useful content that in turn helps to create value in your own business offering.

- Co-creation means allowing customers to collaborate with your business. It encompasses many elements, from allowing prospects and customers to design products and services from scratch, to enabling them to change aspects of the offer, such as delivery, colour, specification, etc.

- Businesses do need to utilize social platforms because, whether it is Facebook, LinkedIn, Google+, Twitter or one of the many others, inevitably these are places that their customers regularly frequent.

- It is important for an organization to understand its social graph. Understanding who a company's connections are, within the social platforms in which it engages, provides a channel for that business to generate more conversations with the 'right people'.

- In any given marketplace there will be key individuals who have more influence over potential buyers than others. These people are known as 'influencers'. Companies should identify who these people are and ways in which they may be able to work with them.

- Identifying the 'key' influencers, whether they are in your prospect target group or not, is vital. In any given market there will be people with more influence than others. Influence is measured in two ways, by reach and resonance.

- Marketing has moved from being a message to being a conversation. Consequently, an important part of a marketing strategy is to give people something to talk about. Building conversation into any offering will inordinately increase the chance of success.

Image to reputation

The Industrial Revolution made it possible to mass-produce products; mass media made it possible to shout about them. It was these phenomena that led to the traditional funnel approach to marketing that became the accepted practice and wisdom.

Goods were mass-produced and distributed. Companies would then shout about them in order to grab people's attention. Constant shouting would ensure that these goods were very much in the public consciousness. As items were required, people would often trust products that were most familiar. Because of this, it was the products that companies paid to shout about that were usually the most successful.

Traditional mass media meant that a company conveyed its message to an audience, who were reduced to being mere passive receivers of the information. Customers did not often interact with any person from these corporations at all. Companies in this world of one-to-many communications needed to try to re-create the feelings that a person had when they bought from someone they knew and trusted.

Take a product like Coca-Cola. The majority of people would never actually have interacted with anyone from the company. People bought the product from distributors: local stores, supermarkets, 24/7 outlets, bars, hotels etc. In these circumstances, companies needed to create a sense of loyalty without having the luxury of a personal relationship with their customers. This resulted in modern branding: that is, giving a label, name or product a personality by which the public could create an emotional attachment, and thereby create loyalty.

Of course, it was not real. Products, labels and logos cannot have personalities. They are merely illusions. With this approach, in traditional marketing image became vital and was the way that consumers were influenced, especially for many companies that had no direct contact with their customers. Businesses spent millions of dollars employing agencies and marketers to devise communications that would create a brand image into which consumers would buy.

Of course, consumers knew that products and labels do not really have personalities. However, there are some simple explanations as to how this form of communication became accepted. First, there was not the transparency of information that there is today. Numerous companies would convey false images about their products. For example, many food manufacturers would use nostalgic imagery of traditional local suppliers delivering a wholesome and natural product. The reality, of course, is that many of these items were produced in large factories and full of chemicals and additives. Although, at a basic level, consumers knew that these adverts were not real, without the wherewithal to easily question the imagery, or the means with which to voice an opinion, most people just accepted the message at face value.

Second, there was nothing else. All companies, to a greater or lesser extent, could only get their message across by shouting. In other words, everyone was playing the same game and by the same rules. As customers, we did not have easy access to information. However far-fetched or tenuous some of the advertising was, it was insightful in informing us about what was available in the market. Therefore, somewhere within these messages, value existed. This being the case, we were more predisposed to accept these communications.

Moreover, a lot of advertising involved attempting to give personalities to labels or inanimate objects. This was an effort to create loyalty in lieu of any personal contact between the company and their customers. Obviously, as consumers, we understood that these objects did not really have personalities. The whole premise was slightly absurd. For example, an excellent and highly successful UK TV commercial from 1974 was for Cadbury's Smash mashed potato.[1] In it, a group of robots recount their visit to planet Earth and speak of their observations regarding human behaviour and their consumption and preparation of potatoes. In a world where adverts included such bizarre scenes as talking robots, any allusions to claims that were not true did not seem quite so incongruous.

Finally, the context of delivery was also very important. Communicating via billboards, magazines, newspapers, radio, television, direct mail, cold calls, etc was all very intrusive. This was because, in essence, you were interrupting people while they were trying to do something else. Because the medium was so crass, people's expectations of the message were not high. In essence, companies did not have to pretend that they were doing anything other than shouting at people to sell their merchandise. With hindsight, one can see that this form of communication was invasive and somewhat obnoxious. However, there were no real alternatives and so everybody was doing it. This, coupled with the fact that there was some value for the consumer, meant that people just accepted it. However, because this shouting was slightly disagreeable, people did not think of holding companies to a higher set of standards. In other words, if you were paying to interrupt and then shout at me, I did not expect anything more than propaganda from you.

How we all became marketers

However, with the onset of technology and the web, all of this has changed. Customers now have an abundance of choice, an abundance of access to information and the ability to have a say. Image and branding were invented to give products a personality, to replace the people-to-people interaction that originally took place before products were mass produced. It was an attempt to create some sort of loyalty. However, today people-to-people communication is once again happening. Marketing is now two-way. Companies have the ability to engage directly with consumers on a highly personal level. Similarly, customers have a variety of accessible communication channels through which to contact a business.

Consider this. There are more people than company representatives. Therefore, there is likely to be more material – that is, blogs, comments and reviews – written by customers or potential customers than from a company itself. Moreover, consumers are more likely to take notice of what other customers say than any communications from a business. As consumers, we believe that something written by another customer is more likely to reflect the reality of the experience. We assume, in most cases, that other customers have the same interests as our own, have no axe to grind, no agenda and nothing to sell. Therefore, although marketing is people to people, the company is often not even part of the conversation taking place, which is a completely new phenomenon.

For example, tripadvisor.com is a website used by travellers to source information on hotels, flights, restaurants and other ideas for excursions. Perhaps, however, the most valuable aspect of the site is the comments written by those who have already experienced the various offerings. With so many choices available, it is unlikely that travellers will book a hotel that has several scathing reviews.

In a world of abundance of choice, we all need to filter the information available, in order to decide on the most appropriate solutions for us. Word of mouth from friends or other people's reviews and comments help distil down the wide amount of material to a manageable level. However, this is no longer about an image that a company creates. Image does not get you good feedback or positive comments and reviews. You achieve that through a good reputation. In other words, modern marketing has moved from being about the image that companies create to the reputation that companies have.

Brand value has been spoken about by marketers for years and is vitally important. Brands can be worth millions of dollars and have real equity. The importance of the brand has not changed, but the ingredients have. Brands have often been a company's greatest asset, based on the image that has been created and reinforced. Today, a brand may still be the greatest asset a business has, but now it is based on a company's reputation.

Marketing is a conversation

Now that communications are many to many, marketing no longer consists merely of a company delivering messages to a passive receiver of information. Rather, it is now an active participant, 'the company', engaging with another active participant, 'the customer'. Moreover, communications can be delivered by one active participant, 'the customer', who, through blogging, writing comments or posting reviews, can convey a message to another active participant, another 'customer'. In other words, customer-to-customer as well as company-to-customer communications.

This means that marketing is undertaken less by traditional messaging and more in the context of conversations and discussions. In reality, this means that much of a company's marketing will be done by others, whether it likes it or not. Today, we know about companies, not because of the image they project but through comments, conversations and discussions. In this world image matters less. Reputation, however, is vital.

Of course, this does not mean that image can be completely neglected. Companies still need to make an effort in this regard. However, the point is this: with image, what was most important was what a company said about itself. In a connected, web-enabled world where conversations matter, the most important factor is what others say. This is not image, but reputation.

Image is directed by a company itself, but a company cannot control the conversation. It can participate, it can add value and comment, it can even facilitate discussions, but it cannot control. For example, Google yourself and see the search results. Did you know everything that is there? Do you know everybody who has written something? You can try to manage your reputation and it is vital to do this, but you must remember that people will participate on their terms and not yours.

One of the ways of greatly influencing your own reputation is by dominating much of the content about yourself. Owning your own profiles on industry networks, eg the Chamber of Commerce, Institute of Directors and any trade association, is vitally important. The same is true for big platforms such as Facebook, Google+, Twitter, LinkedIn and YouTube etc.

Providing great content will not only help you engage with people but will positively enhance the reputation that you have. Winston Churchill once said: 'History will be kind to me, for I intend to write it.'[2] In a web-enabled world this is very apt, and today it could be changed to read: 'People will find good content about me, for I intend to provide it.' While providing valuable content and plenty of it will certainly help in developing your reputation, just as Churchill could not write every history book and control everything that is written about him, neither can you.

Building credibility and demonstrating expertise and knowledge, by supplying good content, will enhance your reputation. It is more important today than any image you may create. As more people produce their own blogs, videos and podcasts, we are willing to put up with a less polished production as long as the content is good. A lot of this home-recorded material conveys authenticity and is therefore often very well received. Thus, where a well-produced, slick image might have been enough before the web, now, even more important than image is content. In fact, producing something too slick can be counter-productive, as it may lose the human element and then may no longer seem genuine.

The move to authenticity

This move towards genuine, authentic and real is another result of the web-enabled world in which we now live, and the move from image to reputation. What customers are buying today are experiences. However, in an experience, the customer becomes part of the offering. For example, think about the crowd at our football match in Chapter 5. Without the crowd, there is no excitement. In other words, the crowd is an important part of the occasion. Delivering an experience requires customers to make more of an emotional investment than is true of products or services. They inadvertently become 'stakeholders' in your business. The result is that companies have to reflect the values of their prospects and customers. They have to match their customers' perception of themselves and who they are.

Think how passionate football supporters become about off-the-field business decisions made by the board. This is because of the emotional investment that supporters make when following their team. The same is true of any experience. For example, Gary Glitter was a very popular musician in the 1970s, with millions of fans. Many of these fans, however, will feel unable to play his music today because he is now a convicted sex offender. Because experiences require an emotional investment by the customer, in a way that products or services do not, a company's values and beliefs will be examined and considered far more closely by customers than they were previously.

Potentially, this can provide a business with the opportunity to have a more loyal and committed client base if the business's values align with those of its customers. However, it also brings risks. Customers will not want to invest emotionally in companies and offerings they feel are fake or based on trickery. Old marketing often relied on companies developing an image that was rarely based on reality. Buying was emotional in that it was aspirational, but it rarely required people to give something of themselves. The few experiences that were on offer, such as football matches or pop concerts, did require this. This, perhaps, goes some way to explaining why we have always been so critical of our pop stars, holding them under a microscope. This is because we feel like 'stakeholders' in their lives, having invested emotionally in them. However, most products or services did not require much of an emotional investment and companies were therefore able to convey a false image purely invented in the marketing department or advertising agency.

However, because customers today are more likely to communicate directly with a business, the traditional marketing approach now seems a lot more like lying than it once did. Companies can no longer pretend to be something that they are not. When businesses went out into the market and shouted about themselves, customers did not expect more than a phoney advertising message. Today however, a lot of customers' interaction with your business will be at their behest. They will have taken the time to ask their network for a recommendation or will have found you by searching online. When customers go to this much trouble, investing time and effort in the process, they expect something genuine.

Moreover, when marketing was purely transactional and existed to grab people's attention, everyday images were not best placed to achieve that. Rather, exaggerated imagery would need to be used. Grandiose claims would frequently be made, often completely removed from reality, in order to seize the attention of the consumer. By its very nature, this is not a genuine approach, and in today's market a company that works this way is unlikely to achieve the successes of yesteryear. For example, Vaibhav Bedi brought a case against Unilever in India[3] for the 'depression and psychological damage' caused by the lack of any 'Lynx effect'. Whether this brings a wry smile to your face because, as a sophisticated consumer, you assumed the 'Lynx effect' never existed, or whether you feel he is right to sue over a product that, in his opinion, has failed to deliver on its promise, it demonstrates the problem with traditional advertising. That is, in order to stand out from the crowd, companies exaggerate the results of using their products or services.

When marketing is about engagement, rather than transactions, it requires a company to provide value rather than just a phoney image. There needs to be substance and content. To produce value requires a genuine approach, something more authentic. This is because marketing is now part of the experience, not separate from it. Previously, marketing was one step removed from the product or service people bought. It was simply a vehicle for driving the customer to the offering and nothing more. However, if you are selling experiences, this changes. Every single interaction and message from your company is part of the experience.

Communications in trusted networks and social platforms

The whole point of 'sticky marketing' is to engage with prospects and customers over a long period of time. This requires a business to constantly provide a valued experience. The way interactions now occur affects the tone of communications and renders the traditional marketing approach irrelevant. Today, an increasing number of conversations are taking place within trusted networks and on social platforms. These are communities where individuals are firmly in control of their profile, the messages they write and the ones to which they respond. Because they are social, companies have to act in a social way. Think of other social places, like a bar or a pub. A company representative would not just walk into a bar and shout about what they do. Needless to say, they cannot do this in the context of social media, which is personal and discussion based. These places require a higher standard of behaviour from business, an honesty and integrity perhaps not required on a billboard or TV commercial. Moreover, niche communities that exist within platforms such as Facebook, or on their own sites, are created around values. Therefore, it is incumbent upon companies to reflect the values of the community with which they would like to become involved. Similarly, companies will not be able to truly engage customers and build their own communities without reflecting the values of those people they are looking to attract.

This becomes increasingly important within the context of word of mouth. We trust other customers, bloggers and reviewers more than companies themselves. There is a plethora of ways for people to access the recommendations of others and for all of us to show the wider community our likes and dislikes. These consist of blogs, forums, apps and a variety of websites where one can post reviews, and platforms that allow people to tag and share videos, photos and other content. Among these are platforms such as Instagram, Pinterest, Tumblr, Flickr and StumbleUpon, to name just a few. The more advocates a company has and the more passionate people are about its business, the more likely it is that positive word of mouth will occur. People will not go out of their way for you unless they feel they know you and like you.

This is the antithesis of old marketing. It requires the stripping away of the outdated obsession with creating desirable, yet unrealistic, imagery that develops expectations that cannot possibly be met. Instead, 'sticky marketing' requires a transparency, honesty and authenticity that, quite frankly, most companies are just not used to offering. With marketing being peer to peer rather than company to prospect, and consumers having more of an influence over people's perceptions of a business than ever before, this is now the only approach that will prove effective. Having advocates, as well as being part of and building communities, will contribute to generating positive word of mouth. It is about establishing a good reputation. This requires substance; it is not about image.

For many companies this also means not being obsessed with trying to be perfect. Businesses that are too slick can put customers off participating. This is because, if something seems complete and perfect, there is little point in anyone else contributing. However, not pretending to have all the answers will encourage engagement and participation. Empowering people, and genuinely asking for their input, makes it more likely that they will want to become involved. Allowing users to generate content and customize offerings is a great way of becoming an experience, as well as being seen as authentic. Crowd participation, by definition, is genuine.

The 'social web'

When the web was being widely adopted in the mid-1990s it was a 'web of things'. That is, most people used the web to look up information and static content, which was delivered almost in the tradition of company brochures on many websites.

With the development of blogging and social networks at the end of the 1990s and into the early 2000s, the web started to move from a 'web of things' to a 'web of people'. With the emergence of MySpace and LinkedIn in 2003 and Facebook in 2004 this trend accelerated. Over the last few years, we have seen the emergence of a new era in the web. It is what Facebook founder Mark Zuckerberg, and Facebook Chief Operating Officer Sheryl Sandberg, have called 'the wisdom of friends'.[4]

Traditionally, if one wanted an electrician, it would have been possible to go online and undertake a search for local electricians. A variety of results would have appeared based on a complex set of algorithms designed to give the searcher the most relevant results. Of course, it would have been perfectly possible to identify an electrician this way. However, in many ways the search would be no more helpful than *Yellow Pages* was before the web. In other words, one could identify a supplier with an online search, but that did not automatically provide the assurance that the particular electrician was honest, reliable and well skilled. Of course, there might be testimonials and other information about a particular electrician online, but finding and accessing this material would require more time and effort from the individual looking.

One could argue, therefore, that many people would find search much more useful if they could look for an electrician and immediately find ones whom their friends liked and recommended. This would take the apparent risk out of any purchase and therefore would assist people in finding a supplier with confidence. In fact, this would make search a more powerful tool for the service providers themselves. Social proof is one of the biggest influencers of human behaviour. That being the case, if one were to identify an electrician whom some friends had liked and recommended, the purchaser would be more likely to buy and less likely to require meetings, references, etc. Therefore, the cost of sale, for the supplier concerned, would be less. This is because it is likely that the sale would happen more quickly and with less need for the supplier to invest as much time in the process.

Quite simply, this is the 'social web'. Whether it's looking at cinema listings, bands to explore, restaurants to eat at or professional service providers to hire, we are increasingly able to utilize the opinions and wisdom of our friends and contacts at the touch of a button.

In July 2013, Facebook opened 'Graph Search' for the general public.[5] In essence this is the beginning of Facebook being able to deliver search results based on the data it collects on people's preferences and likes. Want to buy a new album? Why not explore the recent albums your friends have purchased and recommend? Looking for somewhere to eat in a place you don't know? Now you can identify the restaurants and bars that your friends and connections recommend in this area. Need a car mechanic? See who your friends and colleagues have used and what they have to say about them. Facebook are at the beginning of this journey. Over time, being able to use Facebook and other social platforms – not just to connect with friends, but to learn from their purchasing experience – is a very powerful tool for suppliers and buyers alike.

Meanwhile, in June 2011 Google launched their social platform, Google+.[6] This platform allows Google to add a 'social layer' to all its products and services. In other words Google+ is about making all Google's products, from Gmail to Google Maps, its mobile Android system to Google Search, social. Whether one is searching using Google Search, looking for directions on Google Maps, accessing Gmail or watching YouTube, Google encourages their users to 'log in' to get the most out of these services. Once one is 'logged in' it becomes easy to share anything with your Google+ network. This could be a music purchase on 'Google Play', a video on YouTube or an event in Google Calendar. Google meanwhile can obtain all the data on customer preferences, behaviour, interests, likes and dislikes, and in so doing deliver much more personalized and relevant results to individuals.

So, for example, Google's 'Search Plus Your World'[7] service can feed information from Google+ connections as well as Gmail contacts in order to personalize any search a person makes using Google Search. In other words,

Google+ allows Google to start to personalize the web to make it much more relevant, social and interesting for every single individual. In a 'web of people', much of this is about understanding an individual's connections and interactions with others. In so doing, Google can allow individuals to have access to the preferences and selections made by friends and colleagues, and enable them to seamlessly share ideas and content with them.

These developments have two big implications for businesses and organizations. Firstly, the web is becoming ever more social. Everyone is now becoming more connected online. The result of this is that it is becoming easier to share and access the content, thoughts and preferences posted by others. This activity is increasingly important in search. Companies that don't start to become more social – that is, listen to conversations, share content, post thoughts and participate within the relevant online communities – will find themselves no longer appearing in search results. 'Online' at least, these organizations will become increasingly irrelevant.

Secondly, I have yet to meet a company that has not identified word of mouth as an important business driver: that is, referrals, recommendations and positive mentions about their organization. Businesses now have to understand that word of mouth and 'online' are no longer two distinctly different channels to market. Of course, there will always be word of mouth that takes place offline. However, smart phones and tablets mean that we find ourselves with web access 24/7. As we all become increasingly connected online, it has become the easiest way for many to share information, comments, ideas and events and make future plans.

In other words, word of mouth has gone online. Social proof has always been one of the biggest influencers on human behaviour. However, we couldn't always access the thoughts of friends, colleagues and respected individuals at the time they were needed. The web, however, has made this all possible. This 'social proof' by way of likes, preferences, reviews, comments and shared content online is increasingly influencing our purchasing decisions. Businesses can no longer afford to ignore these digital platforms. Failure to utilize these channels properly, for many companies, will simply mean that they can no longer compete.

Moreover, as the information we access is increasingly that which is disseminated via 'conversations', the biggest influencer on how people perceive a company will be the reputation that it cultivates amongst prospects and customers, as opposed to what it says about itself (image). This paradigm shift forces companies that want to be successful to think in a different way.

The importance of values

This 'different thinking' requires a business to consider its values as never before. In an image-based world, where customers bought products and services, values were not nearly as important as they are today. Now, customers buy experiences and are therefore more emotionally involved in a company's offering. In this environment, reputation is key. For businesses, this means that they have to stand for more than merely making money for their shareholders. There has to be a higher purpose. By a higher purpose we are not necessarily referring to a philanthropic aim, such as feeding the hungry or housing the homeless, although for some companies this may be applicable. Rather, higher purpose refers to a vision, to a company's reason for delivering its solutions.

So, Benny's Burgers' higher purpose could be to assist in making the most stimulating and vibrant activities accessible to every child in its locality. Aspects of this had already been achieved through partnerships with other businesses, such as the local cinema or zoo, which resulted in their being able to provide discounts on these activities. At other times, Benny's Burgers fulfilled this mission itself; for example, by producing activity booklets for children during the winter months. This purpose, while not necessarily stated publicly, would guide the way the company operated. In turn, consumers would have a sense of what Benny's Burgers is about. This is something bigger than simply making money.

Similarly, our small business accountancy firm's aim may be to try to ensure the success of every entrepreneurial start-up within its area. Some of the partnerships it establishes and seminars it hosts may help towards this goal. Its purpose would be something that could excite the small business community in its locality, as well as guide its future actions.

People cannot rally around making someone else money. In order for a business to have meaningful values, it must understand its purpose: that is, what lies at its essence. Today, all companies need to think about their vision at a much deeper level than many have previously. In order to identify what this is, businesses must put the customer at the centre of everything they do. Built into any solution should be the wherewithal to enable people to contribute. Providing consumers with the mechanism to generate feedback and ideas will assist a company in staying vibrant and delivering something authentic and exciting. In so doing, customers will be more likely to want to engage and talk about the business. This is in stark contrast to how companies traditionally operated: that is, looking internally for answers and, on producing them, shouting at consumers, hoping they would buy.

Developing a narrative

One aspect that can help businesses understand who they are and engage customers is their narrative: that is, the company story. Good speakers engage their audience by telling stories. This is because they can often capture the imagination, providing a context and perspective that can be easily remembered and understood. Meanwhile, developing a narrative forces a business to think about its history, the personalities involved, their backgrounds and why the company was started.

What was the bigger picture? Was it about providing a better offering to the market or changing the way a particular product or service was delivered? Alternatively, was the vision to introduce an existing product or service to a new area? Remembering how and why it came into existence can help to articulate the essence of a business. This is not the corporate faceless speak that is routinely regurgitated, but a narrative developed about real people with genuine stories. A good narrative can enhance a company's reputation and demonstrate its authenticity in a way that very few other approaches can achieve.

Today, a business must have clarity about its sense of identity, in order to be able to deliver a consistent message across all the different channels with which it must engage its patrons. These include face to face, on its own website, on blogs, in forums, on other people's websites, on YouTube, on social networks such as Google+, Facebook, LinkedIn and Twitter, and a plethora of other places that exist.

Today, we live in a 'YouTube World' with unparalleled transparency. Increasingly, in one way or another, everything is recorded and documented. For example, individuals sitting in an audience will tweet what is happening, in real time. Similarly, using just a mobile phone, apps such as Vine and Instagram enable people to take pictures or videos of any sudden occurrence of interest and share them immediately. Whether it is expressing a point of view on dedicated areas of a website such as Amazon, disseminating opinions on blogs or providing customer feedback in forums, there are few secrets anymore. In this context, a business that does not know what it stands for is very unlikely to be able to instil enthusiasm in those it wishes to engage.

Today, we are living through the midst of a 'communication revolution'. For the first time in history, everyone has their own media channels to communicate and be heard. The web today gives everyone the potential to have a say. It connects us in an unprecedented way. Marketing is no longer directed at passive consumers by businesses that can pay to control the flow of information. Today, marketing is conducted less by messaging and more by conversations. Some of these are between companies and customers, but many are between the consumers themselves, without any involvement from the business about which they are speaking.

In the context of a conversation, it is no longer a company's image that is vital. Rather, it is reputation that will determine a business's success. In other words, it is no longer what companies say about themselves that matters; it is what others say that really counts.

Key point summary

- Today, marketing is two-way. Companies can engage directly with consumers, but now customers also have access to a variety of communication channels. This can mean that more material is produced by consumers about a business than by the company itself.

- Consumers are more likely to take notice of what other customers say than of any communication from a business. With the plethora of platforms available, this means that conversations in which the company has no part are often taking place.

- Marketing is undertaken less by traditional messaging and more in the context of conversations and discussions. In reality this means that much of a company's marketing will inadvertently be undertaken by others. Consequently, marketing is no longer about the image companies create (what they say) but the reputation that they earn (what others say).

- Customers today are buying experiences, which requires them to make more of an emotional investment. They inadvertently become 'stakeholders' in the business. This results in companies having to reflect the values of their prospects and customers.

- Marketing is part of the experience delivery, not separate from it. Every single interaction with, and message from, a business is part of the experience.

- Today, an increasing number of conversations are taking place within trusted networks and social media. These places require a higher standard of behaviour from companies, an honesty and integrity not required of a billboard or TV commercial.

- By not pretending to have all the answers, companies can encourage engagement and participation from their clientele. Providing consumers with the mechanism to generate feedback and ideas will assist a business to stay vibrant and deliver an experience that is authentic and exciting.

- The web is becoming ever more social. Everyone is now becoming more connected online. The result is that it is becoming easier to share and access the content, thoughts and preferences posted by others. This activity is increasingly important in search.

- Word of mouth has gone online. Social proof has always been the biggest influencer on human behaviour. However, we couldn't always access the thoughts of friends, colleagues and respected individuals when they were needed. The web, however, has made this possible. This 'social proof' by way of likes, preferences, reviews, comments and shared content, online, is increasingly influencing our purchasing decisions.

- One aspect that can aid businesses in understanding who they are and engaging with customers is a narrative. This is not faceless corporate speak, but a narrative developed about real people with genuine stories. A good narrative can enhance a company's reputation and demonstrate authenticity.

- Today, we are living through the midst of a 'communication revolution'. For the first time in history, everyone has their own media channels to communicate and be heard.

Controlling to sharing

The creation of the internet and the world wide web, combined with advances in technology, presents both individuals and companies with unprecedented opportunities. At the same time, however, one could argue that the landscape is more competitive than it has ever been, as many barriers to market have come down and therefore there are more entities trying to compete.

For example, there were 1,186,900 registered companies in the United Kingdom in 1990–91.[1] By 2012–13, this had nearly trebled to 3,044,710.[2] Similarly, in the United States, registered companies grew by over a million from 6,319,300 in 1992[3] to 7,396,628 in 2010.[4] However, this is only a small part of the story. With the collapse of the Berlin Wall and the rise of India and China, the Western industrial economies now find themselves competing with literally billions of extra people. As technology increasingly renders geographical boundaries irrelevant for many purchases, this competition becomes even more fervent. Of course, the same facts also present companies with fresh and exciting opportunities. These territories provide Western industrialized countries with new markets in which to expand, as growing businesses and an emerging middle class look to purchase goods and services. In this global market, however, it is the very nature of competition and the way you respond to it that has really changed.

Before the web, in most areas of our lives we had fewer choices. There was far less access to information or communication channels available. This made locating, contacting and ordering from companies further afield extremely difficult. Therefore, people were much more tied to local suppliers when making a purchase. This resulted in businesses, for the most part, competing with a handful of other providers within the geographical territories they covered. If you did not get the business, a competitor you knew well probably would. This world of relative scarcity made business a zero-sum game.

It encouraged rivals to compete head on and be obsessed with each other's activities. In this environment, companies tried to protect their ideas by limiting access to them in case they were stolen by the competition.

In the main, businesses tried to keep confidential any fresh ideas involving messaging, strategy, new products or services and promotions. Companies would compete by protecting plans and keeping much of their operations secret. For a few industries, where there are still a small number of participants in the market, this approach *may* still work, in sectors where scarcity still exists and customer choice remains extremely limited. However, most companies no longer operate in this environment.

The changing nature of competition

Today, the very nature of competition has changed. Most companies operate in a marketplace that has an abundance of suppliers. When you are competing in a locality with three other rivals, it may make sense to obsess about their activities and go head to head against them. But what happens when three become 3,000 or more? And where the web has enabled the creation of so many mini markets, with whom are you contending anyway? For example, Cafepress,[5] a website that allows individuals to create and sell their own merchandise, has over 11 million visitors to its website each month.[6] Lemonade,[7] a site that lets people create their own virtual stands, recommending products and services, has 65,000 individual stand owners.[8] So if you are selling products or services, are you now up against the over 112.3 million users on eBay?[9] If you are a recruitment agent, are you now trying to compete with craigslist.org[10] where people from all over the world can outsource jobs?

Scarcity thinking led companies to become controlling, protective and restrictive in allowing access to their goods and services. With few choices available, consumers would often enquire about your offering merely because you were one of the few companies supplying their geographical area. Frequently shouting at people, via the traditional marketing channels, would ensure that prospects knew of your existence when they were looking to make a purchase.

In the mass-marketing era, many companies provided very similar products and services. These businesses often had to serve an extremely wide demographic in order for the economies of scale to work. This often meant that decidedly similar companies were trying to win business from the same customers. However, we are now operating in the realm of many mini markets. The new world of abundance means that consumers can always find products and services that are more personal to them. They are no longer forced to compromise in their choice of purchase as they did previously. Now, everyone wants to find something to suit them exactly.

The result is that consumers will no longer settle for impersonal mass products when there are more personalized choices available. Companies are now being forced to think of every customer as an individual and respond to their special requirements, as people are prepared to pay for a more personal experience. Today's consumers are increasingly used to personalizing everything they do, whether it is buying only certain tracks from an album or picking individual subject categories of news streams that are then delivered directly to their inbox. We live in a world of personalization.

As customers find new alternatives that are more appealing to their individual tastes, they develop a greater expectation of this availability in all aspects of their lives. They therefore continue to look for more personal choices. The whole situation then becomes a self-fulfilling prophecy. Technology and the web perpetuate this situation because they enable personalization to be delivered cost effectively.

This has given rise to the idea of 'mass-personalization'. By automating processes, companies can provide every individual with their own bespoke choices, so they can create a product or service particular to them. This automation means a product or service can now be personalized for millions. For example, Nike's service, NIKEiD[11] allows customers to personalize their trainers. Individuals can choose from a range of colours, appending their own choices to almost all parts of the trainer, as well as adding their own personal ID. No two trainers need ever be alike, although the process itself is the same for everyone. Today, businesses can deliver experiences designed just for us, and with us.

These circumstances also create an environment where many more companies can operate, each serving a very specific type of clientele. The result is that companies that would have been in competition years ago are now increasingly likely to be potential collaborators.

For example, in the early 1990s, two high-street accountants, covering a similar area, would have probably been competing for exactly the same clients. Today, if a small accountancy practice wants to thrive it is much better off specializing in certain niche market sectors. So, our two-partner accountancy firm, in earlier chapters, decided to concentrate on small business entrepreneurs. This is where it had a story to tell and specialist expertise it could offer. It is, of course, perfectly possible that both accountants are still competing directly. However, in a working environment comprising lots of mini markets, it is more likely that, although there may be some overlap, each accountant will be working in slightly different domains. If this is the case, there is an opportunity for these accountants to collaborate and pass potential clients to each other. This would have been less likely in the mass market era when both accountants would have been serving a very wide and similar demographic within their locality. In other words, today it is often more sensible to leverage a potential competitor, and work with it, than to compete in the traditional way.

The mindset of abundance

In fact, leveraging partnerships with other aligned businesses is vital. It means thinking collaboratively instead of competitively. It is a completely different mindset. The thinking in this approach is the polar opposite of the attitude that comes with scarcity: that is, control and protect. Today, in the majority of markets people have an abundance of choice. Abundance thinking means understanding that, in most cases, trying to protect and control information is futile. If you have had an idea, it is highly likely that someone else has had it as well.

The big revolution that the web has delivered is that everyone now has a voice. Social platforms are not merely new channels of delivering information. They will continue to force the companies that want to be successful to undergo a change of mindset. Customers, employees and partners alike now have the wherewithal to distribute and disseminate content with ease. Therefore, however reticent you are in sharing your ideas, it is probable that they will find their way to market anyway, just via someone else.

The whole nature of the way information is disseminated is changing. Traditionally, new information would be 'announced' via press conferences, press releases and as news items via traditional broadcast media. Increasingly, many of us are now learning about events and developments through the sharing of information via social platforms such as Facebook and Twitter. Social proof – that is, what our family, friends and colleagues say and do – has always been one of the biggest influencers on human behaviour. For a business wanting to engage and sell its products and services, encouraging people to 'get involved' and talk about their business, both online and offline is invaluable. Far from a company discouraging this trend, in this new age of openness businesses should be doing everything they can to enable these interactions to happen.

Abundance thinking recognizes that today, trying to control and take ownership of information is not a sustainable strategy. As soon as an idea is out in the market, the ease with which it can travel and the tools available that give everyone opportunity to comment, manipulate or alter the idea mean that control is not realistic. Abundance thinking, therefore, is about sharing and collaborating. It recognizes that the web is a fantastic tool for creating opportunities through this very kind of approach.

In the old world of broadcast media, it was the job of marketing departments to try and reach and communicate to all their potential customers. Often, these communications were not deemed to be very persuasive, as savvy customers were fairly cynical about the claims businesses made to make their products and services desirable.

Increasingly, marketing is becoming collaborative. Engaged prospects and customers should be seen as partners in assisting in the communication of a company's message. By creating real 'value' in the marketing, through competitions, insightful videos and articles, and humour etc, and by involving and supporting their engaged prospects and customers, marketers are more artisans in crafting communications that will be embraced by the community. In so doing, any engagement has the potential to be far more powerful when shared by friends and colleagues than anything sent directly from companies themselves. Encouraging prospects and customers to participate and share, is the key to making marketing work in the digital age.

In the old days of scarcity, knowledge gave you power. A business would therefore try to protect this knowledge and use it to draw in customers. The web, however, has made it easy to disseminate knowledge. Consequently, we now have access to it in abundance. There are more ideas available than we could all use in a lifetime. It is no longer having knowledge that gives you power, as it is something to which we all have access. Rather, it is the sharing of knowledge and expertise that gives you the attention of others. In a world where the scarcest resource is customer attention, attracting that attention will lead towards success.

For example, I worked with an association for company chief executives. It had an enormous pool of resources that could be accessed online. However, it was only available for members. At the time, the organization took the view that this fantastic wealth of resources was a member perk and should therefore be protected from anyone else. The information was excellent. It contained an array of expertise and knowledge. However, it was unrealistic to think that similar prowess could not be found elsewhere on the web. While the members of this organization may have appreciated the resources available, I doubt if it was this that either led them to join or retained them. After all, why would people pay for information that could be accessed elsewhere for free?

Meanwhile, consider all the people who, every day, would be searching for this type of expertise online, and could have been using these resources. These potential prospects may have been unaware of the existence of this organization and the value it could offer. By making this information freely available, how many new potential members could the organization have attracted? How many more people would it have actively engaged? How much stronger would this association's reputation and market position have been among its core clientele, chief executives? What considerable word of mouth would this resource have generated?

Scarcity thinking worked when having information was special. At that time, protecting it, and using it to encourage people to join your organization, made sense. However, in a world of abundance, the real power of this material is in sharing it, not keeping it securely away from public consumption. Today, scarcity thinking will actually prevent you from being competitive, rather than making you more so. Those companies that do not share knowledge and expertise will find it harder to engage and gain people's attention. Subsequently, they will find themselves bypassed by others that do. In a world of scarcity, protecting knowledge might have led prospects to seek you out. In a world of abundance, it will mean that they will go somewhere else.

The importance of sharing and collaboration

Technology and the web have made disseminating expertise and cooperating with others easy. 'Crowdsourcing', the idea of utilizing the creativity and expertise of the wider community, cannot be ignored by any company wishing to compete in today's business environment. Right across the world, we are now seeing the sharing of knowledge, collaborations and discussions taking place in unprecedented ways. Failure to participate will result in a business being left behind. Whether it is on social networks, dedicated forums or blogs etc, or using tools such as Skype, it is delusive to think that it is now an option for any company to try to opt out of this trend.

This approach to sharing and collaboration is highlighted by Open Source: that is, communities dedicated to producing all sorts of free products and services by cooperating and working together. This is done on what is called a 'General Public Licence', which means that anyone can use or alter the platform. The Linux operating system was one of the first of these collaborations to have a large impact. It is a real rival to Microsoft, yet, it has been produced completely by experts and enthusiasts collaborating and giving of their time for nothing. Anyone can use the platform completely free of charge. The internet browser Firefox was created in the same way. It currently accounts for around 20 per cent of the market.[12] This is market share that could have gone to Microsoft's internet Explorer, Apple's Safari or Google's Chrome, yet it was not paid for by one large corporation. Rather, it was a collaboration between developers giving of their time for nothing. 'Free' is now competing against some of the biggest companies in the world. Wikipedia is another famous example of mass collaboration in action. It is currently the fifth most visited website on the web,[13] has 30,808,495 pages[14] and entries in 285 languages.[15] There are few businesses that would have succeeded in building and maintaining such a large resource. However, this is happening right now, by way of mass collaboration and the sharing of knowledge.

In fact, there are examples of companies sharing and collaborating all over the web in order to be able to compete. For example, Facebook, Google+, Twitter and LinkedIn have opened up their platforms with APIs (application programming interfaces). This enables others to build online businesses and applications that integrate with these companies. This approach helps to keep these social networks relevant, as they are constantly able to offer their users new tools and functionality through third parties. It also helps them to widen their reach, as every business that chooses to integrate with them becomes a de facto referral and free piece of marketing.

Google's mobile platform is another example. In order to challenge in the market, Google ensured that its Android operating system was on an open development platform. This makes it easily customizable, enabling programmers to develop all sorts of enhancements. In so doing, Google hoped to be unrivalled in the value it could offer the user. In turn, Google wanted to make its Android system the most attractive one to consumers. In fact, the strategy seems to have worked. As of May 2013, the Android platform had a 75 per cent market share.[16] Despite its size and success, Google couldn't hope to achieve this goal without sharing and collaborating with the wider community.

Today, innovation is happening so quickly that it becomes increasingly unlikely that any one company can compete on its own. Therefore, it is imperative that businesses share and collaborate. As the world becomes increasingly complex, and we have more knowledge and choice than ever before, the market becomes more specialized. In order to be able to deliver valued experiences, companies must look to partner with individuals, other businesses and the wider community. Today, in order to stay relevant, businesses must be creative, innovative and fast. While collaboration and the sharing of ideas help this process, keeping everything under your control and protected actually hinders it.

As long as some businesses are willing to share their ideas and cooperate with others, like the communities that make up the Open Source movement, then others will have to do likewise. Otherwise, quite simply, companies will be left behind. Wireless technology, together with laptops, tablet computers and smart phones, means that collaboration no longer has any boundaries. It can happen anywhere and at any time. Social platforms now make it easy to identify and connect with relevant people. Meanwhile, the software now available to manage complex workflow means that any barriers to working with others are all but disappearing, for companies of any size.

Sites like eLance.com make it possible to utilize expertise, anywhere in the world, in order to achieve particular objectives. Sharing information across the globe is a cost-effective way of accessing some of the best minds available. It is often cheaper now for companies to partner, collaborate, share and leverage human resources and knowledge than ever attempt to undertake tasks internally. Companies that do not embrace this new world order will not be able to compete in the marketplace.

Personalization and the new working environment

The move to personalization also provides opportunities for small businesses to offer niche experiences. This comes at a time when the middle market is disappearing, as consumers increasingly move towards two extremes. In a world of personalization and choice, customers who care about a particular product or service look for a highly personal experience, something special. On the other hand, for the purchases that a particular individual simply deems necessary, the acquisition becomes merely a commodity and, therefore, cost and convenience become the biggest issues in making a decision. Consequently, we are witnessing the growth of a highly personalized 'premium experience' being offered at one end of the market, and the expansion of 'no frills' offerings at the other. This is having a polarizing effect and making the middle ground untenable.

This comes at a time when no one has a job for life anymore. Consequently, there is an increase in people working for themselves. We are entering the dawn of a new economy. Companies will progressively be smaller entities that come together for projects, to deliver highly personal specific experiences for niche markets or to work on particular challenges. This may result in the world of work starting to look more like the film industry, where people work on a film collectively and then go their separate ways.

This way of working is not suited to tight controls and the protection of knowledge. Instead, a mindset embracing openness and transparency will be required. Companies are going to find that they need to 'get social' by integrating social platforms into their own working environment. Increasingly, tools such as Yammer, a private social network for a specific company, will need to be utilized and will be as important to a business as the telephone or e-mail. Operating like many public social media platforms, it allows for instant collaboration between employees and the sharing and commenting on all sorts of information, with everyone able to see messages, calendars and activity streams. This ensures everybody is up to date with the latest company knowledge and developments. It makes communication easier, faster and more efficient. With this level of transparency it also gets rid of silo thinking as individuals have a much better understanding of the whole picture within an organization. Traditionally, most organizations' control and decision making has been top down. In this new world paradigm, employees will need to be empowered to collaborate, be informed and get involved.

This collaborative approach is vital when trying to deliver experiences rather than products or services. Experiences require an offering that is much more three-dimensional than a traditional product line or service capability. There are many aspects in being able to provide an experience to customers, and that will often mean operating with others to deliver the promise.

For example, take an experience such as a pop concert. It consists of various elements. The artist or band that everyone has come to see is one entity. The set design will be delivered by another company. The sound will be mixed and operated by a further provider, as will the merchandise and food concessions, which are often rented separately. Roadies, who build and dismantle the set in every venue, need to be employed. Meanwhile, the security required will be supplied by others still. In other words, several constituents share, collaborate and come together to deliver an experience. Increasingly, this is a strategy that more traditional businesses will adopt, albeit in a slightly different way.

Customers will also require your business to collaborate with others as they demand seamless integration of the different products and services they use. This may mean a company sharing information and ideas with a competitor, in order to ensure that their solutions work together for customers that use both. Partnering could mean that each company attracts more business. Conversely, refusing to work with others could lead to customers looking for alternative suppliers. So a software supplier offering both customer relationship management and accounting software may find itself working with a provider that offers more popular customer relationship management solutions. Although these companies are technically competitors, without integrating each other's products they risk frustrating customers of both, who as a result may go elsewhere.

Co-creation with customers

One of the most effective ways for a business to supply a personalized experience and provide value is by co-creating with customers. However, in order for a company to enable customers to contribute, it has to be willing to share and collaborate. It is almost impossible to facilitate this cooperation while trying to control and protect. Businesses that don't embrace this new paradigm are in danger of missing out. We live in a world where the greatest innovations and value will not necessarily come from inside your business. Customers are posting ideas and opinions all over the web, which can be seen by everyone. Social networks, forums and the conversations that take place on these platforms are as rich in great new concepts as anything a business can come up with on its own. In any case, why would a business, today, try and design its next product or service without utilizing the most important resource necessary for its success? That is, of course, its own customers.

Social media has changed the world. It has created an environment whereby highly connected individuals can create incredible value by collaborating and sharing. People can see the contributions of others in real time, and respond and react immediately. This, for many, is incredibly exciting. The opportunity for businesses is to lead, guide and inspire their customers in order to facilitate these ideas and collaborations. In so doing, the innovations and ideas that can be created by people, potentially all over the world, are unrivalled.

The idea of consumers being actively involved in a company's innovations was predicted as far back as 1981 by Alvin Toffler in his book *The Third Wave*. Coining the word 'prosumer',[17] he described a world where the customer is both the producer and consumer in the creation of the product.

Today, co-creation works because customers want to be involved. The web is an active not a passive medium. It provides everybody with a voice and makes it easier for customers to participate in designing products and services in order to create their own unique experience. The increasing importance of co-creation, together with user-generated content where customers provide the content that contributes to the experience of others, eg, on YouTube or Amazon reviews shows that Alvin Toffler's prediction of the prosumer has absolutely come true.

Marketing is now about conversations and engagement, not broadcast and transactions. By its very nature this is a sharing and collaborative process. The scarcest resource that companies require today is customer attention. A business that has this has a huge competitive advantage in any given market. Only a company that is willing to open up and share will be able to engage people sufficiently in order to keep their attention.

Once consumers give your company their attention, it is important not to lose it. Collaborating with aligned businesses, maybe even ones that you have traditionally seen as competitors, can help in ensuring that within your area of competence there is nothing with which you cannot assist. This may be delivering a solution yourself, providing some knowledge or expertise via a third party, or even recommending an alternative supplier. Through this cooperation, you become and remain an information hub for your customers. They are then more likely to engage with you and ask your advice again in the future. In other words, you keep their attention. Without collaborating, it is less likely that this will be achieved.

In creating a hub or community with which customers are frequently engaged, you will start to build a good reputation and generate positive word of mouth. Effective marketing today is about building a community around your business. This can happen only if you provide value that consumers want to share and talk about. Failure to accomplish this will mean they will not engage. The further your business is willing to go in being open and transparent, the more material will be available to aid this process. The greatest risk to a business today is not sharing and giving information away for free. Rather, it is not doing it and being outsmarted by those that do.

A new age of openness

Openness means that employees should also be encouraged to blog, tweet and use social networks. Too many companies still think in terms of protect and control. With this mentality, the potential for missing out is growing all the time. By being transparent, companies have much less to fear on these social platforms than if they are trying to be guarded and secretive. There are still businesses that believe that, because of the lack of control that they can exert in social networks, they are better off not participating at all. Of course, this lack of presence does not preclude others from commenting on that company's industry, products or ability. However, it does prevent that business from having any influence on public perception whatsoever.

It is imperative that companies shift their mindset from control and protection to one of sharing and collaboration. This approach changes the dynamic of a business and provides new opportunities for developing strategic partnerships. In fact, companies should no longer think in terms of customers, suppliers, associates or alliances. Instead, they should think of strategic partnerships where everyone, from a supplier to a customer, is a partner. The two key questions to ask in all these exchanges are:

- Are you providing value?
- Are you receiving value?

For example, with customers, are you keeping them engaged? Are you providing knowledge and information and supplying a great experience? In other words, are they getting value? One of the ways businesses can ensure they are delivering value is to ensure they are listening. Companies must ensure they spend time listening to what customers, prospects and the wider market are saying. In so doing, a business will get new ideas, understand how it can create value and help to ensure that the activities it undertakes are deemed relevant and worthwhile by the community with which it wishes to engage. Monitoring conversations and sentiment – that is, understanding the overall attitude of the marketplace on any particular topic – has become vital for all businesses today. To ignore such an accessible and valuable resource, which can then inform a company's communications, is simply nonsensical.

Conversely, you should look at your clients and see which ones give you value. Who recommends you the most? Who spends the most? Who contributes the best ideas? These customers need to be rewarded. More resources and time should be allocated to looking after them than others. This does not mean neglecting any of your clientele. However, every company has finite resources, and more should go to those customers who help make your business increasingly desirable.

Today, smaller companies can compete with some of the world's biggest by leveraging, partnering and collaborating with others. All businesses, in such a competitive landscape, need to strive to continually get better at what they do. Sharing and collaboration allow for faster innovation with less investment required. All the best companies are now sharing and opening up in order to provide increasing value to their customers.

For example, Amazon encourages its clientele to write reviews. It enables people to become affiliates and receive commission by selling the products that Amazon carries via their own blogs or websites. It also facilitates people in selling their own inventory, by leveraging Amazon's infrastructure. This open approach allows Amazon to offer more value to its own customers by making a bigger product range available through others. This, in turn, makes it less likely to lose out to a competitor. With this approach, Amazon increases the amount of sales channels it has, while raising marketing awareness. This is all achieved without having to invest very much of its own money. Moreover, all this customer interaction means that Amazon is much more likely to stay up to date with market trends. Partnering and leveraging is a very cost-effective mechanism for penetrating new markets. This is an aspect of business that otherwise is often costly and difficult to undertake on your own.

Quite simply, the more you are willing to open up and share, the greater the scope for engagement. Consequently, you are likely to receive an increase in opportunities coming into your business. Being closed and controlling is scarcity thinking, and over the long term will severely damage your business. For example, with the onset of the music file-sharing service Napster in 1999, the music industry started to fight a battle of trying to protect the copyright of its product.[18] That was a battle in which it failed miserably. In 2009, only 5 per cent of all music downloads were paid for.[19] Moreover, one of the only companies that had been able to make music downloads a success was Apple.[20] They, of course, are not even a music company but a technology business. It is only in the last two years, with the introduction of free music streaming services, that illegal downloads have started to decline.[21] While free streaming services in themselves do not provide an income for the music industry, they have finally allowed companies to take some semblance of control. In so doing, they will be able to monetize these services with up-sells and added-value options.

The music industry would have saved itself an awful lot of trouble if, in 1999, it had taken a more open and collaborative approach. Instead of trying to protect copyright, what if the record companies had made their catalogues available on their own websites for free, and then found ways of up-selling and monetizing the situation, rather than taking 10 years to do so? What would the music industry look like today if companies such as Universal or Sony Music had an engaged subscriber base of millions? They would have an incredible amount of data on every customer. The opportunities for partnering with other businesses, hosting unique events and producing special merchandise, all of which could be made relevant to a specific clientele, are unbelievable. The opportunities seem endless. Instead the music industry went through a decade of missed opportunity and lost revenue – a situation it is only now beginning to rectify.

Today, value has shifted. Value now comes from the attention you have from the community with which you engage. In the old economy, value used to be measured by individual transactions. Today, it is created from engaged communities built over the long term. Companies that made money by controlling and protecting information need to find new ways to create an income from their offering. The web is a world of sharing and transparency. Opportunities will be developed by embracing this, rather than trying to put the genie back in the bottle.

Businesses must understand that the world of digital and the web has changed the rules. What once worked for companies – protect and control – will now damage them beyond belief. Conversely, what would have been deemed commercial suicide back in the 1990s and before – that of sharing and collaborating on a scale previously unseen – is now the only way that companies can compete in today's business environment.

Key point summary

- We are now operating in a world of many mini markets. Consumers will no longer settle for impersonal mass products when there are more personalized choices available.

- Marketing is becoming collaborative. Engaged prospects and customers should be seen as partners in assisting in the communication of a company's message. Any engagement has the potential to be far more powerful when shared by friends and colleagues than anything sent directly from a company itself. Encouraging prospects and customers to participate and share is the key to making marketing work in the digital age.

- It is no longer having knowledge that gives you power, as knowledge is now something to which we all have access. Rather, today it is the sharing of knowledge and expertise that gives you the attention of others.

- Technology and the web have made disseminating expertise and cooperating with others easy. Right across the world we are seeing the sharing of knowledge, collaborations and discussions taking place in unprecedented ways. Failure to participate will result in a business being left behind.

- Companies are going to find that they need to 'get social' by integrating social platforms into their own working environments. This allows for instant collaboration among employees, and sharing and commenting on all sorts of information, with everyone able to see messages, calendars and activity streams. Traditionally, most organizations control, and decision making has been top down. In this new world paradigm employees will need to be empowered to collaborate, be informed and get involved.

- The middle market is disappearing as consumers increasingly move towards two extremes. We are witnessing the growth of a highly personalized premium experience being offered at one end of the market, and the expansion of 'no frills' offerings at the other.

- Companies will progressively be smaller entities that come together for projects, to deliver very personal specific experiences for niche markets or to work on particular challenges. Consequently, the world of work may start to look more like the film industry, where people work on a film collectively and then, when finished, go their separate ways. Thus, a mindset of openness and transparency will be required.

- One of the most effective ways for a business to supply a personalized experience and provide value is co-creating with customers. In order for a company to enable customers to contribute, it has to be willing to share and collaborate. It is almost impossible to facilitate this cooperation while trying to control and protect.

- One of the ways businesses can ensure they are delivering value is to ensure they are listening. Monitoring conversations and sentiment – that is, understanding the overall attitude of the marketplace on any particular topic – has become vital for all businesses today. To ignore such an accessible and valuable resource, which can then inform a company's communications, is simply nonsensical.

- Today, value has shifted. Value now comes from the attention you have from the community with which you engage. In the old economy, value used to be measured by individual transactions. Today, it is created from engaged communities built over the long term.

- The greatest risk to a business today is not sharing and giving information away for free. Rather, it is not doing so and being outsmarted by those that do. The more a business is willing to open up and share, the greater the scope for customer engagement.

PART FIVE
It's not about you, it's about the customer

Advertisements to content

When over 8 million people watched Felix Baumgartner become the first skydiver to break the speed of sound live on YouTube, it was not just a triumph for him and his team, but also for Red Bull. The space diving project was known as 'Red Bull Stratos'[1] because it was the energy drink company Red Bull that funded the venture. However, this was just an extension of a strategy Red Bull has followed for many years.

Red Bull Media House, the content arm of Red Bull, was established in 2007 and has since been responsible for producing a plethora of videos covering a wide range of extreme sports. These videos, while entertaining and compelling, also fit with the company's market positioning of enabling people to live life at the extreme. Whether you are an athlete in training, working in an office or partying in a nightclub, Red Bull, as their strap line suggests, 'gives you wings'.

Red Bull is a severe example of a principle that all organizations must learn if they want their marketing to be effective in a digital age. That is, that all businesses are now publishers. Quite simply, every company today has media it owns. Whether it is a website, a blog, a page on LinkedIn, Facebook or Google+, a Twitter, Pinterest or Instagram account, a YouTube channel, or any of the other multitude of communication mediums that can be utilized by a company, every business today is a media business, because every company owns a variety of media channels.

However, these channels are only as good as the content they contain. There are, of course, many different types of content a company can choose to create. Amongst others that may or may not be appropriate are newsletters, articles, case studies, white papers, how-to guides, PowerPoint presentations, photos, podcasts, webinars, infographics, e-books and videos. Whatever the content, there has to be one commonality about all of the material produced. That is, it has to be compelling.

Before the world wide web, companies would create adverts, circulars, messages and other promotional literature. These would then be blasted into the homes and offices of prospects and customers via channels such as the radio, TV, the letterbox and telephone. While many of these promotions were ignored by the majority of the recipients, some would respond. This is because we relied culturally on sales and marketing material to inform us of products and services that were available. In an age where we didn't have much access to information, when we were in the market for a particular solution promotional messages would often be useful.

Today, this is no longer the case. With the ubiquity of smart phones and tablet computers, consumers now have 24/7 access to all the information they are ever likely to require. In this environment, bombarding prospects and customers with promotional material is becoming less effective. Increasingly, people will search online and access their networks to find suppliers. In other words, they will come and find you.

In order to be found, either through search or word of mouth, a business has to become 'attractive'. One important way an organization does this is by creating content of value. Traditional adverts and promotional messages usually only had relevance at the point someone was thinking of making a particular purchase. Valuable content, however, has some 'worth' to the relevant audience, regardless of whether they are interested in a particular transaction at that moment in time.

So, for example, a company producing anti-virus software could produce a fact-sheet delivering the latest tips in ensuring your computer is protected against viruses. This information would be both interesting and valuable to any computer owner, regardless of whether they were currently looking for new anti-virus software. Similarly, a company that builds websites could present a webinar on the five biggest reasons websites are ineffective. This would appeal to many business owners and marketing managers, irrespective of whether they were looking to invest in a new website at that moment in time.

In a business-to-business environment, content will often come in the form of high-level technical expertise or commercial insight and tips. For a business-to-consumer lifestyle brand such as Red Bull, content can be pure recreation. Whoever the audience, however, the principle of 'content marketing' is the same. The material has to be relevant and interesting to the clientele to whom you want to appeal, regardless of how imminent a purchase may be. In 1994, Zen Joseph Player[2] coined a word for this concept when he referred to 'advertainment'. The word fuses the idea of promotions with delivering entertainment or material of value. In other words, don't interrupt: instead, attract people by becoming something that they find interesting.

Good, valuable content, therefore, is rarely about what a company does. Most of the time, people are only interested in the products or services a business provides when they are looking to make a purchase. Generating worthwhile content is about creating value around the company offering. So, our anti-virus provider makes money by selling subscriptions to its software. Traditional promotions would explain the benefits of that particular product. However, this would only be interesting to a person actually looking to buy anti-virus software. On the other hand, in the digital age the approach would be to deliver a more general fact sheet providing tips on how to protect a computer against viruses. This course has wider appeal. It is obviously related to the anti-virus software the company produces, but generates value around the core product. Content marketing thus enables a business to become important in its prospects' and customers' lives, regardless of whether they are currently looking to make a purchase.

By attracting the right audience and potential customers with appropriate content, a business will gain the most precious resource available in marketing terms today: that is, its prospects' and customers' attention. This has two important ramifications. Firstly, if a company's prospects and customers are regularly engaging with content that they find entertaining or useful, it is likely to be shared. This, in turn, will attract more prospects and customers to that business. Secondly, when the prospect is ready to buy, that business will be front of mind.

Content marketing may not guarantee a company business. However, it does help to ensure an organization has a seat at the table when someone within their target market is making a purchase. Ultimately, no company can ask more from its marketing than that, whenever someone is looking to buy, it should be one of the suppliers considered. Unless an organization is doing everything else wrong, any company where the marketing is achieving this goal is bound to win business. Of course, if someone is regularly engaging with an organization's content, it is likely that, over time, the business will have built up a certain degree of credibility and trust with that particular individual. This will certainly provide a distinct advantage to the company if that prospect ever starts to look at the suppliers available within their market, in order to make a purchase.

Content marketing, therefore, is unlike much marketing activity of the past in that it creates value for an organization in its own right. Years ago, a company might have undertaken a direct mail campaign to a database it purchased of 5,000 prospects. It might have received 25 responses from the mailing and these, in turn, might have led to five new customers. In this example, the campaign may or may not have produced a return on investment, but we do know that there would be no residual value. Neither prospects nor customers, or the company itself, would receive any other lasting value from the direct mail piece. With content marketing, this is not the case. The content, because it is not simply promoting a transaction, has wider appeal and lasting value. In encouraging prospects and customers to subscribe, in some form, to the content being produced, the database created also becomes an asset of a business.

CASE STUDY Example case study: LN Lighting

The following is an example case study for a company we will call 'LN Lighting', a manufacturer of lights and lighting products. It started a video channel producing case studies, top tips and interviews with top protagonists covering areas such as health and safety, environmental considerations and interior design. Over time, prospects and customers subscribed to the channel to receive the twice-monthly videos. As more videos were shared, more subscribers joined the channel. As the channel developed, it boasted a comprehensive library of videos and several thousand subscribers.

LN Lighting now had the attention of many of its potential customers and consequently was front of mind when someone was looking to make a purchase. Today, it regularly receives enquiries and wins contracts from viewers of the channel. However, there are many people who regularly watch the videos with no intention of ever buying any of LN Lighting's products. Of course, a few of these individuals may share some of the content and in so doing are helping to attract potential new customers to LN Lighting.

The point is that in the world of digital, *marketing is no longer a means to an end; it is the end in itself.*

Marketing should create an experience in its own right. In this case, the video channel is a great marketing vehicle that generates leads and provides a healthy return on investment for LN Lighting. However, it is also an asset of the business. With a comprehensive library of videos and several thousand subscribers, the video channel provides an experience of its own, regardless of the lighting that the company supplies. It is possible that someone would want to purchase the video channel and subscriber base without ever being interested in buying LN Lighting itself! Marketing was always seen as a cost centre to an organization. Whereas the sales department generated income for a business, the marketing department just spent whatever budget it was allocated. Today, this is no longer the case. Not only does content marketing gain prospects and customers' attention, generate leads and enable a company to win business, it also becomes an asset in its own right.

Understanding your customer's world

Great content can only be delivered if an organization truly learns to see the world from their customer's point of view. In a digital world, people have been empowered. The journey to a purchase is normally initiated by a customer asking their network of family, friends and colleagues and searching online. Too often, companies create content about their business and all the wonderful benefits they can offer. Instead, content has to be about their customers' world, their likes and dislikes, concerns and challenges, aims and objectives.

To this end, there are four main areas a company must examine to be able to create customer-centric content that will appeal to their audience. These are understanding:

- the challenges customers are facing;
- the behaviours that customers exhibit;
- the context in which searches and purchases take place;
- the broad view of the buying cycle to which customers adhere.

The challenges customers are facing

Firstly, a business must recognize the challenges the customer faces in relation to its own product or service. The mechanism for achieving this objective is the Problem Map explored in Chapter 4. Once a business understands some of the issues being faced by its customers, it can produce a variety of different materials to assist with those challenges. For example, a training provider might ascertain from its Problem Map that one of the big challenges faced by some of its prospects in particular industries is high staff attrition. In this scenario, it may choose to partner with a human resource expert to deliver a webinar entitled 'How to build effective teams', designed to appeal to those specific market sectors.

The behaviours that customers exhibit

Secondly, a business has to understand its customers. Of course, not all information is relevant to all businesses. It depends on what they do. For example, in the world of business-to-business trading, a company may well know what its prospect does for a living. However, it may be relevant for a lifestyle brand to understand the sorts of professions in which its customers are engaged. Whatever the information, an organization needs to have a deeper perception of who its customers actually are.

This information should include basic demographics such as sex, age, income, marital status, geographic location and ethnicity but go way beyond this. More interesting for a marketer today is to understand the types of behaviours its audience exhibit.

For example, what type of leisure activities do they undertake? What products and services do they use? What music, books or films do they like? What type of holiday activities do they enjoy? Increasingly, this information is widely available. With so many people posting such a great amount of information on social platforms, 'social media monitoring products', as mentioned in Chapter 7, will allow a business to explore a person's social profiles and, therefore, have a much better understanding of an individual. When this data is applied across the entire customer base, it may be possible for a business to see some useful patterns emerge about the lifestyles and interests of its clientele. Of course, this can provide amazing insights when producing content. So, if a business understands that it has a disproportionate number of golfing fans amongst its customers, it may choose to use golf or golfing analogies as a recurring theme in some of the content it produces.

The context in which searches and purchases take place

One of the most fundamental areas a business has to understand, in order to produce interesting and relevant content, is the context in which someone would start to look for its type of product or service.

No one gets up in the morning and suddenly decides, on a whim, that they want a new accountant, training provider, lawyer, smart phone or car. Of course there are always exceptions, but in the main, every purchase is triggered by an event. It is by understanding these different events that an organization can create and deliver compelling content.

For example, take the purchase of a new car. In reality, there are not many events, in broad terms, that lead to someone looking for a new car. They may have written their car off in an accident, or changed jobs and therefore lost their company car. It may keep breaking down, is old or has become unreliable or too expensive to run. They may change their car every three years or feel that they are missing out on some of the latest techie gadgets and gizmos. Alternatively, they may have a new addition to the family and their current vehicle is not big enough. While this may not be an exhaustive list, there will not be too many other motivations for buying a vehicle. However, once these events are understood, it becomes much easier for an organization to deliver compelling content.

Let us now imagine that I have landed on the home page of a car website. An embedded link reads: 'Change your car every three years?' That is me! Already, by understanding the events that will trigger someone to investigate a purchase, a business can elicit some credibility and trust with a new prospect. Seeing my primary motivation listed on the home page immediately makes me feel that the company understands my requirements. Once I click on the link, the first piece of information delivered is which particular models hold their second-hand value. For many car buyers this information may be irrelevant, but for someone who changes their car every three years it is extremely useful.

Alternatively, let's say that this time I visit the site and see the link that reads: 'New addition to the family?' Immediately I know that the only vehicles I am going to be shown are cars made for families, so there is an immediate relevance. Moreover, the initial information delivered could be a table demonstrating how particular models performed in safety tests, a chart detailing child-seat compatibility, for each car, and a video showing how spacious the back is and how easy it is to fit a buggy and shopping, etc. in the trunk. Of course, for some car buyers this information would be completely useless, but for someone who clicked on the new addition to the family link, it is relevant, interesting and important. Understanding the context of any search is vital to any content marketing strategy. This is because it immediately enables a business to create and deliver information and material that will be highly relevant and engage with a particular target audience.

The broad view of the buying cycle to which customers adhere

The final area a company must understand, in order to create compelling content, is the customer's buying cycle. Of course, for any particular product or service, the buying cycle may be slightly different. However, by understanding the varying iterations a person goes through, before making a purchase, a business can create content that will be engaging and useful at each stage of the process. Below are the type of considerations a business should have in mind when looking to align its content to the customer's buying cycle.

Awareness

In general terms this is the initial stage of letting your audience know you exist. They may not be looking for your product or service at all. However, understanding the challenges and issues they have in their business, that relate to your offering, means that you can produce useful material that engages with them. So, for example, a financial services provider may produce a tip sheet, 'How to make your household budget go further', or an IT company may produce a webinar entitled 'The 10 best apps your business cannot afford to miss'. Neither of these subjects require a person to be looking to make a purchase right now. However, the content is useful and therefore has a chance to engage and create awareness with prospects, before there is a requirement for any particular products or services.

Research

The research stage is the first iteration of buying. This is when a prospect has decided they require some sort of solution. Understanding the context in which they are looking, as in our car example, will enable a business to deliver timely and useful information. In so doing, it will be able to start to build some trust and credibility with the prospect. It is in the research stage that a company has a really good chance of assisting a purchaser in defining their criteria of purchase. This is really important. If a business can help a customer define the most important aspects of the purchase, while demonstrating it can fulfil these requirements, it will help them get a step closer to being the supplier of choice.

In order to achieve this, an organization's content must deliver 'insight'. That is, make prospects aware of an aspect of the purchase that they had not previously considered. It is about providing the 'Aha!' moment to a prospect. Of course, different purchasers will have varying amounts of knowledge on a subject. By having a few of these expert 'insights', a company increases the probability of at least one or two being effective. In the research stage, companies want to create content that answers questions such as: How do I choose? What is the most important consideration? Why should I choose? Who is important?

So, for example, a PR firm may create a fact sheet entitled, 'Top 10 considerations before you hire a PR firm'. This would not be seen as self-promotional by the reader. Instead, it would deliver some important aspects that should be kept in mind. One of the tips offered may be to ensure that any individual working on a campaign has particular experience of working in that industry previously. This would be followed by an explanation as to why. This may not have been something to which a company had given much thought. However, having read the reason why this is important, it resonates, delivers insight (the 'Aha!' moment), and becomes one of their purchasing criteria. Of course, this particular PR firm has individuals with the actual industry experience within the sectors in which it operates. It is now going to be very hard for any PR firm that does not offer this to win the business. This is regardless of whether or not this would affect their ability to undertake the job.

Evaluation

This is where the prospect starts to decide which provider they will use. Listed here is the sort of content that can assist at this stage:

- *Guarantees*: whether it is a money-back guarantee, a guarantee to be the cheapest, fastest, most knowledgeable, most experienced, or a guarantee of the minimum results one can expect, etc. any content that can provide reassurance will help a business in becoming the prospect's preference.

- *Interesting case studies* that will genuinely resonate with specific market sectors or types of customer can positively assist in providing the feeling that you are the most appropriate supplier. The more specific the case study to the prospect's situation, the more likely it will be effective. Therefore, a business with a wide client base should have many different types of case study.

- *Testimonials* from previous customers, put together in an engaging way, can be very effective in giving a prospect confidence that your company should be the provider of choice. Video testimonials are really powerful and can be edited to be fast-moving and interesting. At the evaluation stage, providing prospects with credentials covering areas such as qualifications, experience and achievements, presented in an interesting way, can be very reassuring.

- *Tasters* (try before you buy): any method to allow a prospect to get more of a feel for what they will be buying will help them in their purchasing decision. For example, software providers often allow a free trial of the product. Similarly, service providers may create webinars or other presentations to enable a prospect to have some experience of what engaging with the business will be like.

Purchase

The actual purchase itself can be encouraged with special 'one time only' offers. On an e-commerce site, for example, this may be free delivery if you buy today. In terms of content, a business may offer a free e-book, access to a webinar or seminar, or a free white paper with a particular order.

Continuous engagement

This stage is not dissimilar to the awareness phase of the process. Having bought, the customer may no longer require any more purchases. However, in today's world it is the companies with their customers' attention that are successful. Once a business has acquired a customer, it does not want to lose their attention. Therefore, producing content that frequently engages will enable a business to be front of mind when the next purchase is made. Moreover, by keeping the channels of communication open, a business will be able to promote any special offers or deals that may be relevant for its existing customers. It will also enable them to take advantage of any referrals, recommendations or 'shares' of content that the customer may be inclined to give.

Ensuring 'value' in every communication

Although good content has to be completely customer focused, it has to be created within a framework. This framework is created by the company.

In Chapter 6 we introduced 'customer engagement points' and the importance of a company's market positioning and 'emotional selling proposition'. Chapter 8 stressed the significance of the business narrative: that is, the story a company tells and the vision it has. The vision, of course, is bigger than just what a company does. It is what it stands for, the reason it exists. It is the very essence of the organization. Any content that a business produces has to keep all these aspects in mind. It must ensure that at the very least, its content is consistent with these elements of the company. In an ideal world the content should reinforce some of these messages.

For example, a technology firm whose raison d'être was to be at the cutting edge of innovation would not want to produce content pieces on the more pedestrian aspects of IT. Although these communications might provide their audience with value, they would go against the ethos of the business. Instead, it would want to create material that both provided value and reinforced its positioning. For instance, a Webinar entitled, 'Five innovations that will revolutionize your business in the next two years' would both be something of worth and reinforce the cutting-edge nature of that particular technology business.

Even when working within this company framework, and when a business has a real understanding of its customers' world, content can often miss the mark. In order to ensure the content that a company produces is compelling, every business should ask itself one question before distributing any material: 'Where is the value in this piece of communication for my customer?' This question needs to be answered honestly. We have all signed up to receive regular newsletters, podcasts or videos from a business, only to find that too many of the communications we received were irrelevant or purely self-promotional. Over time, we end up unsubscribing, flagging the particular communications as spam or just deleting them as soon as they are received.

The most precious resource that every business requires today, to be successful, is its prospects' and customers' attention. It is not easy to get attention, but it can be very easy to lose. Producing content with no customer value will be a very quick way for a business to forfeit the customer attention it had. Sometimes it is not just the message that is the problem, but the way it is communicated.

For example, I worked with a business that was moving offices. Although not many of their clients would visit their premises, they felt it important to communicate they would be relocating, albeit that it was only down the road. The first communication they designed was a picture of their brand-new offices with a heading that said: 'We're Moving.' This company was merely trying to inform their prospects and customers of a genuine piece of information of which they should be aware. However, the way this communication piece had been written was that it was all about the company themselves: 'We are moving into our brand new offices.'

The actual communication piece that went out was different. On the front was a picture of a cup of coffee and some biscuits. This time the headline read, 'Fancy a coffee?' On the back the message read: 'Next time you are passing, feel free to drop by for coffee and biscuits. In our new offices we have the room for you to use a desk and access the WiFi if you need to catch up with e-mails etc. Please note our new address is…'. Of course, this is exactly the same message; however, in the second iteration it was communicated in a way that put the customer at the heart of the correspondence. In so doing, it was more likely to resonate and be deemed something of worth. Every business must ensure that all the material it communicates has value and is expressed in a way that is customer, rather than company, focused.

Creating compelling content

Creating great content is not always easy. Like anything, however, a process can be developed that makes it more manageable for a business to generate the content it requires. The first aspect of constructing excellent material is to have powerful ideas. Apart from coming up with its own ideas, there are many other ways an organization can find inspiration.

In Chapter 7 we identified the importance of using influencer marketing software and social media monitoring software. Tracking the key influencers, within the relevant geographical region and market, will produce a plethora of ideas. Once a company can identify the subjects that the main influencers are writing about, it can create its own content around some of these topics. Whatever is concerning the top influencers, almost by definition, must be pertinent.

Monitoring the relevant discussions and topics that come up on social platforms will also provide insight into the subjects in which people are interested. Inputting industry keywords into services such as 'Google Alerts', whereby the latest Google results (based on those keywords) are e-mailed directly to an individual's inbox, is also useful. Keeping track of the latest industry news, key conversations and materials being produced should be enough to provide any business with a multitude of opportunities to create content of its own.

Once the inspiration is present, it needs to be used to generate compelling material. There is, of course, no magic formula for creating amazing content. However, it is often useful to have some mechanisms that can help in channelling one's efforts. In the main, good content falls into one of these five categories: Facts, Fame, Fortune, Freedom and Fun. Think of them as the 'Five Fs'.

Facts

Content that provides really useful facts or information is valuable. However, just reiterating knowledge that is broadly accessible and generally known, is unlikely to create any tangible worth. Great factual material either delivers information that is not widely recognized or provides real 'insight'. Meaningful factual content offers people a new understanding or perspective that they did not have previously.

Fame

In 1968, Andy Warhol famously commented 'In the future, everyone will be world famous for 15 minutes.'[3] The rise of reality TV and social media has certainly made this statement truer than ever. For many individuals, whether it is winning an award, being photographed with someone famous, attending a prestigious event or appearing on a medium that is listened to, watched or read by a vast array of people, any chance to taste fame is often irresistible. This kind of opportunity can often be created by companies in some form of contest or competition.

Fortune

Providing the chance to 'win' something of value is also compelling for many individuals. Whether it is the latest gadget or piece of technology, a holiday, money or a car, people will often go out of their way to take advantage of this type of opportunity.

Freedom

We inhabit a world where people are busier than ever. Juggling jobs and personal lives at the fast pace in which we all now live has become increasingly challenging and complex. Therefore, any information, apps, software or processes that makes life more convenient or easier can be extremely valuable. Whether it is a short cut to a particular outcome, a time-saving opportunity or a more convenient way of achieving something, making life easier is always a popular theme.

Fun

Any material that makes people laugh or that they find amusing or enjoyable will be deemed to have some merit. Of course, lifestyle brands have a history of creating incredibly funny videos to amuse. Take, for example, the Cadbury's Dairy Milk gorilla playing the drums to Phil Collins's *In The Air Tonight*, which has now had over 7 million hits on YouTube.[4]

Apart from the 'Five Fs', there are two other constructs that make producing compelling content easier. These are 'Combined Relevance' and 'Gamification'.

Combined Relevance

'Combined Relevance'[5] is a technique that I learnt from Dan Zarrella. The idea is to combine what a company does, with a subject that will interest its particular audience. For example, the Olympics is a global event watched by billions over the duration of the games. Almost every company can assume, therefore, that during this time, its clientele are also watching the Olympics. So, if a consultancy targeting entrepreneurs produced a video entitled, 'What the Olympics can teach entrepreneurs about success', it is likely to be seen as relevant and interesting by many of that particular consultant's audience. Whether it is a hit TV show, sporting occasion, political event or any other widely talked about phenomenon, by combining the interest in that particular subject with its own business, a company can become more engaging and relevant to those people it is trying to reach.

Of course, it doesn't have to be a big happening. If a business knows the likes and dislikes of their customers, it may be able to use Combined Relevance in an area that would not have wide appeal, but will be extremely interesting to its target market.

Gamification

In 2002 Nick Pelling[6] coined the term 'Gamification'. The idea behind the term is to use gaming techniques to inspire people to engage. This often manifests itself in turning a quite normal activity into a competition, sometimes with others but often with oneself. This is expressed in the collection of badges and rewards for undertaking certain activities. For example, Foursquare is a location-based social network where users 'check in' at the locations they visit and connect with friends. However, as part of the platform, users earn points and collect badges for accomplishing certain milestones. A user who checks into a venue on more days than anyone else in the last 60 days can be made 'mayor' of that venue. Some venues have really embraced this feature. For example, coffee shops that have declared a user to be the current mayor, serves the winner free coffee. Introducing rewards and an element of competition can often transform a fairly ordinary activity into one that becomes compelling. Gamification is a principle that many businesses will be able to use in order to make their communications more effective.

Along with all the mechanisms that have been mentioned, it is important that a company gets into the 'content creation mindset'. Many businesses are inadvertently producing material that could be turned into compelling content all the time. It is important that this is realized and that the information is leveraged. For example, customer service calls can be used to create a frequently asked questions section of a website, or for questions in a forum. If an employee speaks at an event, whether it be in-house or outside, can it be edited into an interesting video or can the material be used for a webinar? E-mails sent to customers in reply to particular queries can often be used as the basis of an interesting article. In order to create the volume of content that a business often requires, it is important that an organization leverages all the useful material it already produces.

However, not all content has to come from a business itself. Companies must look to others within their networks to assist in the creation of a steady stream of relevant and interesting content. Within an organization's connections, content can come from:

- *Suppliers*: Does the business have suppliers that would have something worthwhile to communicate to the company's clientele?
- *Partners*: Are there any organizations with whom the company works that could provide useful material?
- *Industry experts*: Whether these are economists, health and safety consultants, HR practitioners or other specialists, there are often experts working within an industry who can provide interesting information. Experts are always looking to build their own credibility and reputation. Therefore, they are often willing to produce content that provides them with access to another audience.

- *Influencers*: Influencer marketing software will identify those with a lot of reach and resonance, within a particular field. Again, these people are often leveraging their reputations and will therefore be willing to build their own reputations by producing content for a business.

Finally, it is important that businesses involve their own prospects and customers in the creation of content. User-generated content, whereby customers rate content, write reviews, participate in forums or upload their own articles and videos etc, can be a valuable resource for companies. The big communication revolution, with the creation of the world wide web and subsequent digital technology, is that everyone now has a channel. Encouraging people to use it within a particular context can provide a business with amazing amounts of interesting material.

It must also be noted that companies do not need to create every piece of content themselves. Today, there is a lot of value in content 'curation': that is, presenting other people's relevant content to customers in a meaningful way. For example, people may choose to follow a business on Twitter because they always receive links to interesting articles and videos. However, many of these may be re-tweets, rather than the company itself producing new material. With so much information available, and so little time, people will value a source they can trust to deliver the most relevant and important content to them in any particular field. The fact that much of this content is credited to others will not matter. Of course, it is the business doing the curating that will have the engagement and attention of the customer, which is, after all, the desired outcome.

Finally, when it comes to content creation, a business can consider outsourcing some or all of the content to an agency. Like anything, selecting the right supplier is not easy. However, if a business gets it right, it can be the easiest and most cost-effective solution available.

Key point summary

- All businesses are now publishers. Quite simply, every company today has media it owns. Whether it uses a website, a blog, a page on LinkedIn, Facebook or Google+, a Twitter, Pinterest or Instagram account, a YouTube channel or any of the other multitude of communication mediums that can be utilized by a company, every business today is a media business, because every company owns a variety of media channels.

- In order to be found, either through search or word of mouth, a business has to become 'attractive'. One important way an organization becomes 'attractive' is by creating content of value.

- In 1994, Zen Joseph Player coined the word 'advertainment'. The word fuses the idea of promotions with delivering entertainment, or material of value. In other words, don't interrupt; instead, attract people by becoming something that they find interesting.

- Good, valuable content is rarely about what a company does. Generating worthwhile content is about creating value around the company offering.

- Content marketing enables a business to become important in its prospects' and customers' lives, regardless of whether they currently are looking to make a purchase.

- Content marketing is unlike much of marketing activity of the past in that it creates value for an organization in its own right. The point is that in the world of digital, *marketing is no longer a means to an end, it is the end in itself.*

- There are four main areas a company must examine to be able to create customer-centric content that will appeal to its audience. These are: the challenges customers are facing, the behaviours that customers exhibit, the context in which searches and purchases take place, and a broad view of the buying cycle to which customers adhere.

- Understanding the context of any search is vital to any content marketing strategy. This is because it immediately enables a business to create and deliver information and material that will be highly relevant and engage with a particular audience.

- In order to ensure the content that a company produces is compelling, every business should ask itself one question before distributing any material: 'Where is the value in this piece of communication for my customer?'

- It is often useful to have some mechanisms that can help in channelling one's efforts in producing content. In the main, good content falls into one of these five categories: Facts, Fame, Fortune, Freedom and Fun.

- 'Combined Relevance' is a technique that comes from Dan Zarrella. The idea is to combine what a company does with another subject that will interest its particular audience.
- In 2002 Nick Pelling coined the term 'Gamification'. The idea behind the term is to use gaming techniques to inspire people to engage. This often manifests itself in turning a quite normal activity into a competition, sometimes with others but often with oneself.
- User-generated content, whereby customers rate content, write reviews, participate in forums or upload their own articles and videos etc, can be a valuable resource for companies.
- Companies don't need to create every piece of content themselves. Today, there is a lot of value in content curation.

Broadcast to discovery

Once an organization is producing valuable content, it needs to be 'discovered' by the audience for whom it is relevant. Needless to say, a business will put content on its own 'real estate'. So some videos may go on a company's YouTube channel, while others may be put on its website. Some photographs may be placed on a Facebook page, with others located on Pinterest. In order to ascertain which content should be placed where, an organization needs to decide for whom and what they are utilizing each platform.

For example, a car showroom may decide to use Pinterest to place pictures of all the different makes and models currently available. It may also provide a picture gallery of previous models down the years, and their evolution. Meanwhile, its Facebook page may be dedicated to encouraging customers to upload pictures and stories about their own experiences with their vehicles. Twitter may be utilized to re-tweet interesting stories for car enthusiasts and to provide people with useful hints and tips. The car showroom may be running some 'hangouts' on Google+, whilst participating in relevant forums on LinkedIn to address fleet managers and business customers.

Whether a business is using each platform to impart different aspects of its offering or to address contrasting customer groups, or both, it is important that a company understands 'why and what' they are trying to communicate on each medium. In so doing, different content will be positioned in separate places. Generally, it is best advised to avoid duplicate content. Although Google states (at the time of going to print) that it will not generally penalize duplicate content unless it is obviously spammy, it is nevertheless trying to avoid providing searchers with the same content that just happens to exist in different places. Therefore, although there may be no obvious penalties, in general it is worth avoiding duplication if possible. Whatever the content, utilizing social media to assist in getting content discovered is vital. Social platforms are increasingly where people spend time online. Therefore, it is important that an organization is also found in these places.

Keywords and content

As well as understanding the different platforms that a company's audience visit, a business should be aware of the language it uses around its product or service. By understanding the terms and phrases that people identify with, a business can make sure that these are adopted within the content it creates. This is what is known as a 'keyword strategy': that is, making sure content contains the words and phrases a company's audience is likely to use. In so doing, it increases the chances of that business being found in organic searches.

Search engine optimization or SEO is a moving feast. What is a correct strategy today can be wrong tomorrow, with one change of an algorithm by Google. It is therefore futile to detail the intricacies of a keyword strategy in a book like this. However, it is important to at least be aware of 'keywords' as an issue and understand some of the principles for using them strategically.

Google's keyword search tool is probably the best starting point to identify the particular words and phrases that are being used in relation to a particular product, service or topic. It will be able to provide an organization with the words and phrases that are most used. One should be aware that there is a lot of testing and measuring involved with keywords. Simply picking the most popular ones may not be the right approach for a particular organization. By definition, it will be harder to come near the top of a search for some of the most used keywords. A company may find, for instance, that phrases used slightly less often are actually more relevant to the services it provides. Moreover, because there is less competition on these keywords, it may be easier for the business to feature prominently when a search is undertaken.

'Long-tail keywords' can also prove very useful to a business. As web users get smarter they are often typing longer sentences into the search bar. Long-tail keywords are those containing more than three words. There is often less competition for these and, because they are longer, they can be more specific. This often means that the traffic they deliver is an audience for which a company is more relevant.

As well as using keyword search tools, businesses should also be aware of the particular words and phrases their own audience and customers utilize. Depending on a company's niche and target market, this may be different from Google's lists and may perform better for a particular organization. It is also worth noting that if a company is location specific this might be another angle to use with keywords. Depending on the type of business, people are often naturally drawn to suppliers based more locally.

Obviously, if a business has identified appropriate keywords to use, these must be applied within the content to be effective. Mentioning the keyword once in Paragraph 17 of 18 will not be particularly beneficial. Although, therefore, it is desirable to use the keywords on a few occasions, including in the title, these must appear naturally within the content. Ultimately, a company is producing the content for its audience, not for search engines. Creating content that is valueless and difficult to read will not actually help a business to engage with its prospects and customers. Moreover, as search engines become increasingly sophisticated, this type of material is unlikely to perform well in a search. As Google, for example, gets ever more sophisticated in attempting to deliver the best search results for its customers, it is not just keywords that matter. Increasingly, Google is able to ascertain the thematic relationship between words. Therefore, the context and theme that runs through the content will also make a difference to its performance in search.

One of the key questions every business should ask itself is: 'Where do my customers learn?' In other words, aside from social networks, what other websites, forums and hubs does a particular audience utilize? For example, almost every industry and profession has an institute or association to which practitioners belong. Do lawyers use the Law Society website? Are midwives engaging with the Royal College of Midwives site? Is the Chartered Institute Of Personnel and Development's website used by the majority of UK HR professionals? Are local business people accessing information from their local Chamber Of Commerce or The Institute Of Directors?

The point is, once a business knows some of the places online that its customers use, it can look to get some content placed in these relevant locations. If the content is value-based and not obviously promotional, many organizations will be delighted to take content that will add value to their own audience. Today, every business is in the same position. Companies own media channels and require an ongoing stream of good content to keep them vibrant and engaging. A worthwhile article, video or podcast will therefore often be well received. Of course, any material will be attributed to the original author with a link. This drives traffic back to that company's website, providing it with a chance to engage a potential new customer.

Influencer marketing software, discussed previously, will also provide a business with insight as to where it should attempt to get content placed. By being able to identify where the top influencers blog, write and post, a company can decide which channels it should be using. Engaging directly with the influencers themselves may also offer a business the chance of its content being mentioned and talked about.

All of these activities will allow good content to be discovered. Once such content has been found, if it is deemed to be of worth, it may be shared. Ultimately, this is where digital media becomes extremely powerful. 'Birds of a feather flock together,' meaning architects know architects, entrepreneurs know entrepreneurs and people living in a particular locality are likely to have more connections in that area than others. Therefore, once a particular audience starts to share content, it can reach many more potential clients, in

CASE STUDY   Example case study: Drive IT

The following is an example case study for a company we will call 'Drive IT'. Drive IT is an IT firm that provides cloud computing solutions to small businesses in their locality. They understood that some of their prospects were engaged with a very vibrant local Chamber of Commerce. They approached the Chamber with a really good article explaining some of the virtues of moving to a cloud-based system and why it should be considered by small businesses. The local Chamber agreed to place the article on its site. The article was not self-promotional, but solely intended to provide the audience with real insight. At the end, it gave the name of the author and his company with a link back to his website. The link however did not go to the homepage but to a dedicated page for local Chamber members with an offer and call to action. After all, these were the only people who were likely to click on the link. Google Analytics confirmed that over the next few months a significant amount of web traffic came from the article on the Chamber of Commerce site. This led to some enquiries and subsequently new customers.

a most powerful way. That is, content sent to us by friends and colleagues, will have more influence than if it had been sent by a business itself. The 'social proof' and tacit endorsement provided through this channel is worth its weight in gold to an organization.

The 'sharing' of content, whereby a business can reach many more prospects than it directly 'knows' itself, is one of the most powerful ways content marketing can work for a company. It is because of this that, when an organization is creating content, it should not simply be asking where the value is for its customer. Another question it should ask is: 'Why would anyone share this?' If there is no answer to this question, a company might be well advised to have another think about how it can approach the material in order to make it more 'shareable'. This, of course, is not an exact science and a business won't always get it right. However, not addressing the question when creating content means an organization is most likely missing a trick.

Finally, a company should also make sure that every piece of content is posted with mechanisms that allow people to share it easily. If people are not offered a simple way to share, they probably will not bother. Share buttons produced by all the major platforms, such as Facebook's like, Google's +1, LinkedIn's share and Twitter's re-tweet button, amongst others, are therefore vital. Failure to include the relevant share buttons for its particular customers will mean a business misses out on one of the most valuable outcomes of producing content.

It must be noted that one of the effects of all this activity – that is, getting content placed on the relevant websites, platforms and forums, engaging with influencers and having content shared – is that a business will obtain more credible links to its website. Links are important in being found in organic search. However, a lot of the old 'link-building tactics' used by companies no longer work. Google is becoming increasingly smart about how it judges links that are authentic and ones that are not. Therefore today, for most organizations the safest route is to produce content and material of real value to an audience. In turn, the implementation of all the 'right' activities will produce genuine and therefore valuable links.

Listening and measuring

One of the paradigm shifts in the world of digital is that one-way media no longer exists. Before the world wide web, broadcasters would disseminate their programmes via radio and television, while listeners and viewers passively absorbed the content of the show. Meanwhile, businesses would advertise their products and services on everything from billboards to magazines, via the letterbox and through radio and television and so on.

Today, people own their own powerful channels of communication and are increasingly using them. Television is gradually becoming a two-screen experience with viewers sharing messages about the shows they are watching via Twitter and Facebook, etc. People can respond in the most potent way to films, programmes, music and communications from businesses. If I hear something I don't like on the radio, I can respond on Twitter or Facebook or post a video on YouTube. This is true even for something that I hear on the radio while driving my car, but in this case making a response would take some effort. However, consider communications I am receiving within a digital environment when I am on a company's website, reading a post on Twitter, Facebook, LinkedIn or Google + or watching a video on YouTube. Once I am in the digital environment, responding is literally a click away at any time.

A company producing content today must consider it two-way communications. It is not simply a business providing something of worth, but also producing material that will lead to discussion, comments and opinions. In fact, the more people comment and respond, the better it is for an organization. In this scenario, it is more likely people will be sharing the material, and therefore the business's reach is greater. Also, the more customers 'get involved' the more they are engaged and, in the main, emotionally attached to the organization and its offering. Of course, there are times when content is shared for the wrong reasons. Generally however, the more comments, responses and shares a company receives, the better.

If a business is going to produce content and use social platforms to assist it in reaching its audience, it becomes incumbent on that business to listen and monitor the responses it receives. Imagine walking into a bar, going up to a friend and telling them what you thought about last night's football game. Then, before they have a chance to respond, you leave. What would they think? What would they do? They would most likely think you were extremely self-absorbed and rude. They may very well tell others exactly this.

A business that posts content without monitoring and listening to the responses would be guilty of exactly this. Once a company posts content, it must listen to the comments and opinions of their audience and respond. Social platforms are exactly that: 'social'. They are mechanisms to engage rather than broadcast. In order to assist a company with being able to monitor and respond to the comments being made, there are many different social media monitoring products available. A guide to these types of products can be found in Chapter 7.

Listening to the conversations taking place, and responding to individual comments, allows a business to have a deeper engagement with its customers. Moreover, comments can often be diverted to departments in order to create more value for a customer. Sometimes a comment may be redirected to the sales department where there may be an opportunity to provide someone with a product or service. On other occasions a comment may need to be flagged up to customer service, where they may be able to assist a disgruntled client.

A business should monitor and listen to conversations around the content and material it posts. However, it should also listen more widely. This can be achieved by using the social media monitoring software to follow particular keywords, subjects, brands and competitors. In so doing, businesses will create the chance to get involved in interesting and relevant conversations, engage with new prospects and customers alike and, on occasion, be able to drive traffic back to its own website, blog, YouTube channel, etc. This can be done by pointing people to resources and material that may be relevant within the context of the discussion taking place.

Once a business is listening to and monitoring the conversations and responses happening online, it can also start to measure its effectiveness. Thus a company will be able to identify the content that elicits the greatest responses and is shared most widely. In so doing, an organization can keep refining its content strategy in order to create material that is increasingly compelling. A company will also be able to identify those with the greatest propensity to share material. Should a business engage with those individuals more? Should it provide them with exclusive access to new developments and involve them in developing new products and services? This provides an opportunity to turn very engaged customers into fantastic and powerful advocates.

A business will also be able to ascertain which platforms, forums, blogs, websites, etc. are most effective in driving traffic to specific landing pages on its own website. This will allow a company to keep refining its strategy in order to place content where it has the greatest impact. The beauty of digital is that all aspects of a company's activity can be measured in order to keep refining and improving the performance of the marketing activities.

Of course, this relies on a business collating and crunching the numbers. With a decent analytics package on a website, for example Google Analytics, comprehensive social media monitoring software and good customer relationship management (CRM) software, it is perfectly possible to gather real insight in order to consistently improve results.

Ultimately, there are so many possible measurements one can look at. The most important aspect of all of these, however, is that a company measures against its business objectives. For example, a business may want to measure sentiment: that is, are the communications of a company providing its audience with a more positive or negative feeling about the business? Many social media monitoring tools will provide sentiment analysis as part of the software. Sentiment analysis, for example, can be a good indicator for organizations that want to bolster their reputations.

The number of people following a business on Facebook, Google + or Twitter and connecting on LinkedIn, etc. is another measurable indicator of the effectiveness of a company's communications. As well as connections on these social platforms, one of the most potent outcomes of 'content marketing' is to capture data. That means, at the very least, an e-mail address of a prospect. In order to make sense of all this, a company may want to track how many new and returning visitors are coming to its website, how long they stay on the site and what they look at. It can then put a cost against this to ascertain the cost per visitor and cost per lead. Along with these numbers, a business will also want to consider the bounce rate on the site.

An organization can then measure how effective are its calls to action. For example, it may be encouraging visitors to sign up for a free e-book, download a white paper or report, attend a webinar or enter into a competition. In so doing, it has the opportunity to capture the data of a prospect. This allows the business to deliver more value to that individual, increase the engagement with them and, over time, turn the prospect into an advocate and customer.

Data capture is a pure value exchange. In the main, individuals will be unwilling to provide data where there is no value or the value exchange appears unreasonable to them. So firstly, a business has to be offering something that some of their audience will see as having value. Once this has been achieved, the next step is to ask for data that seems reasonable.

If a business is offering a free report containing a lot of exclusive information, a customer may see the value in the offer. If the business asks for a name and e-mail address, that might appear to be a fair value exchange.

However, if a company asks for a name, e-mail, address, telephone number, marital status, age, favourite books, music and films, last holiday destination visited and the three top ways you spend your leisure time, people will quite understandably see this as onerous and unreasonable. They will therefore be less inclined to download the free report. Capturing data is vital in a world where people's attention is so scarce. Therefore, a company must test and measure and refine in order to get this right.

As well as measuring data capture, an organization may then want to measure sales enquiries and conversions. In other words, from the database of 'engaged' prospects, how many sales enquiries is the business receiving and how many convert? Again, the idea is to keep measuring and analyzing where they come from, when they come and how they come, and look to refine the process to consistently improve the numbers. The same is true of existing customers. What content do they look at? What do they ignore? Do they share content and if so, what and when? How often do they buy? What is the attrition rate of customers leaving? Once a business has the numbers, the trick is to keep tweaking the process to improve engagement, sell more and more often (where possible) and stop any attrition that might be taking place.

The content a business creates is there to gain attention, as a tool for engagement, and ultimately to deliver sales enquiries and business. It is often the case that amongst the mass of material available online, a company's audience will discover some content only to click away and forget about it completely. It is up to a business, therefore, to consider its prospects' and customers' journey. The one question every organization must ask is: 'What do I want my customer to do next?'

In other words, having read the article, do I want them to sign up for the webinar? Having attended the webinar, do I want them to try the product? Whatever the outcome, once a business knows what it would like the customer's next step to be, any content should then contain this call to action. Sometimes it will be appropriate to use a rather soft call to action. On other occasions, the call to action may be more stark: for example, it may be an exclusive special offer for that day only. The point is, that once a company's content is discovered, and it is engaging with a prospect, ideally it wants to take that individual on a journey. Without some call to action there is a danger that journey will never start or, if already underway, may not continue. Therefore, every piece of content should contain a suggestion of what the customer can do next.

Key point summary

- Whatever the content, utilizing social media to assist in getting content discovered is vital. Social platforms are increasingly where people spend time online. Therefore, it is important that an organization is also found in these places.

- A 'keyword strategy' makes sure that content contains the words and phrases a company's audience is likely to use. In so doing, it increases the chances of that business being found in organic searches.

- Simply picking the most popular keywords may not be the right approach for a particular organization. A company may find, for instance, that phrases used slightly less often are actually more relevant to the services it provides. Moreover, because there is less competition on these keywords, it may be easier for the business to feature prominently when a search is undertaken.

- Long-tail keywords (those containing more than three words) can also prove very useful. There is often less competition for these and, because they are longer, they can be more specific. This often means that the traffic they deliver is an audience for which a company is more relevant.

- If a company is location specific, this might be another angle to use with keywords. Depending on the type of business, people are often naturally drawn to suppliers based more locally.

- Increasingly, Google is able to ascertain the thematic relationship between words. Therefore, the context and theme that runs through the content will also make a difference to its performance in search.

- Ultimately, one of the key questions every business should ask itself is: 'Where do my customers learn?' In other words, aside from social networks, what other websites, forums and hubs does a particular audience utilize? Once a business knows some of the places online that its customers use, it can look to get some content placed in those relevant locations.

- Influencer marketing software will also provide a business with insight as to where it should attempt to place content. By being able to identify where the top influencers blog, write and post, a company can decide which channels it should be utilizing. Engaging directly with the influencers themselves may also offer a business the chance of their content being mentioned and talked about.

- The 'sharing' of content, whereby a business can reach many more prospects than it itself directly 'knows', is one of the most powerful ways content marketing can work for a company. It is because of this that when an organization is creating content it should be asking itself: 'Why would anyone share this?'

- A company producing content today must consider its two-way communications. It is not simply a business providing something of worth, but also producing material that will lead to discussion, comments and opinions.

- Once a company posts content, it must listen to the comments and opinions of their audience and respond. Social platforms are exactly that: 'social'. They are mechanisms to engage, rather than broadcast. In order to assist a company, there are many different social media monitoring products available.

- The beauty of digital is that all aspects of a company's activity can be measured in order to keep refining and improving its marketing activities. Of course, this relies on a business collating and crunching the numbers. With a decent analytics package on a website, comprehensive social media monitoring software and good customer relationship management software, it is perfectly possible to gather real insight in order to consistently improve results.

- Data capture is a pure value exchange. In the main, individuals will be unwilling to provide data where there is no value to them or the value exchange appears unreasonable. So firstly, a business has to be offering something that some of their audience will see as having value. Once this has been achieved, the next step is to ask for the amount of data that seems reasonable.

- The one question every organization must ask is 'What do I want my customer to do next?'

Static to mobile

Although the history of the internet can be traced back to the 1950s,[1] it was during the 1980s that the concept of a worldwide network that was all interconnected, called the 'internet',[2] was introduced. However, it was in the mid-1990s,[3] with the widespread use of e-mail, Voice over internet Protocol phone calls and the maturing of the world wide web, that the 'internet' started to have a revolutionary impact on the way we all live and work.

When people started to use the internet and the world wide web, it was something people 'dialled into' in order to access information. In many ways, therefore, it was no different from accessing a book, catalogue, newspaper or some other form of information. In fact, in the days of 'dial up' connections, it was often slower and more challenging than using more traditional media.

However, as the internet and world wide web have matured, together with the fast pace of innovation in digital technology, the whole nature of these channels has changed.

As broadband became more widely available, starting in the year 2000,[4] the web was no longer 'dialled into' but 'always on'. However, use of the web was still static. In other words, one had to be in a particular place in order to access the rich array of information available. With the introduction of the Apple iPhone in 2007,[5] the first smart phone to really capture the public imagination, mobile has increasingly become the primary access point to the internet and web. In other words, it is not just always on, but with us all the time.

Mobile devices are now the most common way of accessing the internet and world wide web. In fact, for many people, their mobile phone will be their only way of accessing the internet. Mobile devices are easier to use and cheaper than traditional computers. They are therefore the devices that are becoming ubiquitous throughout the world. There are now 6.8 billion mobile phone subscribers worldwide, from a global population of just over 7 billion.[6] Of course, a lot of these phones are not smart phones, but that is changing fast. Many of the 2.7 billion people who have access to the internet[7] use it solely via their smart phones.

This being the case, it is vital that companies ensure their websites are 'mobile friendly'. If the primary way people access the web is increasingly through their mobile browser, that makes it essential for an organization to provide a good experience on this medium. This requires businesses to either invest in a stand-alone mobile site or use 'responsive web design' to create a site that renders itself appropriate for any device.

The nature of mobile sites is that they need to load fast and be highly relevant. Companies should ask themselves, 'Why are people visiting the website?', 'What are they looking for?', 'What will they want to see?' It is important that the site is easy to use and easy to navigate. Buttons such as 'click to call', social share buttons and maps with location information are particularly important when someone is looking at a site from a smart phone.

Smart phones have enabled users to seamlessly dip in and out of the web during the course of their busy day, without giving it much thought. Consequently, the world wide web has become the major access point for many daily activities, including shopping, accessing information, watching programmes and films, reading books and interacting with business colleagues, family and friends. Moreover, when people were queuing in a store or waiting for a bus or train, they used to read the billboard advertisements or browse the goods left by the checkout. Today, however, they are more likely to be checking e-mails, sending texts or catching up with friends and colleagues in a social network.

Everything that can be social will be social

As social platforms became established and were adopted by the masses, such as LinkedIn (started in May 2003)[8] and Facebook (launched in February 2004),[9] the web began to transition from a 'web of things' to a 'web of people'. The proliferation of smart phones increased the importance of social networks as these platforms became accessible 24/7 from anywhere. For an increasing number of people today, social platforms are the primary way of staying in contact and interacting with friends, family and colleagues. For example, in January 2013 Facebook mobile users overtook desktop users for the first time.[10] Currently more than a third of the UK population logs on to Facebook daily from a mobile device.[11]

Smart phones enable individuals to use the small periods of downtime they have during the day to catch up with friends, make arrangements and find out what is going on. We now live in a world of 'hyper-connectivity' as described by Canadian social scientists Anabel Quan-Haase and Barry Wellman.[12] That is, that smart phones that are 'always on' means we are 'always connected'. Many of us are constantly checking our phones and, as a consequence of this trend, are worried that we might be missing out on the next message or piece of information. Smart phones have removed the time lag that traditionally existed between communications, meaning people communicate with an immediacy not experienced in any previous generation.

This 'immediacy' and constant connectedness is having a profound effect on the way we behave. With news alerts on apps and social platforms such as Twitter, we are increasingly getting our news in 'real time'. More and more information is being disseminated via conversations within networks rather than being published by traditional broadcasters. These conversations however are not restricted to conventional 'news'.

'Constant connectivity' and the media distribution that we all enjoy have resulted in us sharing more of our lives with more people than ever before. As cameras and video cameras have been absorbed into smart phones, more of us are uploading photos to Facebook and Flickr and sharing video on YouTube or apps such as Vine and Instagram. This leads to comments from friends, family and colleagues, as they see our posts, and an opening up of our lives the like of which has never been previously experienced.

However, it doesn't stop there. Services such as Spotify encourage us to share music with others. Location-based apps such as Foursquare and SCVNGR tell people where we are at any given time, and as smart phones become a major gaming device, we can play against individuals all over the world. 'Share buttons' such as the Facebook 'like', Google '+1' and Twitter 're-tweet' encourage us to share a whole plethora of content, products and services that we use and engage with. As the web, social and mobile come together as one, this has serious ramifications for business.

There are very few companies that would not cite 'word of mouth' as a significant route to market. Recommendations and referrals from others are among the most important avenues for organizations to win new business.

With the ubiquity of smart phones and the immediacy they provide, word of mouth has gone online. Posting thoughts and comments on platforms such as Twitter, Facebook, Google+ and LinkedIn etc, has now become one of the major ways people interact. In order to have effective communications, companies have always had to ensure they were in the same place as their customers. Traditionally, this may have meant attending a particular exhibition, featuring in an industry trade magazine or advertising during the commercial break of a particular television show. Today, it means being in social platforms, as this is where the conversations are taking place.

Engaging with customers and prospects on social platforms becomes even more important in an era of hyper-connectedness. With the plethora of choice that we all face when making purchasing decisions, people look for effective filters to reduce the list of suppliers down to a manageable selection. Social proof, that is what others say and do, has an enormous influence on human behaviour. Constant connectivity enables individuals to ask their networks for advice or find out the purchases and choices they have made. Consequently, we are using the 'wisdom of friends' to inform us when making our own acquisitions. In this environment, it is the companies that have our 'attention' and with which we are regularly interacting and 'engaged' that will win business. Those organizations that focus solely on the transaction, rather than create any value around what they do and engaging prospects before they are ready to buy, will find it increasingly difficult to penetrate this 'social world'.

This trend is exacerbated by the fact that social platforms such as Facebook are increasingly looking to be able to deliver search results based on friends' 'likes' and recommendations. Graph Search, launched to the public in July 2013, is Facebook's first real foray into the world of search (see Chapter 8, note 5), but you can be sure it won't be the last. Most people would find it extremely useful when looking for films to watch, music to buy or electricians to hire to see what their friends have liked and recommended. With the data they have from over a billion users, this is something that over time Facebook may well be able to deliver. Similarly Google, with its Google + platform, is also starting to personalize search results on the basis of people's personal preferences, networks and connections.

Increasingly, the 'wisdom of friends' is pervading more of the choices that we make, from the restaurant we select to music we buy, films we watch to business suppliers we choose. While 'word of mouth' has always been important, the instant access to this information, combined with the array of rich information that we all share, means that this is more powerful and more influential than it has ever been before. Businesses that create value around their products and services, and engage customers and prospects, have unprecedented opportunities to reach their audience, as their customers and prospects share content and recommendations with each other. However, companies that don't focus on creating value, and engaging their prospects and customers, will find it increasingly difficult to communicate in this environment.

The sharing of all this personal information provides other opportunities for business. This social, hyper-connected world has led to a loss of privacy as everything 'online' leaves a trail of who you are, where you go and what you do. For many, it is simply a value exchange. The benefits of connecting with friends, sharing information and exchanging views far outweigh any of the disadvantages. For companies, however, this leaves a rich source of data. It is now possible for businesses to understand more about individual customers, and more general information about their whole customer base, than ever before. By using this information, organizations can add more value and become increasingly relevant in their customers' lives.

Maintaining attention

We are living in the era of 'big data': a proliferation of data that is available in abundance and is more complex than anything previously experienced. As more of the products and services we use become digital, information regarding our personal lives, likes and dislikes and buying habits become accessible. If analyzed and utilized properly this allows organizations to engage, with prospects and customers alike, in ways that are more relevant and, therefore, meaningful.

For example, it will be possible for an e-commerce site to know how many tablet computers consumers look at, on average, before they make a purchase. In so doing, the site will become better at feeding a special offer message at the time that a purchase is most likely to take place. This, of course, increases the chances of its getting the deal. Similarly it will be able to see if there are any brands with which people don't make comparisons. For example, those buying Android devices may shop around. On the other hand, those wanting iPads may be more certain they want the Apple device and so less inclined to look at other options. They may therefore be potentially less price sensitive.

There are people who get apprehensive when they think about the understanding companies can glean about them. Yet most people enjoy the benefits of businesses that use this data well. For example, many individuals enjoy the recommendations that Amazon make, based on their previous purchases. For companies the opportunity is clear. Today, all businesses have the ability to deliver a more personalized experience for their prospects and customers. In so doing, they become more relevant and interesting. It is then easier for them to engage and maintain the 'customer attention' that they require to succeed.

From personalizing their website to specific messages to customers, companies can ensure everything they deliver is relevant to an individual. The opposite, however, is also true. Today, the cardinal sin of marketing is 'irrelevance'. People are now handling more information than ever before. They are accessing 24-hour news, watching a multitude of videos from YouTube to catch up TV services and films, listening to podcasts and digital radio, reading books, newspapers and magazines and surfing the web, all from their mobile devices. They are dealing with a plethora of communications from Tweets to Facebook messages, texts to e-mails, as well as phone calls.

In order to cope with this avalanche of communication, people are becoming increasingly clever at screening out irrelevant information. Whether it is a section of a digital magazine in which they are not interested, a track on an album they don't like or e-mails they don't want, individuals have become progressively more savvy at eliminating these from their lives. Consequently, people are becoming more intolerant when they receive irrelevant information from a business. Any company that is guilty of sending people irrelevant communications is very likely to lose their attention extremely quickly.

This is especially true when communicating with someone on a smart phone. Engaging with customers via their smart phone can provide a business with an unprecedented level of attention. For most individuals their smart phone is a very personal device. It is something that is carried with them 24/7, is always on and is not really shared with anyone else. It is these aspects that make communications on this medium so powerful. However, the other side of the coin is that any company that attempts to engage too often in the eyes of the customer, or delivers information that is considered irrelevant, will very quickly be seen as intrusive.

Among the biggest opportunities for businesses to engage with their prospects and customers, on smart phone devices, are mobile applications or 'apps'. Apps are software that is downloaded by the consumer to their device. Like all marketing and communications today, an app must add value and provide a reason why a customer would use it over and over again.

A business may use an app to deliver regular and interesting content in the way of tips, insights and industry updates. Alternatively, other useful information such as traffic reports, weather forecasts or special offers may prove important to an individual. Access to added-value services such as bonus tracks or ways of personalizing an offering, for example an app for a takeaway or shop that remembers your personal preferences, may be compelling for some customers. An app can also just be a more convenient way of undertaking a task: for example, checking in for a flight. Whatever the value, an app can enable a business to provide a very personalized experience and, if it does consistently deliver value, will ensure a company retains some attention from that particular prospect or customer. This makes it less likely people will go elsewhere.

Apps also provide businesses with the opportunity to send 'push notifications' to a consumer who has opted in to receive these. A push notification is a message that is sent to the mobile device through the app, and it can be a very powerful way of communicating. Not only has a customer opted in to receive these messages, but they are also delivered on a device that is always to hand. This means that they are normally read within a short time of being received. Of course, companies can abuse this. However, if an organization ensures it adds value to a customer, these notifications provide it with a potent direct channel of communication.

Of course, companies are not limited to apps. Smart phones provide other opportunities for businesses to engage their customers, including SMS (short message service, often referred to as texts) and MMS (multimedia messaging service – the same as texts but with the capability of sending media such as pictures and video).

SMS and MMS can provide a business with a number of opportunities to engage with customers and add value. For example, because of their immediacy, texts are a great way of providing customers with time-sensitive information and reminders. Thus news updates, price information in markets where pricing is volatile, weather alerts, payment reminders, specific regional information, order status updates, flight delays information or appointment reminders can all provide value to a client. Similarly, highly personalized discounts or rewards, digital coupons and special offers can all be sent by text and be seen as worthwhile, within the right context.

The point, however, is not that smart phones provide companies with the opportunity to broadcast to their prospects and customers whenever they like; rather, it is that people can access a company's marketing at any time they choose. In many ways we have moved from the idea of customer relationship management to customer-managed relationships. In other words, businesses need to provide value to their customers and prospects through the media channels that those people find most convenient. In this way, customers can interact at a time of their choosing. Needless to say, therefore, that SMS and MMS messaging should be used carefully, always provide value and should be opt-in. In other words, prospects and customers should choose to receive information in this way.

SMS and MMS messaging can also be used interactively, as a way of initially engaging a prospect and capturing data with a call to action. An e-book, white paper, webinar, seminar or any other informational forum could offer prospects and customers options to text to receive a call, text to request a sample or trial, text for more information or text to download a particular piece of content. Similarly, videos could encourage viewers to text to vote, and companies can offer texting options so that prospects can enter competitions or receive discount coupons.

Creating richer experiences

Smart phones allow people to integrate the offline and online world seamlessly into their lives. For example, a group of people may be having a coffee together and involve a friend, who cannot be with them, using Twitter or Facebook. During a business meeting, someone may go online to access information that traditionally would have had to wait until people 'got back to the office'. TV is increasingly becoming a two-screen experience for many who, while watching a show, will share their thoughts with others via platforms such as Facebook and Twitter.

In fact, this idea provides TV companies and businesses with opportunities to create much richer experiences. For example, a TV company can show re-runs of an old favourite show but have a live twitter feed with some of the main actors telling funny anecdotes and recalling happenings that took place during the recordings. Businesses already run events, seminars and webinars and encourage industry experts to feed in via Twitter during the session.

This merging of digital technology, cyberspace and the physical world provides businesses with unprecedented ways of engaging prospects and customers and creating richer and more rewarding experiences. One of the major ways this presents itself is in the use of location-based interactions. All smart phones today are built containing global positioning systems (GPS). Consequently, people's smart phones know where they are at all times. This has given rise to a number of mobile apps that provide information or entertainment to users based on their location.

Apps such as FourSquare and SCVNGR allow people to check in and out of locations and qualify for discounts. They also enable people to search on local popular destinations in order to find restaurants, cafes, shopping facilities and sightseeing opportunities etc. This becomes more powerful still when they can see places that their friends, colleagues and connections recommend. Businesses can encourage these interactions by offering deals, rewards and discounts to encourage people to 'check in'. This 'checking in' and sharing helps drive more people to the store. Moreover, it may be possible to meet up with someone if you can learn that they are in a similar location. There are also plenty of location-based apps, such as Around Me, that will allow an individual to find any particular destination of interest depending on their locality.

Meanwhile, businesses will use 'geo-fencing': that is, a virtual boundary that they create around their restaurant, coffee shop or store. Individuals within this boundary can receive messages with special offers to encourage people to come and pay a visit. This is a great way of engaging prospects and customers. A person could be encouraged to opt-in with the enticement of discounts and exclusive offers etc. When a customer is in the area, a business can provide a relevant offer. So, a person may opt in to receive alerts from a flower shop. When they are in the vicinity of this shop on a Friday, they may receive a message, 'Why not get that special someone flowers this weekend? Show this message to receive a 10 per cent discount today.' Alternatively, a restaurant may send a business lunch special offer to those people who pass near their eatery between 12 pm and 2 pm.

Businesses can encourage people to share exciting promotions, special offers and events taking place with their friends by re-tweeting offers etc. Other companies can get more creative. For example, taking a picture of yourself enjoying New York's tastiest Ice Cream Sundae and uploading it to Facebook may mean you are entitled to a free ice cream on your next visit, or a special gift. Apps such as Kapture provide a range of offers from a variety of stores for people who take pictures in their favourite retail outlets and share them.

These types of happenings have led to the idea that some have coined 'SoLoMo'.[13] That is the concept of social, local and mobile all coming together to provide consumers with a richer experience and companies with commercial opportunities. It is because of this that organizations must ensure they register their business on location-based services. This is true even for business-to-business firms. After all, there are still many individuals who will look for a local supplier even when location, in actuality, would not matter. Also, a company does not want anybody else to claim its business on a location-based service.

Encouraging prospects and customers to opt-in to these messages, and become involved by having interesting experiences, is important. For a business to simply blast messages to anyone who happens to be within a certain radius of their location is using old fashioned marketing principles with new technology. There will be a relevance to a business, for it knows an individual is in its area and would like them to come into their shop. However, for the prospects themselves, the message may be completely irrelevant. A restaurant sending me a lunch offer just after I have eaten, or a clothing store sending a promotion when I am late for a meeting with no intention of buying clothes, will just be an irritation. Location on its own does not provide enough relevance for a business to send out cold messages to people's smart phones. However, once people have opted in and engaged with a company, it can be a great way of interacting with customers and driving business. This is especially true if an organization makes it social and encourages its clientele to share with others.

As smart phones proliferate and technology advances, companies will find they have increasing opportunities and challenges. How does a business provide a rich and seamless experience between the information, products and services that they deliver 'online' across laptops, tablets and smart phones? How does this integrate with the 'offline' delivery of products and services? It is the integration of all these platforms that offer companies the opportunity to deliver rich experiences to their customers.

For example, a 2D code is a bar code that allows a smart phone camera to act as a scanner. Quick response codes (QR codes) are perhaps the best-known 2D codes, although there are others. This is one mechanism companies can use to bridge between the physical and online world. A QR code could be placed on a business card, on a gift such as a cup or bag, or at a point of sale display within a store, etc. It allows for rich information to be placed in a small space. By scanning the code people can be taken to a social media page or a website, receive contact info or directions or more information about a product, or watch a special video.

Another technology that allows for the merging of the physical and online worlds is 'augmented reality'. To augment reality means to enhance your existence. This is exactly what this technology does by providing a visual overlay of digital information onto the physical environment. So, if you mount your smart phone on your windscreen, the app iOnRoad Augmented Driving will overlay information, letting you know, for example, if you are driving too close to the car in front. Star Chart is an app that allows you to look at the sky, and it will identify the stars you are looking at.

Of course, for business, augmented reality has a multitude of applications. By hovering a phone over a product, augmented reality can supply the customer with more information. In restaurants and bars, menus could come to life by hovering the phone over particular food or drink items. Museums and galleries could become more interactive as video, pictures and other information could be displayed when a phone is put in front of an exhibit. Meanwhile, businesses could use augmented reality to display more information or a video when a phone is placed over a picture on a leaflet or in a brochure.

The Google Goggles app allows users to undertake a search by taking a picture of an object rather than typing. Whether it is a book or album you want to know more about, a business card to search on a person or a sign in a foreign language that you would like translated, just take a picture and Google will search and deliver.

Meanwhile, Google Glass comes in the form of wearable glasses that allow users to integrate digital technology and information more seamlessly into their lives. It is Google's first attempt at integrating the physical and digital world in a more seamless way. This is a trend that will only accelerate. Integrating the online and physical world provides companies with huge challenges but also incredible opportunities to engage prospects and customers and provide rich and valuable experiences. In some ways, we are moving from the 'internet' to the 'outernet' as the online world increasingly infiltrates our physical world. Embracing 'the outernet' can provide businesses and marketers with fantastic opportunities to provide more meaningful experiences.

Moment marketing

The merging of the online and physical worlds is all about enhancing the customer experience 'in the moment'. People today value immediacy. The mobile web has taught us that instant gratification is possible. Users of smart phones often think in terms of 'now' when accessing the web. Wherever you are, immediate satisfaction is possible. Smart phones mean everything is becoming increasingly contextual as customers tend to search for new products or services, almost at the exact moment they decide they want them. The expectation is that they will be readily available. In fact, consumers are now less tolerant of having to wait for anything at all. The opportunity for a business today is that people are willing to pay more for immediacy. In a world where we are all pushed for time and impatient, we value speed as never before.

In short, we are moving to a world where *who* is buying is no longer necessarily the most important question. Rather, increasingly, the vital detail is *when* they purchase: in other words 'the moment' in which the search, enquiry or purchase takes place.

In the age of mass marketing, most of the shouting in which companies engaged was out of context. For example, a company would shout at me about its new improved washing powder. At the time, I was neither purchasing any powder nor thinking about doing the washing, but trying to relax with my family after a long and busy day. In this scenario, the best chance of a business having a well-received message was to make sure that, at the very least, it went to the right person. Companies would try to break the audience down by demographics such as age, gender, ethnicity, income etc. So literature advertising a luxury new sports car might be sent to men over 40, and mailed to houses in expensive areas. Meanwhile, a perfume created for young women would be advertised during a TV show that they would be expected to watch.

Companies should still have a good idea of the demographic make-up of their customer. However, today, strategies solely based on segmentation such as age, gender, ethnicity, income etc, are no longer satisfactory. The increasing proliferation of smart phones means consumers now engage with your business at the exact moment they feel it is relevant for them.

Today:

- The most important aspect for a company is its ability to solve issues and enhance people's situation, in the moment.

- 'When' is as important as 'who'.
- Segmentation is more about customer behaviour than demographics.
- In short, marketing is increasingly about the moment. It is all about context.

Today, smart phones have provided customers with the opportunity to engage with any business at exactly the moment and in the place they want the interaction to happen. Whatever the situation, prospects will look to communicate with a company at the very moment they feel it is relevant for them. This could be when they are standing in line for a film, killing time at a railway station or in an airport lounge, when sitting comfortably at home or when walking down the high street near the particular shop with which they wish to interact.

The customer journey now starts with them. Consequently, organizations need to be 'attractive' so as to ensure they are approached by their prospects. There is only one reason, however, for people to access marketing and engage with a company. It is that the marketing and communications provide value in the particular context in which a person chooses to interact. Marketing is no longer about the business at all. It is completely about the customer. The only way for marketing to engage and so ultimately be successful is to provide value to the customer in their particular situation. The result is that marketing is no longer a means to an end. It provides an experience, in its own merit, by adding value to the context and situation in which a particular person decides to interact. In other words, 'sticky marketing' is not solely about the product, service or experience you provide. It is an experience, product or service in its own right; or as Steve Jones so aptly identified, 'It's got nothing to do with music, you silly cow!'

Moreover, as products and services become completely commoditized, the value and differentiation that customers receive are in the experience provided, rather than the tangible goods or services themselves. This, in turn, makes the 'when' of a purchase significant in a way it perhaps has never previously been. As digital technology increasingly permeates our everyday lives, this has a huge significance for marketers.

While it has always been true that a certain degree of purchasing has been generated by events, our ability to access information inside these situations has now been enhanced. This means that an increasing amount of purchasing will be triggered within the moment. The result is that, in order to be effective, marketing has to be increasingly contextual.

Marketers are going to have to be much more conscious about when and where people are when they want to engage. This will be more important, and create more opportunities for a business, than just focusing on who the person is.

For example, a fast-food hamburger company might not have wanted to invest in expensive broadcast media in order to market to a high-net-worth business person. After all, it might not have seen that individual as part of its target audience. However, if it is raining and a business person is running late for a meeting and feeling hungry, they might very well, at that moment, choose to engage with a fast-food hamburger restaurant that offers drive-in facilities. It could be them browsing the web for their nearest provider, rather than a young family who are demographically more in line with the restaurant's core market.

Today, far more important for marketers than any demographics is behavioural targeting: that is, understanding the context, situation and ways that potential customers like to engage with your type of offering. If businesses get this right, it gives them the opportunity to become closer to their customers and create more value for them. In turn, this allows the growth of a variety of different revenue streams.

For example, a pizza takeaway or a nightclub will need to identify when most people look for information about their service. Is it when they are at work on a Friday morning or in the high street on a Saturday night? Should the messaging change according to the time of day? On the Saturday night it is possible that people are looking for somewhere to go right now, whereas, on a Friday morning it is more likely that someone is browsing for the different options available over the weekend. Given that these circumstances are different, should the way that a company tries to add value to the situation also change?

Similarly, providers of business-to-business services need to think about when people access their information. Depending on the time of day, are they at work, at home or on the train travelling to the office? Are they researching an expensive solution? If so, what information would provide value within that context? Alternatively, are they trying to make a quick transaction? How can this experience be made sufficiently easy? Today, it is not just the product or service and the demographic of a customer that matter; the context in which somebody engages with an organization is vital. It allows the company to provide added value in the moment, and so deliver a great experience. In turn, this will make an eventual purchase more likely. It also increases the chances that a customer will want to continue the engagement with the business.

Being able to understand the behaviour of consumers, and the context in which they access particular marketing and information, will also allow companies to offer different solutions to the same customers, depending on their situation. This is because people's preferences change, depending on the context of the purchase they are making.

For example, business owners who are travelling for work may look to fly business class. This enables them to check in as late as possible. It makes it easier to sleep and work on the plane, and arrive at their destination relatively fresh and relaxed. When it comes to choosing a hotel, however, they normally select something basic. This is because they spend very little time there and cannot justify the cost of anything more. However, when booking a holiday, the same people have very different criteria. They decide that business class is too expensive and unnecessary. However, they always choose to stay in a much better hotel for their two-week holiday, where there are plenty of facilities and where they can relax. Thus, where demographics may prove to be quite unhelpful in defining the right solution for a customer, context would be much more revealing in understanding the solution they are looking for.

Understanding consumers' behaviour, and the context in which they choose to access a company's marketing, is vital in being able to provide value. For many businesses, customers will choose to access their communications when they are in the moment and/or area. So, a bar/restaurant may find that many people access its information when they are in the vicinity. This is the power of geographically based applications on smart phones, whereby customers can access real-time information, in the moment.

The point is that, today, consumers will decide to access your marketing at their time of choosing. In order to be effective, any communication should make perfect sense to those people in the context of what they are doing. It should provide value by making them laugh or think or by assisting them in some way. Context, however, does not solely have to be about geographical destinations (that is, where people are physically). Instead, it may be a matter of understanding the events that would lead a person to look for a particular organization's products and services. For an accountant, this could be year-end. For a recruitment agent it could be company growth, and for an intellectual property lawyer it could be the launch of a new venture. If companies understand the different events that may lead someone to look for their offering, they can produce communications that add value in the moment, and consequently become compelling.

Incidentally, this is what can make paid search and online display advertising so effective. The biggest sin in marketing today is irrelevance. The problem with traditional advertising is that it is extremely difficult for most industry sectors to reach people at the appropriate time. However, paid search and display advertising has the ability, if used correctly, to deliver an offering to the consumer at exactly the appropriate moment. In so doing, the communication can often add value, and as such prove effective for both customer and company alike.

Convenience – making life easy

Ultimately, the reason people are so attached to their smart phones is they perceive that these devices make their life easier. In mobile, convenience is everything. Smart phones enable people to carry in their pockets almost all the information they will ever require. No matter what the circumstances, the relevant intelligence can be accessed.

Thus business people can obtain knowledge, research, customer records and competitor information instantly. This leads to faster and more informed decision making. Consumers can assess options of where to go, what to do and what to buy, no matter where they are at the time. For example, many consumers will browse products in a store. Once they have decided on an item they will scan the barcode with their smart phone, and immediately be able to see where else the item is available and for what price. They can choose to purchase the item in store then and there, or wait a short time and buy the item cheaper online and get it delivered to their home.

There is an accelerating trend for any product that can, to become software. Consequently, portable computers are becoming the hub for our activities. Today our calendars, rolodex, music, books, games, clock, alarm, compass, films, camera and magazines etc, have all become software that we access from our mobile device. Apps are increasingly automating services. They now allow us to shop, do our banking, pay our bills, make restaurant reservations, book tickets to events, hail taxis or pay train or plane fares, and interact with the many different organizations on which we rely.

This trend is accelerating all the time, especially with the development of payment technology that makes the smart phone our wallet as cash turns digital. Near field communications (NFC) allows for the exchange of data when a smart phone device touches or is waved over an NFC chip. Whether the chip is in a poster, point of sale display or a checkout within close proximity (about 10cm), data can be transferred securely.

As individuals increasingly use their smart phones to make payments, purchase tickets, store coupons and exchange contact info, companies will have new opportunities to integrate into people's lives and create experiences that make life easier and more convenient.

This mobile, web-enabled world provides companies with unprecedented opportunities to create richer and more relevant experiences for their prospects and customers. This in turn will mean organizations can become more integral to the lives of their clientele and consequently have much deeper levels of engagement with them. Moreover, as the smart phone device is now the primary vehicle for communicating with others via phone calls, texts and social networks, businesses can encourage customers to share the experiences they are having 'in the moment'. This social proof allows companies to utilize and benefit from the best marketers they have at their disposal: that is, their clients.

Key point summary

- It is vital that companies ensure the website they have is 'mobile friendly'. As the primary way people access the web is increasingly through their mobile browsers, it is essential for an organization to provide a good experience on this medium.

- We are living in the era of 'big data': that is a proliferation of data that is available in abundance and is more complex than anything previously experienced. As more of the products and services we use become digital, information regarding our personal lives, likes and dislikes and buying habits becomes accessible. If analysed and utilized properly, this allows organizations to engage with prospects and customers alike, in ways that are more relevant and therefore meaningful.

- For most individuals, their smart phone is a very personal device. Therefore, any company that attempts to engage too often in the eyes of the customer, or delivers information that is considered irrelevant, will very quickly be seen as intrusive.

- One of the biggest opportunities for businesses to engage with their prospects and customers, on smart phone devices, are mobile applications or 'apps'. Apps are software that is downloaded by the consumer to their device.

- SMS and MMS can provide a business with a number of opportunities to engage with customers and add value.

- 'SoLoMo' is the concept of social, local and mobile all coming together to provide consumers with a richer experience and companies with commercial opportunities. It is because of this that organizations must ensure they register their business on location-based services.

- A 2D code is a bar code that allows a smart phone camera to act as a scanner. Quick response codes (QR codes) are perhaps the best-known 2D codes, although there are others. A QR code could be placed on a business card, on a gift such as a cup or bag, or at a point of sale display within a store etc. It allows for rich information to be placed in a small space.

- Augmented reality means to enhance your existence. This is exactly what this technology does by providing a visual overlay of digital information onto the physical environment.

- Integrating the online and physical world provides companies with huge challenges, but also incredible opportunities to engage prospects and customers and provide rich and valuable experiences. In some ways, we are moving from the 'internet' to the 'outernet' as the online world increasingly infiltrates our physical world.

- People today value immediacy. The mobile web has taught us that instant gratification is possible. Users of smart phones often think in terms of 'now' when accessing the web.

- We are moving to a world where *who* is buying is no longer necessarily the most important question. Rather, increasingly, the vital detail is *when* they purchase. In other words 'the moment' in which the search, enquiry or purchase takes place.

- Marketing is no longer a means to an end. It provides an experience in its own merit, by adding value to the context and situation in which a particular person decides to interact.

- Today, far more important for marketers than any demographics is behavioural targeting: that is, understanding the context, situation and ways potential customers like to engage with your type of offering.

- Near field communications (NFC) allows for the exchange of data when a smart phone device touches or is waved over an NFC chip. Whether the chip is in a poster, point of sale display or a checkout within close proximity (about 10cm), data can be transferred securely.

- As individuals increasingly use their smart phone to make payments, purchase tickets, store coupons and exchange contact info, companies will have new opportunities to integrate into people's lives and create experiences that make life easier and more convenient.

PART SIX
Epilogue

Customers to communities

We are currently living through a communication revolution greater than any experienced since the invention of Gutenberg's printing press in the 1450s. Then the ability to print many copies of the same text speedily allowed for the dissemination of knowledge on a scale not previously seen. Gutenberg's invention was, of course, a considerable achievement in its own right. However, it was the ramifications of his invention that proved to be even more significant. The Protestant Reformation, Renaissance and Scientific Revolution were unlikely to have occurred without printing that enabled ideas to spread. Thus the invention of the printing press changed the course of history and the world.

Since the invention of the printing press there have, of course, been other developments in mass communication, most notably cinema, radio and television. While no one would underestimate the cultural importance of any of these, in many ways they continued the job that print started: that is, allowing ideas to spread and helping knowledge to disseminate. While print was a mechanism for distributing ideas from one to many, so were cinema, radio and television. Interestingly enough, print never lost its potency. Many people would agree that the major newspapers of the day were just as influential in informing opinions on politics and elections as television ever was.

The development of the internet and the creation of the world wide web have now changed the rules. One could argue that the world wide web has finished the job print started. If the printing press allowed the dissemination of ideas to take place in a more efficient way, the web gives us access to all the information we are ever likely to need, at our fingertips. If this is all the internet and world wide web had achieved, it would be more of an evolution rather than a revolution. However, the internet and world wide web are not just simply facilitating the spread of ideas in the same way as other forms of mass communication.

Whereas print, cinema, radio and television were tools of mass communication from one to many, the world wide web is the first many-to-many form of communication. For the first time in history, everybody has a channel. People no longer need the patronage of a publisher to get their ideas read. There are multitudes of blogs that are followed by thousands, without any media companies being involved. Musicians no longer need to chase record companies in order to distribute their music. Today, everyone has the ability to spread ideas.

What compounds this revolution, making it complete, is the onset of broadband and mobile technology. If the world wide web could only be accessed when someone was sitting at their desk, from a very slow dial-up connection, it still would have changed the world. However, we would not have seen newspapers and books being replaced in the way that they are, as that would have been impractical. Similarly, directories such as *Yellow Pages* would still have been easier to use than trying to dial in every time one wanted to locate a supplier of particular goods and services.

Broadband, however, caused the web to be ready for use in an instant at speeds that have made all types of information accessible. Smart phones, together with WiFi and 3G, now being replaced by 4G technology, mean that today we have the ability to both access and disseminate information from any place, at any time. Just as print changed the course of history and the world, mobile technology together with the world wide web is doing the same. These new tools of communication are changing all aspects of our lives. The ways we shop, work, communicate and interact, make plans, make decisions and entertain, are all changing in unprecedented ways. There is almost no aspect of society that is not being touched by this revolution.

There are some marketers who will tell you it is business as usual. These new communication platforms such as social networks, YouTube, search engines, websites etc, are simply new channels to market. In the same way that one previously sent a direct mail, made some phone calls and placed some advertising in a trade journal, a business may now build a website and blog, put some video on YouTube and create a Facebook page. In other words, these marketers will state that the fundamental rules of marketing have not changed. It is simply that there are now other channels of communication that can be utilized. These marketers are wrong.

Of course, one cannot throw out the baby with the bathwater, and there are some truisms of marketing that will be valid even in a radically different world. However, we are living through a communication revolution. As some of the traditional paradigms of life are being challenged and altered, it is simply nonsensical to suggest that this does not have severe ramifications for marketing, which is, in essence, all about communication.

Stickier Marketing has been written to explain the changes that have taken place and the implications for business communications. It provides a strategic approach to marketing in a digital age, with practical examples of how these strategies are utilized. While this book covers a plethora of ideas and strategies, all of which are important, there are today three golden rules of new marketing. Every organization that wants to have effective communications must understand these new principles and ensure they are applied.

Marketing is about building communities

Value used to be measured by individual transactions. Companies would shout about their products and services via mechanisms such as TV, radio, print advertising or direct mail, and then measure response and increases in customers and sales. In a world where consumers had relatively few choices when they went to make a purchase, and did not have a great degree of access to information, organizations would run regular promotional activities and rely on these communications touching the customer at the right moment.

Today, customers have an abundance of choice and information when they look to make a purchase. In a multi-media world, the most difficult aspect of winning new customers is getting their attention. Moreover, if a business only manages to obtain a prospect's attention at the point of purchase, it becomes extremely difficult to differentiate its offering within the multitude of alternative providers. That being the case, the consumer's primary concern becomes price.

What effective marketing needs to achieve, in the digital world, is to win the attention of the marketplace regardless of when purchases might occur. By consistently engaging with prospects and customers alike, a business will ensure it is front of mind when a transaction happens. This engagement does not guarantee an organization the business. It does, however, give it a seat at the table when a person is in the market. No company can ask more from its marketing. If every time a person within the marketplace a company can serve considers that business when looking to make a relevant purchase, then the marketing is working.

In taking this approach a business allows itself the opportunity to build credibility and trust with its marketplace over the long term. This, in turn, makes it more likely it will win the business when the opportunity occurs.

Moreover, it is the engaged community who become the company's best marketers. In a hyper-connected world, what others say, do and share is increasingly influencing purchasing behaviour. This is because social platforms become one of the primary ways people communicate, and these interactions increasingly influence results in search engines. Therefore, the higher the levels of engagement that a business has with the prospects and customers in its network, the more people will share, comment on and absorb the content, messages and communications it delivers.

Today, therefore, value has shifted. Of course a company needs to have customers buying its products and services. However, effective marketing is no longer focused on those individual transactions. It will be an outcome of the marketing, but it is not the focus. Today, the value in marketing is created by obtaining the attention of the marketplace that the organization serves. In other words, effective marketing is about engaging communities over the long term. If that is achieved, the customers and transactions will follow.

Marketing communications should focus on people

Marketing generally used to focus on the products and services that companies provided. In the main, this was true of consumer products when we were told about an advanced improved washing powder, a breakthrough shampoo formula or the wonderful distinct features and benefits on the launch of a new car. This was even more applicable in business-to-business communications, where companies tended to merely list the benefits they could provide.

However, we now live in a world where products and services are ubiquitous. Within the gamut of products available, virtually no businesses now offer a USP of any consequence. Whereas breakthrough products may have had first mover advantage for a number of years, these days, this tends to be days or months at best. Consider Samsung demonstrating its tablet device merely five months after Apple launched the 'revolutionary' iPad. Meanwhile, in the service sector there is nothing a business can offer that cannot be copied immediately.

This does not mean that organizations cannot differentiate themselves; they can. However, differentiation is now in the experience a business provides, rather than simply the products or services it delivers. Consequently, a company that markets itself only by communicating messages about its products and services will struggle to get across the aspects of the business that make it distinct. In order to express its differences, a company will need to enlighten prospects and customers as to the experience it provides. By definition, experiences are not done *to* people but *with* them. Therefore, communications have to be as much about people, as products or services.

Moreover, the best marketers any company has today are their engaged community of prospects and customers. The digital environment means that effective communications must engage, and in turn be commented on and shared. People don't get excited about products or services. What touches and excites individuals are emotions, stories and understanding how something will affect them and make a difference to their lives. This requires communications to focus on people rather than products or services.

For example, Coca Cola's 'Share a coke' campaign,[1] whereby individual names have been put on Coke bottles, achieves exactly this outcome. The focus is not on the product at all. Rather, people go to the shops looking for their name or the names of their friends. People have posted up pictures on social media sites of them with their Coke bottle or the Coke bottles containing the names of all their family members. People have seen their friend's name and bought it so they can give it to them. People have even complained when their names have not been included in the campaign.

The point is, this campaign is about people finding their own names, going out of their way to find friends' and family names, and the shared experience in taking part in all this activity. The core marketers in all this become Coca Cola's customers. Coca Cola themselves are merely facilitators. The reason people are prepared to get involved is that the one thing the campaign has very little to do with is the product itself! Rather, it is about them, the customers – people. A similar approach was undertaken with 'Fiesta Movement',[2] where 100 agents are the focus of the activities around their new car. The campaign is about the agents and the 'missions' they undertake, rather than anything to do with the Fiesta itself. Again the focus is on people rather than product.

This rule applies whether you are a business-to-business company or an organization focusing on selling to consumers. It also doesn't matter whether you are in an 'exciting' field such as promoting a new car or whether you are a manufacturer of plastic widgets. The principle is the same. In business to business the application, of course, will be different. Nevertheless, the focus of communications has to be people. This can be achieved by focusing on case studies and producing content such as webinars, articles and videos that are more about answering customer challenges than exemplifying the wondrous products or services the company provides.

Marketing is no longer a means to an end, but an end in itself

In many ways, this final rule is an outcome of the first two. Traditional marketing had no worth for prospects unless they were in the market to make a purchase. So the travel brochure was only useful if I was looking to book a holiday. Moreover, once the holiday was organized I would normally throw the brochure away as it had no residual value.

The same was true for the business actually undertaking the marketing activity. The company might send out 5,000 direct mails, but the only aspect of the campaign that mattered was the 15 responses it received. The other 4,985 were irrelevant. Moreover, once those responses had been followed up, the direct mail itself became immaterial to prospect and company alike. Marketing was therefore a means to an end. It was a mechanism purely to drive responses and transactions. However, this is no longer the case.

If marketing is now about building communities and engaging with them over the long term, marketing cannot purely be focused on the transactions. It now has to create value around what a business does, in order to be able to engage when a relevant audience is not in the market to buy. Moreover, for marketing activity to be people focused and not solely about products or services, it has to create value around its core deliverables.

So a recruitment agency may record a series of videos on how to attract, interview and retain staff within a particular market sector. Many individuals may find these videos useful and choose to watch them and apply some of the tips they contain. However, they never have to use this agency's services. In other words, these videos have a value regardless of whether an individual chooses to employ the agency or not. However, how many of these people will share the videos with colleagues and friends? Maybe some of these people will end up as customers of the agency. Meanwhile, at some point, some of the original viewers themselves may require a recruitment agent. In this scenario, they are likely to at least consider an agency that produced some videos that they found useful. In other words, marketing now has become a product in its own right. The videos are interesting to the appropriate prospects regardless of whether they require an agency at that moment, and whether they become customers or not.

For the agency, however, the marketing also has value. Unlike a direct mail piece, these videos will not be thrown away after being viewed once. Obviously, some of the content may need updating over years, but nevertheless these videos can be shared and engage new viewers for a considerable length of time. Moreover, if the recruitment agency decides to add videos, for example, on a monthly basis, and people subscribe to receive them, over time, the agency will have created a real asset. A video channel with 50 to 60 videos and several thousand subscribers does not just generate leads and new business; it also has a value in its own right.

This is perhaps one of the most remarkable changes in marketing today. Traditionally, marketing used to be seen only as a cost centre for a business. It was a necessary evil on which money had to be spent. In the business-to-business world the sales departments were the heroes, as they brought in new customers. Meanwhile, marketing just spent money. Today, this is not the case. Marketing, by creating value and engaging and building a community, establishes a business asset, rather than being a pure cost. Therefore, not only is marketing not a means to an end for the customers, it is also no longer a means to an end for the company itself. Marketing is now an end in its own right. It is a product that has value for prospects and customers alike.

Traditional marketing was seen by many as purely tactical. Once a company had designed the products and services for which it wanted customers, a certain amount of budget would be allocated to marketing activities. Today, marketing is fundamentally strategic.

In order to win customers in a digital age a business has to understand the experience it provides, and create communications that assist in delivering that experience. In so doing, it can start to engage and build a community of prospects and customers. Some of this community will comment on and share the information, content and messages that the company creates. These people become an organization's most effective marketers. By undertaking these activities, marketing no longer becomes a means to an end, but an end in itself. No longer is marketing purely about the products and services a business provides. As Steve Jones, of the Sex Pistols, expressed it back in 1977, 'It's got nothing to do with music, you silly cow!'

Notes

What the Sex Pistols taught me about marketing

1 More information about Paul Mex, record producer, can be found at: www.paulmex.co.uk.

Chapter 1

1 Bill Clinton quote [accessed 13 May 2013] Australian politics: Bill Jefferson Clinton, 42nd President of the United States, excerpt from full text 'The struggle for the soul of the 21st century', BBC, *The Dimbleby Lecture 2001*, broadcast 14 December 2001[online] http://australianpolitics. com/2001/12/14/bill-clinton-struggle-for-the-soul-of-the-21st-century.html.

Very briefly, what are the main benefits of the modern world? The global economy; it's lifted more people out of poverty in the last twenty years than at any time in history. It's been great for Europe and the United States, in the last few years I was President. It led to huge declines in poverty even as more people were getting rich. Second, the information technology revolution: when I became President in 1993, there were only fifty sites on the worldwide web – unbelievable – fifty. When I left office, the number was three hundred and fifty million and rising. Even before the anthrax scare, there were thirty times as many messages delivered by email as by the postal service in the United States.

2 *Yellow Pages* origins [accessed 13 May 2013] About.com: The history of the *Yellow Pages* [online] http://inventors.about.com/od/xyzstartinventions/a/yellow_pages.htm.

The very first time the term Yellow Pages was used was in 1883. A printer working on a regular telephone directory ran out of white paper and used yellow paper instead.

In 1886, Reuben H. Donnelly produced the first Yellow Pages directory featuring business names and phone numbers, categorized by the types of products and services provided.

In 1909, St. Louis produced the first Yellow Pages directory with coupons.

3a *Yellow Pages* UK [accessed 18 June 2013] Companies / Jobs in Yell [online] http://www.jobandtalent.com/uk/company-yell-uk.

Yell began life in 1966 as a 'Yellow Pages' section in the Brighton telephone directory. Yellow Pages, as part of BT, grew to become the UK's leading provider of classified directory advertising and associated services. In April 2000 the Yellow Pages division of BT became Yell and in June 2001 Yell was purchased from BT by a consortium of private equity investors. In July 2003 Yell was listed on the London Stock Exchange and became Yell Group plc.

3b *Yellow Pages* update [accessed 22 August 2013] Big yellow book closes on Hibu as it is handed over to creditors, by Gabriella Griffith, Friday, 26 July 2013 [online] http://www.managementtoday.co.uk/go/news/article/1193051/big-yellow-book-closes-hibu-handed-creditors/.

Oh how the mighty fall. Just six years ago, Yell was a member of the FTSE 100 with shares at a high of 603p. Now it has been handed over to its creditors, suspending trading and making shares worth less than a faded copy of the Yellow Pages...

Hibu posted group revenue of £1.35bn, which was down 16 per cent on last year, thanks to the dwindling income from print directories. Despite its earlier refusal to acknowledge 'the age of the internet', Hibu has recently invested heavily in online business services, a part of the business which now shows some promise. Its digital services division managed to grow revenues by 34 per cent to £174m, mostly down to Hibu Business, which helps business to create online stores and websites.

4 Google [accessed 13 May 2013] Google corporate information: Google Milestones [online] http://www.google.com/corporate/history.html.

Our company has packed a lot in to a relatively young life. We've captured some of the key milestones in Google's development... August 1998: Sun co-founder Andy Bechtolsheim writes a cheque for $100,000 to an entity that doesn't exist yet: a company called Google Inc. September 1998: Google sets up workspace in Susan Wojcicki's garage at 232 Santa Margarita, Menlo Park.

5 Loot [accessed 13 May 2013] *The Independent*, Sunday 30 April 1995: Impulse led to a £50 paper group [online] http://www.independent.co.uk/news/business/impulse-led-to-a-16350m-paper-group-1617602.html.

EVERY would-be entrepreneur needs a stroke of luck. David Landau's came at Milan airport in 1984. An art historian and enthusiastic picture collector, he bought a copy of a magazine, *Secondamano* ('Secondhand'), to read on the flight back to London. 'I assumed it was an antiques magazine,' he recalls... Landau's copycat product, *Loot*, hit the London news-stands less than a year later.

6 eBay [accessed 13 May 2013] Who we are? History timeline [online] http://www.ebayinc.com/list/milestones.

On Labor Day weekend in 1995, computer programmer Pierre Omidyar wrote the code for what he called an 'experiment': What would happen if everyone in the world had equal access to a single global marketplace? Pierre tested his new auction website by posting a broken laser pointer, which he was about to throw away. And to his surprise, a collector bought it for $14.83. The sale of a broken laser pointer was the beginning of a radical transformation in commerce.

7 SKYPE [accessed 13 May 2013] gigaom.com: Yep, Skype is still taking business away from telcos, by Stacey Higginbotham, 13 February 2013 [online] http://gigaom.com/2013/02/13/yep-skype-is-still-taking-business-away-from-the-telcos/.

The popularity of Skype and other IP-based international calling options has continued to take market share away from the international minutes, according to research firm Telegeography. The analysis firm reports that while telco voice minutes increased in 2012 to 490 billion in total—or by 5 per cent—Skype saw its share of Skype-to-Skype calls grow by 44 per cent to 167 billion minutes.

Skype's increase of nearly 51 billion minutes in 2012 is more than twice that achieved by all international carriers in the world, combined. This is not a new story. As far back as 2009 Skype became the largest carrier of international voice traffic worldwide.

8 WWW [accessed 13 May 2013] World Wide Web Consortium, 10th Anniversary: Pre W3C Web and internet Background [online] http://www.w3.org/2005/01/timelines/timeline-2500x998.png.

End 1990: Development begins for first browser (called 'WorldWideWeb'), editor, server, and line-mode browser. Culminates in first Web client–server communication over internet in December 1990.

9 Gutenberg Bible [accessed 13 May 2013] British Library: Treasures in full, Gutenberg Bible [online] http://www.bl.uk/treasures/gutenberg/background. html.

Printing was one of the most important technical advances in history. It was invented by Johann Gutenberg, a German from Mainz, in the 1450s. An account of his life can be found on this website.

Much earlier, books such as the *Diamond Sutra* had been produced in China and Korea with type made first of wood and later of bronze. Gutenberg's invention was different: it was possible to print many copies of the same text speedily. It had great commercial potential, but it did not make Gutenberg a rich man.

10a Cinema [accessed 13 May 2013] The history of film, by Tim Dirks, Film history of the pre-1920s. Part 1 [online] http://www.filmsite.org/pre20sintro .html.

On April 14, 1894, the Holland Brothers opened the first Kinetoscope Parlor at 1155 Broadway in New York City and for the first time, they commercially exhibited movies, as we know them today, in their amusement arcade. Each film cost 5 cents to view. Patrons paid 25 cents as the admission charge to view films in five kinetoscope machines placed in two rows. The first commercial presentation of a motion picture took place here.

10b Radio [accessed 17 May 2013] PBS: People and discoveries, KDKA begins to broadcast, 1920 (USA) [online] http://www.pbs.org/wgbh/aso/databank/entries/dt20ra.html.

In 1920, Westinghouse, one of the leading radio manufacturers, had an idea for selling more radios: It would offer programming. Radio began as a one-to-one method of communication, so this was a novel idea. Dr. Frank Conrad was a Pittsburgh area ham operator with lots of connections. He frequently played records over the airwaves for the benefit of his friends. This was just the sort of thing Westinghouse had in mind, and it asked Conrad to help set up a regularly transmitting station in Pittsburgh. On November 2, 1920, station KDKA made the nation's first commercial broadcast (a term coined by Conrad himself). They chose that date because it was election day, and the power of radio was proven when people could hear the results of the Harding–Cox presidential race before they read about it in the newspaper. KDKA was a huge hit, inspiring other companies to take up broadcasting. In four years there were 600 commercial stations around the country. To keep up with the cost of improving equipment and paying for performers, stations turned to advertisers. In August 1922, the first radio ad, for a real estate developer, was aired in New York City. Networks of local stations developed to share programming and became big business. In 1926, RCA (Radio Corporation of America) formed the first national network, called NBC (National Broadcasting Company). Their first nationwide broadcast was the 1927 Rose Bowl football game from Pasadena. The burgeoning industry made the airwaves so jammed and chaotic that the Federal Radio Commission was established in 1927 to assign frequencies to broadcasters.

10c TV [accessed 13 May 2013] BBC: History of the BBC: The BBC story, 1930s, BBC TV [accessed 13 May 2013]: [online] http://www.bbc.co.uk/historyofthebbc/resources/factsheets/1930s.pdf.

The world's first regular TV service: John Logie Baird had given the first public demonstration of low-definition television back in 1925. There had been experimental transmissions from a studio in Broadcasting House since 1932. On 2 November 1936 the BBC opened the world's first regular service of high-definition television from Alexandra Palace in North London, known affectionately as 'Ally Pally'.

11 Tennis [accessed 22 May 2013] BBC, BBC Sport: What are tennis racquets made of? [online] http://news.bbc.co.uk/sportacademy/hi/sa/tennis/features/newsid_3000000/3000836.stm.

Racquet frames were made of wood until the 1970s. Now, they're made of graphite, fibreglass and other man-made materials. It means racquets are a lot lighter – but just as strong. Tennis legend Bjorn Borg won 11 Grand Slam titles in the 1970s and 80s using a wooden racquet. In 1991 he made a comeback wanting to prove his old-fashioned wooden racquet was still good enough. But he was blown away by little-known Jordi Arrese using a modern graphite racquet. When big hitter Mark Philippoussis compared the speed of his serves using wood and graphite racquets, they were found to be almost the same. The difference was that the graphite racquet was far more accurate.

12 *Pet sounds* [accessed 22 May 2013] Album Liner Notes.com: Paul McCartney comments, interview with David Leaf 1990 [online] http://albumlinernotes.com/Paul_McCartney_Comments.html.

It was later… it was Pet Sounds that blew me out of the water. First of all, it was Brian's writing. I love the album so much. I've just bought my kids each a copy of it for their education in life – I figure no one is educated musically 'til they've heard that album. I was into the writing and the songs.

The other thing that really made me sit up and take notice was the bass lines on *Pet Sounds*. If you were in the key of C, you would normally use – the root note would be, like, a C on the bass (demonstrates vocally). You'd always be on the C. I'd done a little bit of work, like on 'Michelle,' where you don't use the obvious bass line. And you just get a completely different effect if you play a G when the band is playing in C. There's a kind of tension created.

I don't really understand how it happens musically, because I'm not very technical musically. But something special happens. And I noticed that throughout that Brian would be using notes that weren't the obvious notes to use. As I say, 'the G if you're in C – that kind of thing. And also putting melodies in the bass line. That I think was probably the big influence that set me thinking when we recorded Pepper, it set me off on a period I had then for a couple of years of nearly always writing quite melodic bass lines.

13a United Airlines [accessed 22 May 2013] *The Economist*: Did Dave Carroll lose United Airlines $180m? Jul 24 2009, [online] http://www.economist.com/blogs/gulliver/2009/07/did_dave_carroll_cost_united_1.

UNITED AIRLINES has tried to draw a line under Guitar-gate by paying for repairs to Dave Carroll's damaged instrument, and offering him $1,200–worth of flight vouchers. Mr Carroll, a musician, has told the airline to give the money to charity.

You may remember that Mr Carroll's guitar was apparently rendered unusable as a result of rough handling during a United flight last year. He tried and failed to get recompense from the carrier, and finally decided to have his revenge by writing a song. That tune, *United Breaks Guitars* has had over 3.6m hits on YouTube. Gulliver particularly enjoyed the Daily Mail's angle:

When airlines damage or lose their passenger's luggage, they normally – perhaps grudgingly – end up paying back compensation of a few hundred pounds.

But United Airlines are much more out of pocket in this case.

The company has lost 10 per cent of their share value – a massive $180million – after being blamed for damaging a musician's guitar.

That's right, folks. United's share-price plunge is all attributable to Dave Carroll.

13b Dave Carroll [accessed 23 June 2013] You Tube YouTube.com: United *Breaks Guitars* '13,165,110' [online] http://www.youtube.com/watch?v=5YGc4zOqozo.

14 Jim Hanrahan [accessed 22 May 2013] *Daily Telegraph*: New York plane crash: Twitter breaks the news, again, by Claudine Beaumont, 11:29AM GMT 16 January 2009 [online] http://www.telegraph.co.uk/technology/twitter/4269765/New-York-plane-crash-Twitter-breaks-the-news-again.html.

Within minutes of US Airways flight 1549 ditching in New York's Hudson river, the blogosphere was buzzing with the news. Emails, Twitter messages, mobile phone photos and hazy videos about the crash flitted across cyberspace. Some reassured friends and loved ones that all was well; others simply documented the unfolding drama as all 155 passengers and crew made their way to safety using the jet's inflatable emergency chutes.

Twitter, the increasingly popular microblogging service, was, as ever, leading the pack. When dozens of New York-based Twitter users started sending 'tweets' about a possible plane crash in the city, the news spread like wildfire across the Twitterverse. Indeed, Twitter users broke the news of the incident around 15 minutes before the mainstream media alerted viewers and readers to the crash. The first recorded tweet about the crash came from Jim Hanrahan, aka Manolantern, four minutes after the plane went down, who wrote: 'I just watched a plane crash into the hudson riv [sic] in manhattan.'

15 Arab Spring [accessed 22 May 2013] *Huffington Post*: Social media and the Arab Spring: What have we learned? Raymond Schillinger, posted: 09/20/11 03:59 PM ET [online] http://www.huffingtonpost.com/raymond-schillinger/arab-spring-social-media_b_970165.html.

For the legions of critics who had previously dismissed platforms like Facebook and Twitter as vapid troughs of celebrity gossip and self-aggrandizement, the toppling of regimes in Tunisia and Egypt suggested that these tools were as effective for organizing protests and revolutions as they were for organizing keg parties. The movements throughout the Arab world appeared to have imbued social media with an irrevocable sense of legitimacy as a tool for fomenting change.

16 Sohaib Athar [accessed 22 May 2013] *BBC News*: Technology: Bin Laden raid was revealed on Twitter, 2 May 2011, last updated at 10:49 [online] http://www.bbc.co.uk/news/technology-13257940.

The raid that killed Osama Bin Laden was revealed on Twitter.

An IT consultant, living in Abbottabad, unknowingly tweeted details of the US-led operation as it happened.

Sohaib Athar wrote that a helicopter was hovering overhead shortly before the assault began and said that it might not be a Pakistani aircraft.

He only became aware of the significance of his tweets after President Obama announced details of Bin Laden's death.

Mr Athar's first posting on the subject came at around 1am local time (9pm BST).

He wrote: 'Helicopter hovering above Abbottabad at 1AM (is a rare event).'

Soon after, he reported the sound of an explosion, now known to have been US forces blowing up their damaged helicopter.

'A huge window shaking bang here in Abbottabad Cantt. I hope it's not the start of something nasty :-S'

Throughout the raid, Mr Athar was drawing on information from friends in the local area who were also online.

17 Guardian Witness [accessed 22 May 2013] Mashable.com: The *Guardian* calls for citizen journalists via app, by Lauren Indvikapr, 16 April 2013 [online] http://mashable.com/2013/04/16/the-guardianwitness/.

Vanishing are the days when readers' contributions to the papers they read are limited to the 'letters to the editor' section. The latest publication to open its arms to reader contributions—in the form of videos, photos and stories—is The Guardian which launched Tuesday a program called 'Guardian Witness.'

Guardian Witness, available, online and as an app for iPhone and Android devices, asks users to supply staff journalists with videos, photos and stories for both breaking news events and less pressing features, which could then appear on The Guardian's website and/or in print...

The initiative is similar to that of CNN iReport and ProPublica's Get Involved which ask readers to contribute stories and footage for specific assignments, as well as ideas for coverage.

18 CNN Facebook [accessed 22 May 2013] *Guardian*: Technology Blog, posted by Kevin Anderson, Wednesday 21 January 2009 16.53 GMT [online] http://www.guardian.co.uk/technology/blog/2009/jan/21/barackobama-television.

Facebook meets TV, literally. CNN integrated Facebook with a live video stream of their coverage of Barack Obama's inauguration. This might just jump start more social video experiments... CNN.com said it has served more than 21.3m live video streams, including 1.3m simultaneous streams before Obama gave his address, according to CNET.com. Facebook had 1.5m inauguration-related updates, and Facebook provided these figures:

600,000 status updates have been posted so far through the CNN.com Live Facebook feed

There were an average of 4,000 status updates every minute during the broadcast

There were 8,500 status updates the minute Obama began his speech.

19 Barack Obama [accessed 22 May 2013] Mashable.com: Obama's 'Four More Years' tweet is most popular of all time, by Stan Schroedernov, 7 November 2012 [online] http://mashable.com/2012/11/07/obama-four-more-years-tweet/.

President Barack Obama's celebratory tweet after winning the U.S. election surpassed 500,000 retweets, making it the most retweeted post of all time, according to reports.

The tweet, which simply says, 'Four more years' accompanies a photo of Obama and First Lady Michelle Obama embracing. At the time of writing, it garnered more than 510,000 retweets — and that number is still rising rapidly.

20 Common Market [accessed 22 May 2013] History.com: This day in history: general interest, 25 March 1957, Common Market founded [online] http://www.history.com/this-day-in-history/common-market-founded.

On March 25, 1957, France, West Germany, Italy, the Netherlands, Belgium, and Luxembourg sign a treaty in Rome establishing the European Economic Community (EEC), also known as the Common Market. The EEC, which came into operation in January 1958, was a major step in Europe's movement toward economic and political union... In early 1990s, the European Community became the basis for the European Union (EU), which was established in 1993 following ratification of the Maastricht Treaty.

21 Berlin Wall [accessed 18 June 2013] BBC: On this day: 9 November 1989 [online] http://news.bbc.co.uk/onthisday/hi/witness/november/9/newsid_3241000/3241641.stm.

1989: The night the Wall came down

The 28-mile (45 km) barrier dividing Germany's capital was built in 1961 to prevent East Berliners fleeing to the West.

But as Communism in the Soviet Republic and Eastern Europe began to crumble, pressure mounted on the East German authorities to open the Berlin border.

The Wall was finally breached by jubilant Berliners on 9 November 1989, unifying a city that had been divided for over 30 years.

22 Globalization [accessed 20 June 2013] *Bloomberg Business Week*: Global economics, 5 November 2009, Fall of the Berlin Wall: A victory for Europe, by Gabriele Suder [online] http://www.businessweek.com/stories/2009–11–05/fall-of-the-berlin-wall-a-victory-for-europebusinessweek-business-news-stock-market-and-financial-advice.

Two decades after the collapse of the Iron Curtain, Europe and the world have gained enormously from democratic and economic integration.

...For business, far-reaching changes in the global economic environment kicked off at that time: The transition to market-based economies in most Central and Eastern European countries created significant opportunities for markets, resources, supplies, and manufacturing. We saw a huge increase in cross-border trade and foreign direct investment, including in services. Almost simultaneously, the emergence of the digital revolution brought with it a decrease in international transaction costs and led to offshore service advantages. Innovations in both developed and developing countries and the emergence of the Asian tigers and the BRIC countries – Brazil, Russia, India, and China – increased the speed of product life cycles and market opportunities, with accelerating globalization taking hold of our economies. Companies turned to cross-border mergers and acquisitions in an effort to improve their global competitiveness, boosting multinational activity in locations until then untouched by market capitalism. From an EU business standpoint, the fall of the Berlin Wall brought a revolution of a unique kind. German reunification expanded the common market in size and population; now, thanks to EU enlargements in 2004 and 2007, the market encompasses 500 million people, with yet more set to join in future years. Indeed, it could be argued that the fall of the Berlin Wall set in motion steps that have solidified Europe's position in international affairs.

Chapter 2

1 The web [accessed 22 May 2013] World Wide Web Consortium, 10th Anniversary: Pre W3C web and internet background [online] http://www.w3.org/2005/01/timelines/timeline-2500x998.png.

End 1990: Development begins for first browser (called 'WorldWideWeb'), editor, server, and line-mode browser. Culminates in first Web client–server communication over internet in December 1990.

2 Sky [accessed 22 May 2013] Sky TV timeline [online] http://corporate.sky.com/about_sky/timeline.

1989 Sky launches a 'Direct to Home' satellite television service via the Astra satellite with four free-to-air channels including Sky News, Europe's first 24-hour news channel. 1990 Sky and rival broadcaster BSB agree to merge and form BSkyB. Sky Movies uses encryption technology to become a subscription service.

3 European air industry [accessed 22 May 2013] Parliament: Liberalization of aviation in the EU, Select Committee on European Union Seventeenth Report [online] http://www.publications.parliament.uk/pa/ld200203/ldselect/ldeucom/92/9203.htm.

14. Within the European Community, the liberalization process began in 1987 with the adoption of a first package of measures aimed at opening up the traditionally restrictive bilateral arrangements. A second package agreed in June 1990 built on this foundation, and a third package of measures was agreed in June 1992. As a result, a single market in air transport in the European Community came into being on 1 January 1993.

4 EasyJet [accessed 22 May 2013] Our timeline 1995–2010 [online] http://traveller.easyjet.com/features/2010/11/easyjet-timeline-1995–2010.

1995 – easyJet is founded by Sir Stelios Haji-Ioannou in March to offer low-cost flights in Europe. In October, easyLand, our first home, opens at Luton Airport. Our inaugural flights take off from London Luton to Glasgow on 10 November, and to Edinburgh on the 15th.

5 Ryanair [accessed 18 June 2013] About us: History of Ryanair [online] http://www.ryanair.com/site/EN/about.php.

1986: Ryanair obtains permission from the regulatory authorities to challenge the British Airways and Aer Lingus' high fare duopoly on the Dublin–London route. Services are launched with two (46-seater) turbo prop BAE748 aircraft. The first flights operate in May from Dublin to London Luton. The launch fare of £99 return is less than half the price of the BA/Aer Lingus lowest return fare of £209. Both British Airways and Aer Lingus slash their high prices in response to Ryanair's. Ryanair starts the first fare war in Europe. With two routes in operation, Ryanair carries 82,000 passengers in its first full year in operation.

6 UK telephony [accessed 18 June 2013] *The Independent*: Mercury available from any telephone, by Mary Fagan, Friday, 1 October 1993 [online] http://www.independent.co.uk/news/uk/mercury-available-from-any-telephone-1507928.html.

Although Mercury has more than 10 per cent of the telecommunications market by revenue, it has made limited inroads into the residential sector. Almost 500,000 households are connected to Mercury via BT local lines and about 200,000 through cable television companies. This compares with a total of 20 million residential customers in the United Kingdom.

7 Gas & electric privatization [accessed 23 June 2013] Energylinx: UK gas and electricity milestones [online] http://www.energylinx.co.uk/milestones.htm.

1986 British Gas privatised...

November 1988 Electricity Bill presented to Parliament...

May 1998 Domestic gas marketing fully open to competition...

May 1999 Domestic electricity market fully open to competition.

8 Deregulation [accessed 18 June 2013] OpenLearn: Personal finance: Debt and borrowing in its wider context. > 1.3 Liberalization in the financial services industry [online] http://projects.kmi.open.ac.uk/role/moodle/mod/page/view.php?id=2136.

there are other aspects of the social and economic context relevant to understanding debt. One of the most important is the liberalization of the UK financial services industry. This process has brought about great change within financial services, dating back to legislation passed in the 1980s. This included the Financial Services Act 1986, the Building Societies Act 1986, and the Banking Act 1987. Together with policy changes by lenders, these acts prompted the diversification by financial institutions into various new activities; relaxed rules on the use by lenders of borrowing from other financial institutions in the world's financial markets to finance their personal lending, and encouraged greater price competition among lenders.

9 Mobile phone ownership [accessed 18 June 2013] Mobile Operators Association (MOA): Mobile phone usage 1990 [online] http://www.

mobilemastinfo.com/history-of-mobile-cellular-communication/history-of-cellular-mobile-communications.html.

Mobile Phone Subscribers: 1990 = 1.14m.

10 UK population [accessed 18 June 2013] Optimum Population Trust: UK Population 1990 [online] http://populationmatters.org/documents/uk_population_growth.pdf?phpMyAdmin=e11b8b687c20198d9ad050fbb1aa7f2f.

UK population mid 1990 = 57.561m.

11 SMS texting [accessed 18 June 2013] *New Scientist*, Tech: The pioneering messages made possible by technology (part 2) 12:40 16 October 2008, by Colin Barras. First text message [online] http://www.newscientist.com/article/dn14958–the-pioneering-messages-made-possible-by-technology-part-2.html.

'Merry Christmas' texted Neil Papworth of Sema Group to Richard Jarvis of Vodafone on 3rd December 1992. Papworth actually sent the message from a PC. Riku Pihkonen of Nokia claims to be the first to have physically 'texted' from a phone, in 1993.

12a Demon internet [accessed 18 June 2013] *Guardian*, Technology Series: The internet at 40: Forty years of the internet: How the world changed for ever, by Oliver Burkeman, the *Guardian*, Friday 23 October 2009 [online] http://www.guardian.co.uk/technology/2009/oct/23/internet-40–history-arpanet.

In October 1969, a student typed 'LO' on a computer… The spread of the internet across the Atlantic, through academia and eventually to the public, is a tale too intricate to recount here, though it bears mentioning that British Telecom and the British government didn't really want the internet at all: along with other European governments, they were in favour of a different networking technology, Open Systems Interconnect. Nevertheless, by July 1992, an Essex-born businessman named Cliff Stanford had opened Demon internet, Britain's first commercial internet service provider. Officially, the public still wasn't meant to be connecting to the internet. 'But it was never a real problem', Stanford says today. 'The people trying to enforce that weren't working very hard to make it happen, and the people working to do the opposite were working much harder.' The French consulate in London was an early customer, paying Demon £10 a month instead of thousands of pounds to lease a private line to Paris from BT.

After a year or so, Demon had between 2,000 and 3,000 users, but they weren't always clear why they had signed up: it was as if they had sensed the direction of the future, in some inchoate fashion, but hadn't thought things through any further than that. 'The question we always got was: "OK, I'm connected – what do I do now?"', Stanford recalls. 'It was one of the most common questions on our support line. We would answer with "Well, what do you want to do? Do you want to send an email?" "Well, I don't know anyone with an email address."' People got connected, but they didn't know what was meant to happen next.

12b AOL [accessed 18 June 2013] Living internet: Email history, by Dave Crocker, AOL, Online Services [online] http://www.livinginternet.com/e/ei.htm.

In 1993, the large network service providers America Online and Delphi started to connect their proprietary email systems to the internet, beginning the large scale adoption of internet email as a global standard.

13a TV ratings 1990 [accessed 18 June 2013] BARB Top 10 UK TV programmes 1990 [online] http://www.barb.co.uk/resources/tv-facts/since-1981/1990/top10.

Average viewing figure of Top 10 programmes viewed in 1990: 17.62m

No. of reported channels: 12.

13b TV ratings 2010 [accessed 18 June 2013] BARB Top 10 UK TV programmes 2010 [online] http://www.barb.co.uk/resources/tv-facts/since-1981/2010/top10.

Average viewing figure of Top 10 programmes viewed in 2010: 14.14m

No. of reported channels: 286.

14 Digital advertising [Accessed 23 June 2013] FreshPita: TV v Onlinevideo advertising: the heat is on, by Emily Cretella, 4 April, 2013 [online] http://blog.thepitagroup.com/2013/tv-vs-online-video-advertising-the-heat-is-on/.

U.S. consumers spent 3.8 billion minutes streaming video advertising in February, according to Online Media Daily. That's 9.9 billion video ads in one month, with Google sites (YouTube) serving an all-time high of 2.2 billion ads.

Online video advertising continues to break records. While digital video ad spending was projected to increase 46.5 per cent in 2012, TV ad spending was only projected to rise 6.4 per cent. And that's only one of the many impressive stats gathered in an infographic by Prestige Marketing...

Not sure if online video advertising makes sense for your brand? Here are some of the top takeaways to consider:

25 per cent of all viewed video content was advertising

11+ billion online ads were streamed in June 2012

Social media users are 5x more likely to click on videos and photos

Brand recall increases nine times with ad campaigns on multiple screens (TV, online video, etc)

81 per cent of marketers used online video in 2011.

15 Broadband [Accessed 18 June 2013] *The Independent*: Broadband: The first decade, by Kate Youde, Sunday, 28 March 2010 [online] http://www.independent.co.uk/life-style/gadgets-and-tech/news/broadband-the-first-decade-1929515.html.

Telewest launched home ADSL – asymmetric digital subscriber line, as it was known – in the UK on 31 March 2000, with Goldsmith Road in Gillingham, Kent, the first street to receive the technology after the trial at Mr Bush's home.

TABLE 2.1 BARB Top 10 UK TV Programmes 1990
Average viewing figure of Top 10 programmes viewed in 1990:
17.62m. Number of reported channels: 12.

Rank	Programme	Date	Channel	Audience (millions)
1	Neighbours* aggregated, lunchtime + teatime showing	26 Feb 1990	BBC1	21.16
2	Coronation Street	01 Jan 1990	ITV	19.20
3	Only Fools and Horses	25 Dec 1990	BBC1	17.97
4	It'll Be Alright on the Night	01 Dec 1990	ITV	17.92
5	Film: E.T.	25 Dec 1990	BBC1	17.50
6	Film: A View To A Kill	31 Jan 1990	ITV	16.93
7	The Generation Game	25 Dec 1990	BBC1	16.73
8	World Cup 1990: England v West Germany	03 July 1990	BBC1	16.69
9	Inspector Morse	w/e28 Jan 1990	ITV	16.16
10	World Cup 1990: England v Ireland	11 Jun 1990	ITV	15.96

Source: TV Ratings 1990 (accessed 18 June 2013) BARB Top 10 UK TV Programmes 1990 [online] http://www.barb.co.uk/resources/tv-facts/since-1981/1990/top10).

TABLE 2.2 BARB Top 10 UK TV Programmes 2010
Average viewing figure of Top 10 programmes viewed in 2010:
14.14m. Number of reported channels: 286.

Rank	Programme	Date	Channel	Audience (millions)
1	The X Factor Results	12 Dec 2010	ITV1	16.55
2	Eastenders	19 Feb 2010	BBC1	16.41
3	World Cup 2010: England v Germany	27 June 2010	BBC1	15.81
4	The X Factor	03 Oct 2010	ITV1	14.51
5	Strictly Come Dancing	18 Dec 2010	BBC1	14.28
6	Coronation Street	06 Dec 2010	ITV1	14.10
7	Britain's Got Talent	05 June 2010	ITV1	12.83
8	Come Fly With Me	25 Dec 2010	BBC1	12.47
9	I'm a Celebrity - Get Me Out of Here	04 Dec 2010	ITV1	12.37
10	Dr Who	25 Dec 2010	BBC1	12.11

Source: TV Ratings 2010 [accessed 18 June 2013] BARB Top 10 UK TV Programmes 2010 [online] http://www.barb.co.uk/resources/tv-facts/since-1981/2010/top10.

16 iPhone [Accessed 18 June 2013] Macworld.com: Apple unveils iPhone, by Mathew Honan, PC World, 9 January 2007 [online] http://www.macworld. com/article/1054769/iphone.html.

After more than two years in the making, Apple CEO Steve Jobs Tuesday announced the company's intention to enter the mobile handset market, unveiling the new Apple iPhone. The iPhone brings together several features of the iPod, digital camera, smart phones and even portable computing to one device, with a widescreen display and an innovative input method.

17 Robert Stephens [accessed 18 June 2013] thebrandgymblog: Advertising is a tax for having an unremarkable product, by David Taylor, 28 November 2006 [online] http://wheresthesausage.typepad.com/my_weblog/customer_experience/.

This quote is by Robert Stephens, Founder and 'Chief Inspector' of the Geek Squad, from his speech at last week's Marketing Society Conference in London. He has been able to grow his computer repair business from a one-man start-up to a company employing 15 000 'agents' in the USA, and secure a UK launch with Carphone Warehouse, all without the need for advertising. How? By designing every single bit of the Geek Squad experience to maximize impact and create word-of-mouth.

Chapter 3

1 Mobile apps [accessed 23 June 2013] FuturePlatforms: Domino's Pizza [online] http://www.futureplatforms.com/case_study/dominos-pizza/.

E-commerce – In 2012 we have surpassed our original goal for Domino's e-commerce, when they announced that over nearly 60 per cent of all sales are now being ordered online.

Mobile – Domino's now takes 20 per cent of digital sales from mobile devices, and reported that m-commerce shoppers tend to buy more frequently and loyally.

2 Relationship marketing [accessed 23 June 2013] The dark side of relationship marketing, by D Ramkumar and S Saravanan [online] http://webcache.googleusercontent.com/search?q=cache:http://dspace.iimk.ac.in/bitstream/2259/340/1.

For academicians it is a paradigm shift in marketing philosophy urging the importance of long term relationship and retaining existing customers over getting new customers; since a bird in hand is better than the two in a bush. For practitioners Relationship marketing is a competitive advantage... a tool to reduce the customer churn... a tool to overcome service failures... an opportunity for marketing additional products and services to a more receptive customer base...

Evolution of Relationship Marketing. In 1983 Leonard L. Berry, distinguished professor of Marketing at Texas A&M University, coined the word Relationship Marketing when he presented a paper entitled Relationship Marketing at the American Marketing Association's Services Marketing Conference. The paper was published in the conference proceedings and for the first time the phrase Relationship Marketing appeared in the Marketing literature.

3 RSS feeds [accessed 23 June 2013] DRC Consulting: RSS feeds. What is RSS all about? [online] http://www.drcc.com/home.nsf/rssfeeds.

Really Simple Syndication (RSS) is a lightweight XML format designed for sharing headlines and other Web content. Think of it as a distributable 'What's New' for your site. Originated by UserLand in 1997 and subsequently used by Netscape to fill channels for Netcenter, RSS has evolved into a popular means of sharing content between sites (including the BBC, CNET, CNN, Disney, Forbes, Motley Fool, Wired, Red Herring, Salon, Slashdot, ZDNet, and more). RSS solves myriad problems webmasters commonly face, such as increasing traffic, and gathering and distributing news. RSS can also be the basis for additional content distribution services.

Chapter 4

1 JFK quote [accessed 24 June 2013] BBC, *On This Day*: 20 January 1961: John F Kennedy sworn in as US President [online] http://news.bbc.co.uk/onthisday/hi/dates/stories/january/20/newsid_2506000/2506929.stm.

Ask not what your country can do for you – ask what you can do for your country.

2 Problem Maps® were first introduced in Grant Leboff's 2007 book, *Sales Therapy®: Effective selling for the small business owner*, Capstone Wiley. They are available for download at www.stickymarketing.com> Lessons> How to create effective sales messages>. Scroll down to Problem Map PDF. You need to login or register as a free member to access this page.

Chapter 5

1 The service economy [accessed 27 June 2013] About.com:Economics: The Post War Economy:1945–1960; From the US Department of State: Changes in the American Workforce [online] http://economics.about.com/od/useconomichistory/a/post_war.htm.

During the 1950s, the number of workers providing services grew until it equalled and then surpassed the number who produced goods. And by 1956, a majority of U.S. workers held white-collar rather than blue-collar jobs.

2 IBM [accessed 27 June 2013] Economy Watch.com: Service economy [online] http://www.economywatch.com/economy-articles/service-economy.html.

IBM is an unique example. In spite of being a manufacturing company it tends to call itself a services company. This has been the scenario since it realized that the price elasticity of demand for business solutions is less elastic than for hardware. The company now benefits from the revenue of the elongated contracts rather than receiving payment in a single mode.

3 Henry Ford quote [accessed 27 June 2013] Corporate Ford: Heritage: The Model T put the world on wheels >Mass production begins [online] http://corporate.ford.com/our-company/heritage/heritage-news-detail/672–model-t.

In October 1913, mass production of the Model T began at Ford's Highland Park, Michigan, Assembly Plant. Henry Ford had previously organized men and components to enhance Model T production, but the moving assembly line quickly improved chassis assembly speed from 12 hours and eight minutes to one hour and 33 minutes. In 1914, Ford produced 308,162 cars, more than all other automakers combined. It was also in 1914 that the Model T, in the interest of streamlining production, was no longer available in red, blue, green or grey; it was now available in 'any color so long as it is black.'

4a *X Factor* [accessed 27 June 2013] The radiator: Social media can influence *X Factor* and *Strictly Come Dancing* votes [online] http://www.the-radiator.com/blog/social-media-can-influence-x-factor-and-strictly-come-dancing-votes/.

Media agency Carat studied how influential Facebook and Twitter are when deciding who to vote for on reality shows *X Factor* and *Strictly Come Dancing*. The research derived from data of 13,000 people found that the *X Factor* and *Strictly* judges are equally as influential in forming viewer's opinions as Twitter, with 17 per cent of respondents saying that is what establishes their vote. It was discovered that Twitter is 42 per cent more powerful than other main news sources in deciding voting behaviour. 66 per cent of viewers also say they trust what they read on the site about *X Factor* and *Strictly Come Dancing* when deciding how to vote. Despite Twitter being most influential, only 14 per cent of respondents claim to use the site whilst watching the shows compared with 51 per cent who use Facebook at the same time.

4b *X Factor* [accessed 27 June 2013] Digitalspy.co.uk: #fagashbreath among top The *X Factor* Twitter trends, Friday 7 December 2012, by Andrew Laughlin [online] http://www.digitalspy.co.uk/tech/s103/the-x-factor/news/a443759/fagashbreath-among-top-the-x-factor-twitter-trends.html.

There have been more than 13 million tweets about the ITV1 talent show's latest series from August 18 to December 2, peaking in week eight, according to data compiled by SecondSync.

5 Heineken [accessed 27 June 2013] Creative Review: Heineken launches live football game StarPlayer, posted by Eliza Williams, 27 April 2011 [online] http://www.creativereview.co.uk/cr-blog/2011/april/heineken-starplayer.

Heineken has launched a brand new live game, StarPlayer, which allows players to predict what will happen at key moments in the UEFA Champions League matches to score points.

The game, which was created and devised by creative agency AKQA, taps into a growing 'dual screen' habit amongst audiences: the tendency to watch TV while also chatting with mates via social media networks on computers or mobile phones. StarPlayer works in real-time, with players invited to forecast the outcome of corners, free kicks and penalties by choosing between a number of options. Different point scores are awarded depending on the likelihood of the outcome. Players also have the chance to guess when goals will take place – at the start of the game they are given eight chances to predict whether there will be a goal in the next 30 seconds, with points awarded on a sliding scale depending on how early the goal is anticipated.

Chapter 6

1 USP [accessed 27 June 2013] Wikipedia: Unique selling proposition [online] http://en.wikipedia.org/wiki/Unique_selling_proposition.

The Unique Selling Proposition (also Unique Selling Point) is a marketing concept that was first proposed as a theory to explain a pattern among successful advertising campaigns of the early 1940s. It states that such campaigns made unique propositions to the customer and that this convinced them to switch brands. The term was invented by Rosser Reeves of Ted Bates & Company. Today the term is used in other fields or just casually to refer to any aspect of an object that differentiates it from similar objects...

Definition. In *Reality in Advertising* (Reeves 1961, pp 46–48) Reeves laments that the U.S.P. is widely misunderstood and gives a precise definition in three parts:

1 Each advertisement must make a proposition to the consumer. Not just words, not just product puffer, not just show-window advertising. Each advertisement must say to each reader: 'Buy this product, and you will get this specific benefit.'

2 The proposition must be one that the competition either cannot, or does not, offer. It must be unique—either a uniqueness of the brand or a claim not otherwise made in that particular field of advertising.

3 The proposition must be so strong that it can move the mass millions, ie, pull over new customers to your product.

2a Netbooks 2008 [accessed 27 June 2013] Engadget: ASUS Eee PC given away with T-Mobile mobile broadband package, by Darren Murp, posted May 8th 2008 [online] http://www.engadget.com/2008/05/08/asus-eee-pc-given-away-with-t-mobile-mobile-broadband-plan/.

We're calling this right now: ASUS' Eee PC is the new MP3 player. But only in the context of giveaways. Anyhow, just days after RBC announced that it would dish out free subnotes if prospective customers joined in, PowerUp Mobile is now offering a similar deal for UKers who sign up for T-Mobile's Web n Walk mobile broadband package. In short, folks comfortable with inking their name on a two-year contract at £35 per month will net a free USB modem and a Eee PC 2GB Surf. Better hurry – the deal expires on June 15th.

2b Netbooks 2009 [accessed 27 June 2013] PC World: Office hardware, 6 July 2009, 2:00 pm: Netbooks offered virtually free with mobile contracts, by Agam Shah, IDG News Service [online] http://www.pcworld.com/

businesscenter/article/167929/netbooks_offered_virtually_free_with_mobile_
contracts.html.

Netbook prices in the U.S. are tumbling as retail stores are offering the machines
virtually for free, but with caveats attached to them. Retail store Best Buy is selling
Hewlett-Packard's Compaq Mini 110c-1040DX netbook, which has a 10-inch screen,
for $0.99, but with a two-year mobile broadband contract from wireless carrier
Sprint. The contract limits subscribers to 5GB of internet data usage per month, with
extra fees if the limit is exceeded. Sprint's 3G mobile broadband plans start at around
$60 a month. HP's netbook is available without a contract for $389.99. Consumer
electronics store RadioShack is offering an Acer Aspire One with an 8.9-inch screen for
free with a two-year AT&T mobile broadband contract, according to the retailer's Web
site. AT&T's 3G mobile broadband plans start at $60 a month. RadioShack's offering
goes on 'while supplies last.' The netbook is priced at $349.99 without the contract.
Both netbooks have basic configurations, making them good for word processing and
Web surfing, but weak on graphics capabilities... Telecom providers started offering
netbooks with wireless contracts last year in Europe and Asia, which helped spike the
shipment numbers of the low-cost devices. The trend reached the U.S. late last year,
when RadioShack announced it would offer an Acer netbook for $99 with a two-year
mobile contract from AT&T. Worldwide netbook shipments totaled around 11 million
in 2008, with the number expected to double this year, according to research firm IDC.
Netbook distribution through telecom companies has found a sweet spot in Western
Europe, where telecom companies have accounted for 25 percent to a third of the
netbook shipments, said David Daoud, research manager at IDC.

3   Apple iPad [accessed 27 June 2013] Apple.com: Apple Press Info: iPad
    Available in US on April 3, 'CUPERTINO, California – March 5, 2010'
    [online] http://www.apple.com/pr/library/2010/03/05iPad-Available-in-US-
    on-April-3.html.

Apple® today announced that its magical and revolutionary iPad will be available in
the US on Saturday, April 3, for Wi-Fi models and in late April for Wi-Fi + 3G models.
In addition, all models of iPad will be available in Australia, Canada, France, Germany,
Italy, Japan, Spain, Switzerland and the UK in late April.

4   Samsung Galaxy [accessed 27 June 2013] Telegraph.co.uk: Technology: IFA
    2010: Samsung launches Galaxy Tab iPad rival, by Matt Warman, Consumer
    Technology Editor, in Berlin, 2 September 2010 [online] http://www.
    telegraph.co.uk/technology/samsung/7977216/IFA-2010–Samsung-launches-
    Galaxy-Tab-iPad-rival.html.

Samsung has launched the long-awaited Galaxy Tab tablet computer. The device,
officially called the GT-P1000, is powered by Google's Android 2.2 operating system
and makes an explicit pitch for the market staked out by the Apple iPad.

5   The Bible [accessed 27 June 2013] Guinness World Records: Best-selling
    book of non-fiction [online] http://www.guinnessworldrecords.com/
    records-1/best-selling-book-of-non-fiction/.

Although it is impossible to obtain exact figures, there is little doubt that the Bible is the world's best-selling and most widely distributed book. A survey by the Bible Society concluded that around 2.5 billion copies were printed between 1815 and 1975, but more recent estimates put the number at more than 5 billion.

By the end of 1995, combined global sales of Today's English Version (Good News) New Testament and Bible (copyright for which is held by the Bible Societies) exceeded 17.75 million copies, and the whole Bible had been translated into 349 languages; 2123 languages have at least one book of the Bible in that language.

6 McDonalds / Coke [accessed 27 June 2013] Coca-Cola: Our company: Operating group leadership [online] http://www.thecoca-colacompany.com/ourcompany/bios/bio_113.html.

Javier C. Goizueta is Vice President, The Coca-Cola Company, and President of the global McDonald's Division. He leads a worldwide organization that is responsible for building the strategic alliance with McDonald's in over 31,000 restaurants located in 119 countries.

7 Virgin [accessed 27 June 2013] About Virgin [online] http://www.virgin.com/about-us.

Virgin is a leading international investment group and one of the world's most recognized and respected brands. Conceived in 1970 by Sir Richard Branson, the Virgin Group has gone on to grow successful businesses in sectors ranging from mobile telephony, travel, financial services, leisure, music, holidays and health & wellness. Across its companies, Virgin employs approximately 50,000 people, in 34 countries and global branded revenues in 2011 were around £13bn ($21bn).

Virgin believes in making a difference. We stand for value for money, quality, innovation, fun and a sense of competitive challenge. We strive to achieve this by empowering our employees to continually deliver an unbeatable customer experience.

Chapter 7

1 Guardian Witness [accessed 22 May 2013] Mashable.com: 'The Guardian' calls for citizen journalists via app, by Lauren Indvikapr, 16 April 2013 [online] http://mashable.com/2013/04/16/the-guardianwitness/.

Vanishing are the days when readers' contributions to the papers they read are limited to the 'letters to the editor' section. The latest publication to open its arms to reader contributions—in the form of videos, photos and stories—is The Guardian which launched Tuesday a program called 'Guardian Witness.'

Guardian Witness, available, online and as an app for iPhone and Android devices, asks users to supply staff journalists with videos, photos and stories for both breaking news events and less pressing features, which could then appear on The Guardian's website and/or in print...

...The initiative is similar to that of CNN iReport and ProPublica's Get Involved which ask readers to contribute stories and footage for specific assignments, as well as ideas for coverage.

2 YouTube [accessed 27 June 2013] *The Telegraph*: Eight years of YouTube, 23 April 2013 [online] http://www.telegraph.co.uk/technology/internet/10011915/Eight-years-of-YouTube.html.

With millions of videos uploaded and over one trillion views in its eight year history, YouTube has become part of many people's everyday lives...

YouTube was created in February 2005 by three former PayPal employees, Chad Hurley, Steve Chen and Jawed Karim, who based it in San Bruno, California.

In 2013, roughly 60 hours of new videos are uploaded every minute, and the site has over 800 million unique users a month, according to YouTube.

Gangnam Style, the music video with the distinctive dance by South Korean pop star Psy, is the most viewed upload in YouTube's history. It has been viewed over 1.5 billion times since July 15 2012.

3 New products [accessed 27 June 2013] *Bloomberg Business Week*: Technology: Advertising: Now a conversation, Ted Shelton, 18 January 2008 [online] http://www.businessweek.com/stories/2008–01–18/advertising-now-a-conversationbusinessweek-business-news-stock-market-and-financial-advice.

In a 2006 study, researchers found that only 53 per cent of consumers said they believed ads were a good way to learn about new products. That was down from a 78 per cent response in 2002.

4 Starbucks [accessed 27 June 2013] Mark Shaw: Twitter and customer service – Starbucks style, 31 January 2010, by Mark Shaw [online] http://www.markshaw.biz/twitter-and-customer-service-starbucks-style/.

It is fair to say, that I do love a latte. In fact I would say that I am addicted to them. It is rare that a day goes by, without my fix of a good latte. For the last 18 months or so, I have been a massive Costa Coffee fan. In fact, I think that I have probably single handedly put Costa Coffee Barnet on the map. I talk about them so much, that I am sure that most peeps think they pay me, or I have shares in their business. Both of which I can state are not true... Every day, I talk about Costas in Barnet, I have many of my business meetings in there, and the Oxford Circus branch, and yes I do like their latte's. I am very well known by their staff, and over this time, have often suggested ideas to them on how to improve things. I have also contacted them via Twitter... And the result... Nothing. Nada. Zero response. I am an amazing customer for them, I have not added up what I have spent over the last 18 months, but a latte 5 days per week, at least 3 almond croissants each week, and many a toasted sandwich... all must add up to a fair amount... Enter Starbucks. So there I was on Sunday having just collected my daughter Jessica. She lives near to London Colney, so we often go to the Starbucks in Sainsburys, have a drink, she has a marshmallow twizzler, and then we buy a few things in Sainsburys. This morning was no different, I sat down for my drink, and tweeted.

Approx 3 mins went by… when I checked my phone, I noticed that I had received a message from Starbucks, in fact it was from the MD of Starbucks UK and Ireland… Darcy Wilson–Rymer. Now imagine how I felt… 18 months blasting Costas, spending a fortune, talking about them, being a top customer… and in one message they may well have lost me. During the course of the day, myself and Darcy exchanged more messages. He seemed genuinely interested in me, and [my] experience of his brand. Exactly as I would have hoped. He wanted to know what I thought of his shops, and was all ok. Now I don't know about you, but to me that is what great customer service is all about. Oh and don't forget the most important thing… What have I now done, I have written about my experience and will tell others… They have created a great advocate for their brand, and all in 1 message that may well have taken Darcy 10 seconds…

Never, never underestimate great customer care and service. Oh and Costas, I really do hope that you are reading this blog post, but somehow, I strongly doubt it.

5 Lego [accessed 27 June 2013] Covolet Marketing: LEGO – A global connector, Liz Kaufman [online] http://www.covalentmarketing.com/our-thinking/mkt_innov8/everyday-innovators/lego/.

Both in stores and in homes, LEGO is always finding new ways to interact with its customers. The LEGO Digital Designer not only allows customers to create their own models and purchase them, but also creates social interaction by allowing the users to share their models with others.

6 Starbucks [accessed 27 June 2013] Businesswire: Starbucks Celebrates Five-Year Anniversary of My Starbucks Idea, 29 March 2103 [online] http://www.businesswire.com/news/home/20130328006372/en/Starbucks-Celebrates-Five-Year-Anniversary-Starbucks-Idea.

MyStarbucksIdea.com has welcomed more than 150,000 ideas from customers, leading to the implementation of 277 new innovations for Starbucks

SEATTLE–(BUSINESS WIRE)–Today, consumers can walk into a Starbucks to order a 'skinny' beverage, receive digital rewards for using their Starbucks Card and enjoy the free Wi-Fi. These innovations, and hundreds more, have enhanced the Starbucks experience because of customer ideas shared on MyStarbucksIdea.com.

'For five years, our passionate customers and partners have been sharing their ideas with us on My Starbucks Idea, and we have listened and acted upon many amazing innovations that we have received from this online community.'

This month, Starbucks celebrates a five-year milestone of innovation on MyStarbucksIdea.com, an online community for people to share, vote, discuss and put into action ideas on how to enhance the Starbucks experience. The site was founded to create an open dialogue and collaborative environment with consumers to share their thoughts and ideas and allow them to play a vital role in how they interact with Starbucks, both in and out of stores.

7 Walkers Crisps [accessed 27 June 2013] *Marketing Magazine*: Builder's Breakfast crisps wins Walkers' flavour competition, by Gemma Charles, 6

May 2009 [online] http://www.marketingmagazine.co.uk/article/903478/
builders-breakfast-crisps-wins-walkers-flavour-competition.

LONDON – Builder's Breakfast has emerged as the winner of Walkers' multi-million
pound 'Do us a flavour' campaign which saw consumers cast a total of more than one
million votes. 'The winning flavour – which tastes like egg and beans – received 232,336
votes or almost 22 per cent the votes cast via the Walkers' website, SMS, facebook,
mobile and e-mail. It will now become a permanent flavour and the inventor, Emma
Rushin from Belper, Derbyshire wins a £50,000 prize and 1 per cent of future sales.

'Do us a flavour' kicked off in July 2008, when Walkers challenged consumers to
invent a brand new crisp flavour. The nationwide search received over 1.2 million
entries from the British and Irish public. The six finalist flavours were then selected by
chief judge Heston Blumenthal and a panel of judges from Walkers.

8 Nintendo [accessed 27 June 2013] Gonintendo: Wii marketing blitz – the
rundown, 13 November 2006, by RawmeatCowboy, Ambassador Program
[online] http://gonintendo.com/viewstory.php?id=8448.

Hands-on Sampling

Wii Ambassador Program: The yearlong initiative identified ambassadors in markets
throughout the country. These ambassadors are of three categories: multigenerational
families, hard-core gamers and modern moms. During the initial phase, Nintendo
hosted events for each ambassador and 30 of his or her closest friends and relatives.
The events offered an opportunity for everyday people from all walks of life to play
Wii for the first time and share their experiences with others.

Chapter 8

1 Cadbury Smash [accessed 1 July 2013] BBC News, Monday, 20 December,
1999: Martian ad a Smash hit. Smash hit: The 1970s aliens won the ad
industry's heart too [online] http://news.bbc.co.uk/2/hi/
entertainment/572903.stm.

A TV commercial for mashed potato featuring a group of talking robotic Martians
has been named advertisement of the year by a trade magazine. *Advertising Weekly
Campaign* named the 25-year-old Cadbury's Smash commercial its favourite in its top
ten of the century. The spots featured the creatures chortling as they heard how the
'Earth people' peeled their own potatoes, 'boiled them for 20 of their minutes,' then
'smashed them all to bits' – instead of using Smash instant mash. Viewers were not
insulted at being called 'a most primitive people' by the metallic creations – sales soared
and the Martians received so much fan mail the agency which made the commercials,
now known as BMP DDB, had to prepare special literature to reply to them. Now BMP
DDB is celebrating the accolade by showing the original 1974 commercial in Channel
4's final advertising slot of the year at 2355 GMT on 31 December.

2 Winston Churchill quote [accessed 1 July 2013] Wikiquote: Sir Winston Leonard Spencer-Churchill, KG, OM, CH, TD, FRS, PC (Can) (1874-11-30-1965-01-24) was a British politician. He was Prime Minister of the United Kingdom from 1940 to 1945, and again from 1951 to 1955. He received the Nobel Prize for Literature in 1953 [online] http://en.wikiquote.org/wiki/Winston_Churchill.

'For my part, I consider that it will be found much better by all Parties to leave the past to history, especially as I propose to write that history.' Speech in the House of Commons (January 23, 1948), cited in *The Yale Book of Quotations* (2006), ed. Shapiro & Epstein, Yale University Press, p. 154, ISBN 0300107986. This quote may be the basis for a statement often attributed to Churchill: 'History will be kind to me. For I intend to write it.'

3 Lynx Effect [accessed 1 July 2013] *Daily Record*: Man sues Lynx after failing to pull in seven years, 31 October 2009, Ben Spencer [online] http://www.dailyrecord.co.uk/news/weird-news/2009/10/31/man-sues-lynx-after-failing-to-pull-in-seven-years-86908-21786843/.

A LUCKLESS Romeo has sued cosmetics firm Lynx after he failed to land a girlfriend during seven years of using their products. Indian Vaibhav Bedi, 26, is seeking £50,000 from parent company Unilever for the 'depression and psychological damage' caused by the lack of any Lynx effect. Court officials in New Delhi have accepted dozens of half-used body washes, shampoos, anti-perspirants and hair gels for forensic tests. Lynx – marketed as Axe in India – is famous for its saucy ads showing barely clothed women throwing themselves at men. Vaibhav said in his court petition: 'The company cheated me because in its advertisements, it says women will be attracted to you if you use Axe. I used it for seven years but no girl came to me.' Unilever refused to comment on the case.

4 Mark Zuckerberg [accessed 1 July 2013] CNET: Facebook COO: Search to harness the 'wisdom of friends', Donna Tam, 1 October 2012 [online] http://news.cnet.com/8301-1023_3-57523521-93/facebook-coo-search-to-harness-the-wisdom-of-friends/.

When you're looking for information, the question is who do you want it from. Do you want it from the wisdom of crowds or the wisdom of friends? Our answer to the information that's most relevant for users – it's really about friends… if I'm looking for a restaurant to go to in New York this week, I'd rather get a recommendation from a friend.

5 Facebook Graph Search [accessed 1 September 2013] *Business Insider*: Facebook's new Graph Search launches today – here's how it works, Kevin Smith, 8 July 2013 [online] http://www.businessinsider.com/facebook-graph-search-walkthrough-2013-7?op=1.

Today, Facebook is finally launching its new Graph Search feature.

The new search tool uses your Facebook connections and interests to come up with relevant results for people, photos, places, and interests.

These are generally results for which a regular Web search would come up empty — like 'places I visited in 2010' or 'photos of my friends taken before 1980' or 'restaurants my friends like.'

6 Google+ [accessed 1 September 2013] *Guardian*: Google+ launched to take on Facebook, Charles Arthur and agencies, guardian.com, Wednesday 29 June 2011 [online] http://www.theguardian.com/technology/2011/jun/29/google-plus-facebook-social-networking.

Google is challenging Facebook domination by unveiling a new project called Google+ that it says will try to make online sharing more like real life.

More than a year in the works, Google+ lets users share things with smaller groups of people through 'circles'. This means only university friends, workmates, or families – but not necessarily all at once – would be able to see photos, links or updates.

Another feature called 'sparks' aims to make it easier to find online content you care about, whether fishing or recipes. That can then be shared with friends who might be interested in it. In an online video, Google calls it 'nerding out' and exploring a subject together.

Early reviews also suggest that the 'hangout' and 'huddle' elements of Google+, which enable video and mobile chat, could be aimed at challenging Skype, which was recently bought by Microsoft for $8.5bn (£5.3bn).

7 Google's Search Plus Your World [accessed 1 September 2013] Google's Search Plus Your World: What it means for users, by Ian Paul, *PC World*, 11 January 2012 [online] http://www.pcworld.com/article/247835/googles_search_plus_your_world_what_it_means_for_users.html

Get ready for more Google+ data in your Google searches as the company aims to personalize your results by including more Google+ profiles, business pages, posts, and Google+ and Picasa Photos. The search giant recently announced the significant change to its search engine, calling it Search Plus Your World. The new feature is baked right into Google and aims to personalize your search results by including Google+ data when you are signed into your Google account.

Search Plus Your World surfaces content that has been shared with you on Google+, as well as public information from the social networking site that is related to your search, and integrates this data into typical Web search results. The new opt-out feature is currently rolling out over the next few days to all users searching Google in English.

Chapter 9

1 UK company registrations 1990–91, Companies House [from an e-mail supplied 8 July 2013] UK: Company Registrations. Companies in data management information.

Year: 1990–91; 1,186,900

2 UK company registrations 2012–13, Companies House [from an e-mail supplied 8 July 2013] UK: Company registrations: Companies in data management information.

Year: 2012–13; 3,044,710.

3 US company registrations, US Census Bureau [accessed 17 July 2013] 1992 Statistics of US Businesses (SUSB) Data US businesses: All industries – 1992 [online] http://www.census.gov/econ/susb/data/susb1992.html.

Establishments; 6,319,300.

4 US company registrations. US Census Bureau [accessed 17 July 2013] 2010 Statistics of US Businesses (SUSB) Data US businesses: All industries – 2010 [online] http://www.census.gov/econ/susb/data/susb2010.html.

Establishments; 7,396,628.

5 Cafepress. [accessed 6 August 2013] *Guardian*. Cafepress: Jack Schofield, 18 August 2008 [online] http://www.guardian.co.uk/technology/2008/aug/18/cafepress/print.

Not many shops stock 150 million products. Cafepress not only manages this amazing feat, it adds around 45,000 new ones every day. This is only possible, of course, because the products don't exist until someone orders them. Your T-shirt, poster, cap, bag, book, mug or whatever is produced and shipped on demand.

But that is only half the Cafepress story. The other half is that its business is based on that old Web 2.0 standby, 'user-generated content'. Instead of buying a T-shirt printed with someone else's design, you can create your own. And if it's really good, you might even make a bit of money by letting Cafepress sell it to everybody else. If you fancy trying your hand, you can set up a small business using Cafepress to collect the money, produce the goods, mail them out, and handle customer service. All you need is access to a computer and some graphics software that can save your design in, for preference, the PNG (portable network graphics) format. The site provides web space and has a Learning Center to help you get going.

Cafepress, founded in a garage in 1999, has now grown to the point where it has more than '6.5 million independent shopkeepers and members in addition to syndicated and corporate stores', including geek favourites Dilbert and Wikipedia.

6 Cafepress – current users. [accessed 6 August 2013] Cafepress about us [online] http://www.cafepress.com/cp/info/about/.

Through some 2 million shops, customers can choose from over 300 million products on every subject imaginable — many available on over 600 product SKUs (from apparel and drinkware to posters, electronic accessories and more). Plus users can make their own designs with our easy online design tools, then buy them, share them or sell them in their own online shops. CafePress.com today ships over 6 million products annually, and has over 11 million unique visitors to our website each month.

7   Lemonade [accessed 6 August 2013]: *Time*: Top 10 websites 2007, by
Catherine Sharick # 1Lemonade.com [online] http://www.time.com/time/
specials/2007/article/0,28804,1686204_1686305_1691135,00.html.

Making extra cash through lemonade-stand sales isn't just for kids anymore. You, too,
can now get in the game at Lemonade.com by setting up a virtual 'stand' filled with
products you'd recommend to friends. Add the widget to your Facebook, MySpace
or blog pages and when purchases are made through your site, you receive 5 per cent
to 15 per cent of the cost of the item. The stands are a win–win for everyone: Online
retailers get free advertisements, social networkers are recommended good products,
and you get paid if the deal goes through.

8   Lemonade – current users [accessed 1 March 2010]: Lemonade Stand™
owners [online] http://www.lemonade.com/.

Thank you so much for being part of the Lemonade Stand social commerce network
with over 65,000 users. We currently not allowing new registrations.

9   eBay users Q4 2012 [accessed 6 August 2013] eBay Inc: Corporate fact
sheet: Q4 2012 [online] http://legacy.ebayinc.com/content/fact_sheet/ebay_
inc__corporate_fact_sheet_q4_2012.

112.3 million active users on eBay.

10   Craigslist users [accessed 8 August 2013] Statistic Brain – Source Craigslist.
com: Date verified 26 March 2012 [online] http://www.statisticbrain.com/
craigslist-statistics/.

Total number of local Craigslist sites 700

Number of countries that have a local Craigslist site 70

Number of Craigslist daily queries worldwide 50,000,000

Number of job listings posted to Craigslist each month 1 million.

11   NIKEiD [accesed 8 August 2013] Crossroad innovation: Nike ID – the first
example of mass customization driving revenue? 10 September 2010, David
Dencker [online] http://www.crossroadinnovation.com/nike-id.

NIKEiD is a service provided by the sportswear company NIKE allowing customers
to customize clothing purchased from Nike. The customer becomes the designer as
they change and add a personal look and feel to a selected item. The service can be
accessed both online from their homepage and in select physical branches. The service
was launched initially in 1999 and could only be accessed through their website. It
provided customers the ability to choose from a limited range of different material and
colors to develop their own style of tennis shoe.

NIKE iD is a fantastic customer experience (try it at nikeid.nike.com) and their online
community has recently reached 15 million people. In the same period Nike's market

share has grown from 48–61 per cent. The most interesting fact is that I learned recently is that NIKE iD now is 20 per cent of store revenue.

12 Firefox market share [accessed 6 August 2013] The Next Web: IE10 passes IE9 in market share, Firefox falls back below 20 per cent but Chrome manages to gain the most, by Emil Protalinski, Monday, 1 July 2013 [online] http://thenextweb.com/insider/2013/07/01/ie10–passes-ie9–in-market-share-firefox-falls-back-below-20–but-chrome-manages-to-gain-the-most/.

The first half of 2013's browser war is now over. June saw the third full month of IE10 availability on Windows 7, as well as the release of Firefox 22 and first full month of Chrome 27 availability. The latest market share numbers from Net Applications show Firefox was the biggest loser and Chrome was the biggest winner last month.

Between May and June, internet Explorer gained 0.16 percentage points (from 55.99 percent to 56.15 percent), Firefox lost a whopping 1.48 percentage points (from 20.63 percent to 19.15 percent), and Chrome grabbed 1.43 percentage points (from 15.74 percent to 17.17 percent). Safari meanwhile gained 0.09 percentage points to 5.55 percent and Opera dipped 0.19 percentage points to 1.58 percent.

13 Wikipedia internet rankings [accessed 6 August 2013] eBizMBA: Top 15 most popular websites, August 2013 [online] http://www.ebizmba.com/articles/most-popular-websites.

1 / Google… 900,000,000 Estimated Unique Monthly Visitors

2 / Facebook… 700,000,000 Estimated Unique Monthly Visitors

3 / Yahoo… 500,000,000 Estimated Unique Monthly Visitors

4 / YouTube… 450,000,000 Estimated Unique Monthly Visitors

5 / Wikipedia… 350,000,000 Estimated Unique Monthly Visitors.

14 Wikipedia pages [accessed 8 August 2013] Wikipedia: Statistics. [online] http://en.wikipedia.org/wiki/Wikipedia:Statistics.

Number of pages: 30,808,495.

15 Wikipedia language editions [accessed 7 August 2013] Language editions [online] http://en.wikipedia.org/wiki/Wikipedia.

There are currently 285 language editions (or language versions) of Wikipedia; of these, eight have over one million articles each (English, Dutch, German, French, Swedish Wikipedia, Italian, Spanish, and Russian), five more have over 700,000 articles (Polish, Japanese, Portuguese, and Chinese Wikipedia), 33 more have over 100,000 articles, and 73 more have over 10,000 articles… The largest, the English Wikipedia, has over 4.2 million articles. As of June 2013, according to Alexa, the English subdomain (en.wikidedia.org; English Wikipedia) – receives approximately 56 per cent of Wikipedia's cumulative traffic, with the remaining split among the other languages (Spanish: 9 per cent; Japanese: 8 per cent; Russian: 6 per cent; German: 5 per cent;

French: 4 per cent; Italian: 3 per cent)… As of April 2013, the five largest language editions are (in order of article count) the English, German, Dutch, French, and Italian Wikipedias… The coexistence of multilingual content on Wikipedia is made possible by Unicode, whose support was first introduced into Wikipedia in January 2002 by Brion Vibber after he had similarly implemented the alphabet of Esperanto.

16 Android market share [accessed 7 August 2013] PC Advisor – Android takes 75 percent of the smartphone market, by Chris Martin, *PC Advisor*, 15 May 2013 [online] http://www.pcadvisor.co.uk/news/mobile-phone/3447268/android-dominates-smartphone-market/.

Smartphones running Google's Android are dominating the market, according to the latest figures.

Gartner's numbers show that during the first quarter of 2013 Android smartphones accounted for 74.4 percent of global sales. This represents more than 156 million devices and a jump of nearly 20 percent in market share year-on-year.

17 Prosumer [accessed 6 August 2013] Jeffrey Mark: Culture, politics, and religion from a theological-historical frame of reference, Prosumer, 16 June 2007 [online] http://jeffreymark.typepad.com/myfolder/2007/06/prosumer.html.

Recently Gartner Fellow Ken McGee interviewed Alvin Toffler. During the exchange McGee asks Toffler about the concept of 'prosumer'…

We invented the word prosumer many years ago in my book *The Third Wave*. It's a composite of production and consumption, obviously, and we argue that there [were], prior to the invention of money, people who lived without money. Everybody was a prosumer, growing their own lunch, sewing their own clothes, building their own shack and so on. So it was a pre-monetary or a nonmonetary economy. However, more and more prosuming populations [moved over to] become part of the [consuming or] money system.

18 Napster [accessed 6 August 2013] History: This day in history: Music, 6 March 2001: The death spiral of Napster begins [online] http://www.history.com/this-day-in-history/the-death-spiral-of-napster-begins.

In the year 2000, a new company called Napster created something of a music-fan's utopia—a world in which nearly every song ever recorded was instantly available on your home computer, for free. Even to some at the time, it sounded too good to be true, and in the end, it was. The fantasy world that Napster created came crashing down in 2001 in the face of multiple copyright-violation lawsuits. After a string of adverse legal decisions, Napster, Inc began its death spiral on March 6, 2001, when it began complying with a Federal court order to block the transfer of copyrighted material over its peer-to-peer network.

Oh, but people enjoyed it while it lasted. At the peak of Napster's popularity in late 2000 and early 2001, some 60 million users around the world were freely exchanging digital mp3 files with the help of the program developed by

Northeastern University college student Shawn Fanning in the summer of 1999. Radiohead? Robert Johnson? The Runaways? Metallica? Nearly all of their music was right at your fingertips, and free for the taking. Which, of course, was a problem for the bands, like Metallica, which after discovering their song 'I Disappear' circulating through Napster prior to its official release, filed suit against the company, alleging 'vicarious copyright infringement' under the US Digital Millennium Copyright Act of 1996. Hip-hop artist Dr Dre soon did the same, but the case that eventually brought Napster down was the $20 billion infringement case filed by the Recording Industry Association of America (RIAA).

19 BBC News Channel. [accessed 7 August 2013] Page last updated at 06:02 GMT, Friday, 16 January 2009. Legal downloads swamped by piracy [online] http://news.bbc.co.uk/1/hi/technology/7832396.stm.

Ninety-five per cent of music downloaded online is illegal, a report by the International Federation of the Phonographic Industry (IFPI) has said.

20 Apple iTune downloads [accessed 7 August 2013] Charting The iTunes store's path to 25 billion songs sold, 40 billion apps downloaded and beyond, Darrell Etherington, Wednesday, 6 February 2013 [online] http://techcrunch.com/2013/02/06/charting-the-itunes-stores-path-to-25–billion-songs-sold-40–billion-apps-downloaded-and-beyond/.

Apple today announced a new sales milestone for its iTunes digital music store, with 25 billion songs sold. The news follows an announcement made earlier this month that the App Store has had over 40 billion app downloads since its founding. For the iTunes music store, the new record comes just shy of its 10 year anniversary, but for the App Store, the growth has been quicker, with the larger number accumulated over approximately four and a half years.

...Some other interesting tidbits to put these numbers in context: Apple's iTunes growth means that were you to average out the number of songs downloaded across the entire global population, it'd come out to 3.57 songs per person, and 25 billion songs also adds up to a daily average of 7,002,585 songs downloaded per day over the 9 years, 9 months and 9 days of the iTunes Store's existence.

21 Legal / Illegal Downloads [accessed 7 August 2013] The NPD Group: Music filesharing declined significantly in 2012 [online] https://www.npd.com/wps/portal/npd/us/news/press-releases/the-npd-group-music-file-sharing-declined-significantly-in-2012/.

Increased use of free music streaming services takes a bite out of illegal peer-to-peer music file sharing activity.

PORT WASHINGTON, NEW YORK, February 26, 2012 – According to The NPD Group, a global information company, illegal music file sharing declined significantly in 2012. Last year the number of consumers using peer-to-peer (P2P) services to download music declined 17 percent in 2012 compared to the previous year.

Chapter 10

1 Red Bull Stratos, Felix Baumgartner [accessed on 1 September 2013] PandaWhale: Red Bull Stratos may be the most successful marketing campaign of all time, Adam Rifkin, 16 October 2012 [online] http://pandawhale.com/post/7638/red-bull-stratos-may-be-the-most-successful-marketing-campaign-of-all-time.

Janean Chun of HuffPo writes: More than 8 million people worldwide watched YouTube's live stream on Sunday as Felix Baumgartner became the first person to break the sound barrier, starting in a freefall 128,000 feet above the Earth that reached a high speed of 833.9 miles per hour.

Meanwhile, Red Bull broke the traditional barriers of marketing, sponsorship and social media, skyrocketing from an energy drink known for providing a quick buzz to a big-time generator of international buzz that makes the endeavors of other marketing innovators like Apple look small by comparison.

2 Zen Joseph Player [accessed 22 August 2013] From Wikipedia, the free encyclopedia – Advertainment [online] http://en.wikipedia.org/wiki/Advertainment#cite_ref-1

Advertainment is a term invented by Zen Joseph Player (aka Zen Joseph, Zen Player, Izen Player) in October 1994, first published in an industry white paper entitled 'The future of advertising is called ADVERTAINMENT', later summarized in an interview and appearing in *MEDIAWEEK* (ADWEEK media supplement) below.

An excerpt from the article reads: Advertainment – advertising that seduces by engaging users' game-playing instincts and immersing them in worlds of embedded content, using prizes, coupons and other enticements.

Description – Advertainment is both a System and Methodology that combines elements of Entertainment, Information and Reward in a precisely calibrated algorithm ('Primary Equation') which, when applied to any kind of marketing or advertising content (for any product, service, brand, offering, audience etc, using any type of media), renders the content highly 'magnetic' – and prone to audience response. That is, the combination of these elements (within a permission-based structure) compels an individual with an resonant interest or passion, to engage with the content with a significantly higher level of attention and response, measurably more than any traditional or current solution known to the author.

3 Andy Warhol [accessed 22 August 2013] quote investigator: in the future everyone will be famous for 15 minutes [online] http://quoteinvestigator.com/2012/04/04/famous-15-minutes/.

Warhol's notable maxim about the transience of fame has been popular for much longer than the standard allotment of fifteen minutes. The earliest evidence QI has located for a version of the phrase is in an issue of *Time* magazine dated October 13, 1967 [TIAW]:

Whole new schools of painting seem to charge through the art scene with the speed of an express train, causing Pop Artist Andy Warhol to predict the day 'when everyone will be famous for 15 minutes.'

4 Cadbury ad YouTube [accessed 22 August 2013] Cadbury's gorilla advert, 31 August 2007 [online] http://www.youtube.com/watch?v=TnzFRV1LwIo.

Views 7,366,692.

5 Dan Zarrella [accessed 22 August 2013] Combined Relevance [online] http://danzarrella.com/zombie-marketing-how-to-use-combined-relevance-to-go-viral.html#.

I did a survey a little over a year ago where I asked people why they shared content online, both one-to-one (as emailing or IM'ing a link to a single person) and broadcast (like Tweeting a link to thousands of followers). In both cases the faraway most common answer was relevance. Respondents often said things like 'I saw something and it made me think of one of my friends,' or 'It seemed right up my friend's alley.' When talking about broadcast sharing, the answers were similar: 'I knew my audience would find it interesting.'

And if you take a second to think about why you send links to people this seems pretty obvious, but how as a marketer can we capitalize on this?

The answer is Combined Relevance.

6 Nick Pelling [accessed 22 August 2013] PMLive: Guide to Gamification: Faisal Ahmed [online] http://www.pmlive.com/pharma_intelligence/guide_to_gamification_442439.

History of Gamification

Nick Pelling, an English programmer, first coined the term in 2004 as part of his work with consultancy business Conundra. However, the principles are based on basic game design that has been around for centuries...

So what is Gamification? Gamification is a way of using technology to be more engaging, by giving the user certain actions to complete in return for rewards.

It has become popular due to the fact that its principles contain the fundamental human desires, such as recognition, reward, competition, gifting and status.

Elements of Gamification There are hundreds of game mechanic principles and behavioural theories that can be used to fully build an idea of successful Gamification, but there are five simple elements that stand out:

Progress paths – The use of challenges and evolving narratives to increase the likelihood a task will be completed.

Feedback – Instant feedback on the user's actions. In business this is usually slow, however in Gamification you need to feedback in real-time to help the user on their journey.

Rewards – Think of the best way to give the user a pat on the back, such as a target they can increase. This can include power, leadership or responsibility.

User experience – In 2012, there is no excuse to for users to be unsatisfied with how a game looks or functions. Develop engaging, straightforward graphics and an intuitive interface that helps users on their journey.

Social elements – The social viral loop has to be built into your platform. For centuries, games have been played with friends and family, and Gamification and social media help to amplify this. Think about the ability to challenge people or have the ability for the user to boast about their score via Twitter, Facebook and other social platforms.

A great example of Gamification that contributes to society is the Recycle Bank. First launched in the UK by Royal Borough of Winsdor and Maidenhead, residents receive points for recycling waste that can be redeemed against vouchers to spend on the high street.

In the US, Zamzee is tackling obesity by using Gamification to get people off the couch and to lead a healthier lifestyle. Just imagine a solution like this for people with diabetes or in improving adherence programmes.

The UK's Department of Work and Pensions is also making use of this trend by challenging its workforce to come up with new ideas using a website called Idea Street. The site includes points and leaderboards, offering staff a reward for good suggestions.

Chapter 12

1 Internet 1950s [accessed 1 September 2013] Netvalley: History of the internet: Timeline, by Dave Marshall [online] http://www.netvalley.com/archives/mirrors/davemarsh-timeline-1.htm.

   1957 USSR launches Sputnik, first artificial earth satellite. Why is this relevant?

   The start of global telecommunications. Satellites play an important role in transmitting all sorts of data today. In response, US forms the Advanced Research Projects Agency (ARPA) within the Department of Defense (DoD) to establish US lead in science and technology applicable to the military.

2 Internet 1980s [accessed 1 September 2013] *Newmedia*: History of the internet – 1980s [online] http://www.newmedia.org/history-of-the-internet.html?page=3.

   1980–1982: At a meeting of computer scientists determined to expand accessibility to the ARPANET, Dave Farber reveals how a project which he and his colleagues at the University of Delaware are working on aims to build an inexpensive network by using dial-up phone links rather than radio or satellite as the means of connection. In 1982, after funding from the National Science Foundation, computer scientists build the

PhoneNet system and establish internet connections between the PhoneNet system, the ARPANET, and the first commercial network, Telenet. This CSNET system broadens overall access to the internet and allows almost any school to access the network through less costly PhoneNet service. CSNET also greatly expands the geographic reach of the internet by allowing e-mail between the United States, Germany, France, Japan, Korea, Finland, Sweden, Australia, Israel, and the United Kingdom. This incarnation of the internet would continue to grow at an increasing rate by way of the increase in the number of networks that were attached to the internet.

3 Internet mid-1990s [accessed 1 September 2013] *Newmedia*: History of the internet 1990s [online] http://www.newmedia.org/history-of-the-internet.html?page=4.

1995: Bill Gates authors the now famous memo, The Coming Internet Tidal Wave. By 1995, the bulk of US internet traffic is routed through interconnected network service providers and Microsoft Windows 95 is launched. 1995 proves to be an eventful year in the formation of contemporary internet culture because it also sees the official launch of the online bookstore Amazon.com, the internet search engine Yahoo, online auction site Ebay, the internet Explorer web browser by Microsoft, and the creation by Sun Microsystems of the Java programming language which allows for the programming of animation on websites giving rise to a new level of internet interactivity.

4 Broadband 2000 [accessed 1 September 2013] DTI: BROADBAND UK National Broadband Strategy 2004 [online] http://www.dti.gov.uk/files/file13444.pdf.

The UK made a late start with broadband, but has been catching up very fast. In a worldwide league table compiled by the OECD, at the end of 2000 the UK was ranked 21st out of 30 countries. In recognition of this and of the importance of broadband for the economy, in 2001 the Government adopted an ambitious target to have the most competitive and extensive broadband market in the G7 by 2005 and published its first national strategy for broadband. In the past two years, the rate of growth of broadband has been one of highest in the G7, with 40–50,000 additional connections per week in recent months.

5 iPhone launch [accessed 1 September 2013] BBC: Apple's 'magical' iPhone unveiled, Tuesday 9 January 2007 [online] http://news.bbc.co.uk/1/hi/technology/6246063.stm.

US firm Apple has confirmed its move into the telecoms industry, unveiling the long-awaited iPhone.

Users will be able to download music and videos with the phone, demonstrated by Apple boss Steve Jobs at the annual Macworld Expo in San Francisco.

Mr Jobs praised the phone's design and told the audience the 'magical device' would 'revolutionize the industry'.

The phone, which will cost from $499 (£257) to $599, will be launched in the US in June and Europe later this year.

6 Mobile phone users [accessed 1 September 2013] *Mobithinking*: Mobile subscribers worldwide [online] http://mobithinking.com/mobile-marketing-tools/latest-mobile-stats/a.

'At the end of 2012, there were 6.8 billion mobile subscriptions, estimates The International Telecommunication (February 2013). That is equivalent to 96 percent of the world population (7.1 billion according to the ITU). And is a huge increase from 6.0 billion mobile subscribers in 2011 and 5.4 billion in 2010.

7 Internet access [accessed 1 September 2013] BBC: Facebook's internet.org aims to get billions online, by Dave Lee, 21 August 2013 [online] http://www.bbc.co.uk/news/technology-23779172.

Mr Zuckerberg said the goal was to make 'internet access available to those who cannot currently afford it'. The group's statement said only 2.7 billion people – just over one-third of the world's population – had access to the internet. Adoption was growing by less than 9 per cent a year, which was not fast enough.

8 LinkedIn launch [accessed] 1 September 2013: LinkedIn press centre [online] http://press.linkedin.com/about.

The site officially launched on May 5, 2003. At the end of the first month in operation, LinkedIn had a total of 4,500 members on the network.

9 Facebook launch [accessed 1 September 2013] Facebook: The complete biography [online] http://mashable.com/2006/08/25/facebook-profile/.

Facebook is the second largest social network on the web, behind only My Space in terms of traffic. Primarily focused on high school to college students, Facebook has been gaining market share, and more significantly a supportive user base. Since their launch in February 2004, they've been able to obtain over 8 million users in the US alone and expand worldwide to 7 other English-speaking countries, with more to follow. A growing phenomenon, let's discover Facebook.

10 Facebook becomes mobile [accessed 1 September 2013] *Cellular News*: Facebook sees daily traffic from mobiles overtake desktop for first time, published on 31 January 2013 [online] http://www.cellular-news.com/story/58390.php.

Facebook says that it saw its daily mobile user base exceed its conventional desktop users for the first time in the last quarter of 2012.

Daily active users (DAUs) were 618 million on average for December 2012, an increase of 28 per cent year-over-year. The monthly mobile were 680 million as of December 31, 2012, an increase of 57 per cent year-over-year

Mobile DAUs exceeded web DAUs for the first time in the fourth quarter of 2012, but mobile revenue still represented less than a quarter (23 per cent) of advertising revenue for the company.

'In 2012, we connected over a billion people and became a mobile company,' said Mark Zuckerberg, Facebook founder and CEO. 'We enter 2013 with good momentum and will continue to invest to achieve our mission and become a stronger, more valuable company.'

11 Third of population use Facebook [accessed 1 September 2013] More than a third of the UK population logs on to Facebook daily, site says, by Lara O'Reilly, Wednesday, 14 August 2013 [online] http://www.marketingweek.co.uk/news/more-than-a-third-of-the-uk-population-logs-on-to-facebook-daily-site-says/4007634.article.

In June Facebook's daily active user figure in the UK reached 24 million – more than a third of the country's entire population. The majority (84 per cent) – of those users, visit the site daily via their mobiles. Facebook has also today (14 August) broken out other country-by-country daily active user figures for June and revealed its UK monthly active user figure reached 33 million.

12 Hyperconnectivity [accessed 1 September 2013] P2P Foundation: Definition [online] http://p2pfoundation.net/Hyperconnectivity.

Hyperconnectivity is a term invented by Canadian social scientists Anabel Quan-Haase and Barry Wellman, arising from their studies of person-to-person and person-to-machine communication in networked organizations and networked societies. The term refers to the use of multiple means of communication, such as email, instant messaging, telephone, face-to-face contact and Web 2.0 information services.

13 SoLoMo [accessed 1 September 2013] solomosummit: What is SoLoMo and why is it important to marketers? [online] http://solomosummit.net/solomo-and-why-its-important-to-marketers/.

SoLoMo is an acronym for Social, Local/Location-Based and Mobile marketing. It allows marketers to 'hyper-target' – reach the right customer, with the right message, in the right time and place.

Marketers who approach today's SoLoMo consumer with a new mindset are delving into exciting territory with plenty of opportunity. Technology is finally at a point where we can see how consumers behave at that pivotal moment when they are ready to make purchasing decisions.

Epilogue

1 Share a Coke [accessed 1 September 2013] theguardian: What the Share a Coke campaign can teach other brands, by Tim Grimes [online] http://www.theguardian.com/media-network/media-network-blog/2013/jul/24/share-coke-teach-brands.

The success of the campaign lies in offering an affordable personalised product that exists in the real and virtual world. In the last few months there has been a growing trend for friends and colleagues to spam Twitter and Facebook feeds with pictures of Coca-Cola bottles and cans. As you probably already know, the world's largest beverage company has replaced its usual branding with 150 of the UK's most popular names. Each of these carried the hashtag #shareacoke to encourage users to promote the brand online.

The campaign was originally trialled in Australia in 2011 and produced some impressive results. Young adult consumption increased significantly, up by 7 per cent. The campaign also earned a total of 18,300,000-plus media impressions, and traffic on the Coke Facebook site increased by 870 per cent, with page likes growing by 39 per cent.

Since the UK campaign was launched on 29 April, its [sic] proven to be just as big a hit in the UK. From a social perspective, Coca-Cola has seen its Facebook community grow by 3.5 per cent and globally by 6.8 per cent. The hashtag has also been used 29,000 times on Twitter (Brandwatch, 2013). A study by YouGov in May this year, using its BrandIndex, highlighted that Coca-Cola had also increased its Buzz score, moving it from negative to positive.

2 Fiesta Movement [accessed 1 September 2013] Forbes: Ford remixes the Fiesta Movement For 2014, David Vinjamuri, 2 February 2013 [online] http://www.forbes.com/sites/davidvinjamuri/2013/02/19/ford-revives-the-fiesta-movement-to-launch-the-2014–fiesta/.

When Ford launched the Fiesta for 2011, they had a head start. Two years earlier in 2009, they'd brought 100 European Fiestas to the US and created the Fiesta Movement. Thousands of consumers submitted entries to be chosen as one of 100 digital influencers given the keys to a Fiesta for six months. These Fiesta agents completed monthly challenges, posted video and blogged about their experiences. The campaign, masterminded by new Ford social media head Scott Monty, was called the Fiesta Movement. It was spectacularly successful.

The campaign did an exceptional job of exposing the Fiesta name to a new generation of users (the name had been defunct in the US for over a decade), gaining 6.2mm YouTube views, 750,000 Flickr views and 40mm Twitter impressions. Most importantly, it singlehandedly brought top-of-mind awareness for the Fiesta name to a new generation of drivers. 132,000 drivers signed up for updates on the new Fiesta and over 6,000 pre-ordered the Fiesta, an exceptionally strong showing for a new economy car.

Four years later, Ford is resurrecting the Fiesta Movement for the launch of the 2014 Fiesta.

INDEX

(*italics* indicate a figure or table in the text)

CPSIA information can be obtained at www.ICGtesting.com
Printed in the USA
LVOW10s1559190214

374387LV00006B/257/P

9 780749 471088